Praise for The Time Paradox

"[Zimbardo] has become in effect a lobbyist for time. . . . Zimbardo does admit that he is perhaps writing a 'self-help book' and if this is true—and I think it is—there is no reason to be embarrassed. We want to help people gain control over their brains and lives. We want them to be more conscious and intelligent. We want them to improve themselves. And this is indeed one of the important goals of the psychologist: attain the knowledge of ourselves, the required knowledge, and then strive to improve our position in society as well as society itself. Zimbardo is surely an authentic and bold psychologist. There is no domain in the mental and psychological realms that he is afraid to explore."

—World ‸⁓

"Makes the intriguing case that e
ity . . . the goal being to help you r

"So little self-help material based on ᴧ ⁔ published that, when something like this comes along, we ow᷈ ᴊᴛ to our patrons to make sure it is readily available."

—Library Journal starred review

"Cogent insight into all of time's elements. . . . They blend scientific results into a straightforward narrative. . . . A compelling and practical primer on making every moment count."

—Publishers Weekly

"Fascinating new theories about how your time perspective shapes your life . . . [and] how understanding those attitudes can bring success, better health and greater fulfillment—but this is not just another self-help book. The conclusions are based on real science."

—St. Petersburg Times (Florida)

"The Time Paradox reveals how to better use your most irreplaceable resource, based on solid science and timeless wisdom."

—Martin Seligman, author of *Authentic Happiness*

"Informed by the world's foremost expert on the psychology of time, *The Time Paradox* combines solid science, compelling stories, and crisp prose to illuminate how time . . . pervades every aspect of our lives. Reading this book will yield insights into your own motivation and behavior, and help you be happier, healthier, and more successful. It will also help you understand the source of many of the world's greatest triumphs and most pressing problems. Zimbardo and Boyd have hit a home run."

—Sonja Lyubomirsky, author of *The How of Happiness*

"The Time Paradox explores a very important topic from a fresh, practical, and entertaining perspective. Since time is limited for all of us, this book is well worth your time."

—Daniel Amen, M.D., author of *Change Your Brain, Change Your Life* and *Healing the Hardware of the Soul*

"In this important book, Zimbardo and Boyd call our attention to [time] . . . explain[ing] the profound effect that our attitude toward time has on our habits, our happiness, our likelihood of success . . . and offer key advice on shifting perspectives. It's one of those rare and illuminating books that can change the way you think. And quite possibly the way you live."

—June Cohen, Director, TED Media

"Boyd and Zimbardo have set the new gold standard for books about time. *The Time Paradox* is a provocative, informative treatise that combines cutting-edge research with practical, hands-on guidance for self-change. In the hands of these two experienced scholars, time becomes a tool for helping us understand and better control . . . the way we live our lives."

—Robert V. Levine, Ph.D., Professor of Psychology, California State University, Fresno, and author of *Journeys in Social Psychology*

"Phil Zimbardo, a master at making complex ideas and discoveries in psychology, including his own, not only intelligible but fun and personally relevant for nonspecialists, has done it again, this time with the fascinating topic of time perspective. Bravo!"

—Walter Mischel, Ph.D., Columbia University Niven Professor of Humane Letters in Psychology

"At long last we have been offered this essential book, which is not only an examination but an understanding of . . . time. Uniquely, Zimbardo and Boyd offer genuine insights into how time is personally experienced, with . . . affecting and memorable personal narratives. It's not only a must-read, it's a must-know. I'm so happy at last to know that the spark that prompted my own doctoral writing decades ago has inspired such gifted researchers and writers."

—Ann L. Weber, Ph.D., Professor of Psychology,
University of North Carolina at Asheville

"This book would change Silicon Valley if we only took the time to read it. As such, you will gain a significant competitive advantage if you read it, so fork over the price and get going."

—Guy Kawasaki, cofounder of Alltop and
author of *The Art of the Start*

Also by Philip Zimbardo

The Lucifer Effect: Understanding How Good People Turn Evil
Shyness: What It Is, What to Do About It
The Shy Child: A Parent's Guide
Psychology: Core Concepts, Discovering Psychology
Psychology and Life
The Psychology of Attitude Change and Social Influence

the
Time
Paradox

The New Psychology of Time
That Will Change Your Life

Philip Zimbardo, Ph.D.,
and John Boyd, Ph.D.

FREE PRESS
NEW YORK LONDON TORONTO SYDNEY NEW DELHI

*f*P

Free Press
A Division of Simon & Schuster, Inc.
1230 Avenue of the Americas
New York, NY 10020

Copyright © 2008 by John Boyd and Philip Zimbardo

Zimbardo Time Perspective Inventory (ZTPI) © 1999 by
Philip Zimbardo and John Boyd

All rights reserved, including the right to reproduce this book or
portions thereof in any form whatsoever. For information address
Free Press Subsidiary Rights Department,
1230 Avenue of the Americas, New York, NY 10020.

First Free Press paperback edition July 2009

FREE PRESS and colophon are trademarks of
Simon & Schuster, Inc.

For information about special discounts for bulk purchases,
please contact Simon & Schuster Special Sales at
1-800-456-6798 or business@simonandschuster.com.

The Simon & Schuster Speakers Bureau can bring authors to your
live event. For more information or to book an event contact the
Simon & Schuster Speakers Bureau at 1-866-248-3049 or visit our
website at www.simonspeakers.com.

Designed by Level C

Manufactured in the United States of America

10 9 8 7

The Library of Congress has cataloged the hardcover edition as follows:
Zimbardo, Philip G.
    The time paradox: understanding and using the revolutionary new
science of time / Philip Zimbardo and John Boyd.
        p. cm.
    Includes bibliographical references.
    1. Time—Psychological aspects.   2. Time perception.   I. Boyd, John.
II. Title.
    BF468.Z56   2008
    153.7'53—dc22   2008002149

ISBN: 978-1-4165-4198-1
ISBN: 978-1-4165-4199-8 (pbk)

To my son, Adam, and my brother, Don,
who have taught me much about how and why time
used wisely and well really matters and enhances
the quality of our lives.

—*Philip Zimbardo*

To my parents:
All that I am, and ever hope to be,
I owe to you.

To Nancy:
You fill my present with love
and my future with purpose.

—*John Boyd*

Contents

Prologue

by Philip Zimbardo and John Boyd

We welcome you to what we hope will be an exciting journey of discovery as you learn new things about yourself and about more effective ways of living. Since the first publication of *The Time Paradox*, many readers and reviewers have shared with us their enthusiasm for its insights. In this book, we make apparent a rather simple lesson about the role of time in our lives and the enhanced self-understanding that stems from this knowledge. In this new prologue, and later in the epilogue, we want to mention some recent discoveries that have been made since we wrote the book that will tie together some of the themes of our book and point to what the future may hold in these very uncertain times.

Life is all about making decisions: some big, some little, some mundane, some vital to your existence. Important decisions move from being internal mental processes to triggering overt actions. The core of your life can be reduced to two types of actions: those taken and those not taken. Each action—whether taken or not taken—is associated with positive and negative consequences, with specific emotions, and with a sense of self-regard. We are filled with **joy and pride** by our actions that turned out to have good consequences. We are filled with **regret and distress** for actions we avoided—but realize that we should have taken. Similarly, we feel **wise and prudent** for having decided to avoid taking action that proved to have negative consequences for others. Finally, we feel **dumb and foolish** when we have done something that we later realize we should not have done.

What is missing from these mental calibrations are the mental *decisions* that generated our Go / No Go Actions. What caused us to do one thing and not another? We all want to feel joy, pride, wisdom, and prudence and we don't want to act in regrettable or dumb ways, so it is vital that we understand the mental dynamics that influence our underlying decisions.

ACTION	GOOD OUTCOME	BAD OUTCOME
Taken	Joy & Pride	Dumb & Foolish
Not Taken	Regret & Distress	Wise & Prudent

Imagine now that almost all of your mental decisions are influenced by something else that's going on in your mind but you are totally unaware of it—YOUR BIASED TIME PERSPECTIVE! Time perspective is the psychological term for the process by which each of us sorts out our personal experiences into temporal categories, or time zones. It is one aspect of psychological, or subjective, time that contrasts with objective, or clock, time. Other types of psychological time include our sense of the duration that events seem to take, our sense of rate of change of time, our sense of rhythm, and our sense of feeling pressured by time commitments.

In this book, we explain how you partition all of your life experiences into the three broad categories of what was, *The Past,* what is, *The Present,* and what will be, *The Future.* We show you how and why many people come to overuse one of these three major time zones while underutilizing the others. You may develop these time-perspective biases just as you learn most of the other biases you carry around in your head: from personal experiences, cultural influences, education, social class, religion, geography and climate in which you live, and from still more sources. And of course, you learn them from social models, from your families, peer groups, and from school and work settings. The number of these influences acting on you in subtle but pervasive ways from childhood on throughout adolescence and adulthood is so large that you are often not aware of how you have come to prefer and think in terms of one of these time categories over another.

Consider any decision you had to make recently: Do I keep working or go out to play; take one more drink before driving home; take a chance and cheat on my taxes or an exam; practice safe sex or just do it; resist or give into temptation? As you contemplate what you will do, you are influenced by a number of factors. For some people, the world is limited to all the forces they perceive in their immediately present situation, their biological urges, their social setting and that which others are doing or urging them to do, and the sensuous appeal of the stimulus itself. Those folks who usually limit their decision-making by referring only to the current circumstances are Present-oriented. Other people making a decision in the same setting downplay the present and search their memories for similar past situations; they recall what they did in the past and how these decisions turned out. These folks are Past-oriented. Finally, a third type of person makes up her or his mind entirely based on imagined future consequences—the costs and benefits—of an action. If anticipated costs outweigh anticipated benefits or gains, they won't go forward. They only go forward when they expect gains to predominate.

We have discovered through decades of research that each type of person routinely makes these time-based decisions without being aware that their choices are temporally biased. They do so because such decision-making has become a mental habit practiced over and over. As you will discover in the coming chapters, these three main time frames are subdivided into very different pairs. Present-orientation can be Hedonistic, focused on pleasure, risk taking, and sensation seeking; or it can be Fatalistic, focused on not taking control of situations because of a belief that life is fated to play out a certain way, no matter what one does. Past-orientation is divided between a Positive focus on the memories of the good old days, family, and tradition, or a Negative focus that recalls abuse, failures, and regrets over missed opportunities. Future-orientation can entail working for goals, meeting deadlines, and achieving objectives, or it can entail a Transcendental Future in which spiritual life after death of the body is what matters most. These six time frames—or time zones—map out most of what is meant by time perspective. We discuss later on, but have not developed a way to measure, what might be called the Holistic Expanded Present, which is the Zen-like focus on the power of the present moment, the NOW. Eckhart Tolle's best-selling book, *The Power of Now,* focuses only on that particular aspect of time perspective.

The first time paradox arises from our assertion that time perspective is one of the most powerful influences on our decisions, yet we are typically unaware of its role. The second paradox is that some of these specific time-perspective categories have many good features, but when one category is too heavily favored, its negatives will undercut its virtues. Specifically, the virtues of being Past-Positive, Present-Hedonistic, or Future-Oriented are strong, but only when one doesn't rely too heavily on one time perspective over the others to make decisions. Past-Negative and Present-Fatalism are mainly damaging time perspectives, so we encourage you to make major changes in your life if you are high on either dimension. Talking about change, we should make clear up front that we believe time perspectives are learned, not inborn, and, like all learned behaviors, they can be relearned and modified to make them work in a more ideal way. We all have the power to adjust our time biases to optimize our decision-making processes and improve our lives.

We hope that by reading our book, you will gain these significant take-home messages: become aware of your personal time-perspective profile; become more sensitive to the ways in which your decisions have been and are influenced by that profile; realize how your social and business relationships are affected unconsciously by it; and finally, appreciate the ideal profile for which we should all strive. This ideal time profile is a balance of being high on the past-positive, moderately high on the present-hedonistic and future, and low on the past-negative and present-fatalistic time perspectives. Such a balance generates the combined strengths of these time frames without any of the negatives of their excesses. Further, such an optimally balanced time perspective will enable you to flexibly shift your time focus depending on the demands of each situation you face, freeing you from being a slave to a fixed time focus.

How will you discover what your time-perspective profile is? It is easy, quick, and simple to find out. Your authors have developed a unique inventory that gives you a score on each of the six time dimensions. The scales were developed and refined over many years, and they have proven to be both reliable (they give similar results each time they are taken) and valid (they enable testable predictions of actual behavior and relationships with a host of psychological and social measures). You can get your scores in two ways: Go to page 53 to take the ZTPI and Transcendental Future scales. Or go to our website to answer the scale items and have it scored for you immediately: **www.TheTimeParadox.com.**

EXCITING NEW DEVELOPMENTS IN THE PAST YEAR SINCE FIRST PUBLICATION OF *THE TIME PARADOX*

Conscientious People Live Longer.

Of all the outcomes of psychologically related traits, the most important is longevity. If having some psychological trait can be proven to influence one's lifespan, you obviously want to know about it and to understand how and why it does this. Recent research published in the September 2008 issue of *Health Psychology* indicates that higher levels of conscientiousness are associated with living longer.[1] Conscientious individuals are less likely to die regardless of their age. Conscientiousness is a composite of responsibility, self-control, achievement, order, and responsibility. This research was conducted by Howard Friedman, best known for his pioneering work on Type A personalities and cardiac problems, and co-investigator Margaret Kern, both of the University of California, Riverside.

Their investigation analyzed data from twenty independent studies with nearly nine thousand participants from six different countries, using various measurements of conscientiousness. The highly significant results are quite robust, especially for the components of achievement and order. So why do time-perspective researchers like us care about such a finding? Consider that the strongest characteristic of Future-Orientation is conscientiousness. In fact, the two measures have a very high correlation of 0.70, which is rare in psychological research on personality, where the typical correlation between personality measures is a modest 0.30 association level. In other words, conscientious people regularly think about future consequences before making a decision. How does our research on time perspective help explain this newly developed link between conscientious life and death? We found and report here in *The Time Paradox* that future-oriented people are more likely than all others to engage in positive health behaviors, such as getting regular medical and dental checkups, breast cancer testing and Pap smears, eating healthy foods, exercising, and wearing seat belts. They are also more likely than others not to engage in health-threatening behaviors, like taking drugs, smoking, drinking alcohol, taking risks while driving or in sports, or getting into arguments and fights. These negative health-related behavior patterns set the stage for an individual to die sooner. Future-oriented, highly conscientious individuals can be expected to live longer because of their positive health actions and attitudes. They also become more educated and may thus gravitate to less physically dangerous occupations. However, excessively future-oriented business people sacrifice sleep, friends, family, and personal fun in order to get their work done. That could mean a longer, but more boring, isolated, unfulfilling life—again, unless they work at achieving better time-perspective balance.

Time-perspective Metaphors Reduce PTSD in Veterans.

Following a recent lecture (October, 2008) on time perspective that Phil Zimbardo gave to clinical psychologists at the Hawaii Psychological Association, a therapist reported dramatic effects from using some of our ideas in treating military vets suffering from Post-Traumatic Stress Disorder (PTSD). Dr. Richard Sword, who is in private practice in Maui as well as on the Maui Memorial Medical Center staff, has been providing psychology therapy to vets with PTSD for many years. His e-mail note was filled with amazement at the new results he was achieving utilizing time-perspective concepts to help these patients deal more effectively with their PTSD. We quote from a personal e-mail communication to Phil (November 4, 2008):

The main aspects I've been using in my Time Perspective therapy with veterans are:

1. The importance of time and how we take time for granted. I emphasize that time can neither be saved nor borrowed; that we must make the best with it as it progresses. This makes time our most precious resource. Without time, other resources have no value whatsoever.

2. The fact that there are really only three times zones: the past, the present, and the future, and how we relate to them. If we are not careful we can get stuck in any one of them at the expense of the others and our overall well-being.

3. Therefore our most important asset is our time perspective (TP). We must learn to identify whether or not we may be stuck in any particular TP at the expense of other TPs.

4. It is very predictable and reliable that war vets with PTSD are stuck in the past-negative TP and present-fatalistic, at the expense of both present and future TPs. I explain in order to arrive at a new place you must first leave the old. If you have one foot stuck in the past and one foot planted in the present, you have to unstick the foot that is stuck in the past, lift it up, and stand on the other foot in the present, so you can move/project the past foot forward to the future.

5. Once the vets realize that living in the past negative/present fatalistic TP cost them their future, they begin to realize how expensive it is to live in the pains of the past. It is incredible when speaking about this to the veterans, as it never occurs to them that they are trading their most valuable resource . . . their future, for their past, by not control-

ling their present. I believe present transcendence and future hopefulness are essential components of a successful therapeutic intervention.

6. When they come to this realization, they begin to understand the importance of Time Perspective (TP) and how it crafts our lives. This is how I get their attention in order to motivate them to actually examine their TP and begin working toward balance and a more dynamic TP.

We have encouraged Dr. Sword to follow up this exciting development in a controlled investigation with pre-post assessment and independent observers. It could represent a vital breakthrough in treating this debilitating syndrome, which has had such a negative impact on the lives of so many young men and women (and their families) who have served their nation well, but who suffer long and deep the scars of wartime experiences.

Time Perspective Goes Global Across Thirty-two Nations.

The primary audience for *The Time Paradox* is the general public. Nevertheless, we still feel as if we are time-perspective missionaries, as we are eager to bring our ideas and ways of measuring different time perspectives to our colleagues. Our goal is to encourage, support, and collaborate with researchers who are open to exploring these basic ideas in more breadth and depth and with new visions. One of the most encouraging consequences of this outreach has been the development of an international time-perspective group of researchers from thirty-two nations (Australia, Belgium, Brazil, Bulgaria, China, Croatia, Czech Republic, Denmark, France, Germany, Greece, India, Italy, Japan, Latvia, Lithuania, Mexico, Moldova, Netherlands, Pakistan, Poland, Portugal, Russia, Serbia, Slovenia, South Africa, Spain, Sweden, Turkey, UK, Ukraine, and the USA). Many of them presented their original research using the ZTPI at the International Congress of Psychology in Berlin (July, 2008), and many young international researchers will present new time research at the European Congress of Psychology in Oslo,

Norway (July 2009). Anna Sircova from Moscow State University of Psychology and Education and Nicolas Fieulaine of the University of Lyon, France, have taken leading roles in organizing dozens of translations of our scale, and compiling a twenty-nation cross-cultural compendium of the emerging research. In addition, a wonderfully rich website has been developed for this international group, which readers of *The Time Paradox* may wish to visit: www .timeorientation.com—"A Website on Future Thinking, Time Psychology & Time Perspective." (Created and maintained by Wessel van Beek Vrije University, Netherlands.)

We authors are delighted that you are reading our book and are about to embark on your adventure into the new world of time perspective. We hope you will be entertained along the way, while you learn the profound ways that shaping your time perspective will enrich your life and your well-being.

part one

THE NEW SCIENCE OF TIME
How Time Works

one

WHY TIME MATTERS

YOUR TIME IS FINITE

In the eighteenth century, a secretive sect of men created a gruesome memorial to the importance of time in the dim, dusty basement of Santa Maria della Concezione, a nondescript church at the top of the Spanish Steps in Rome. Like the great St. Peter's, which towers nearby, the cramped walls of Santa Maria della Concezione are covered with individual tessera from which transcendent mosaics emerge. Unlike those in St. Peter's, the decorative tessera adorning the narrow confines of Santa Maria della Concezione are made not of colored glass but of discolored human bone. Hundreds of stacked skulls form Roman arches. Thousands of individual vertebrae create intricate mandalas. Smaller bones, perhaps from hands and feet, form chandeliers replete with lightbulbs. The complete skeleton of a small boy dangles from the ceiling holding the scales of justice in its bony hands. And fully dressed monks with withered skin still intact wait in reflective poses for eternity. The sheer spectacle is at once terrifying and enthralling.[1]

Capuchin monks, better known for giving the name of their distinctive hats to coffee topped with foam, or cappuccino, reinterred four thousand of their deceased brethren in this basement because their earlier "final resting place" had become the site of new construction. Despite its solemn content, the almost surreal Crypt of the Capuchin Monks with its posed corpses has the feel of a Hollywood movie set or an exceptionally well-done Halloween display.

Rooms in Santa Maria della Concezione

For most visitors, the crypt is a sight to be seen, not a site for serious contemplation, and tourists shuffle through it each year paying less homage to the dead before them than they do to works of art in the nearby Vatican museum.

To someone who is not eager to rush off to the next wonder on his itinerary, a deeper message reveals itself. For instance, when one of your authors, John Boyd, had an unexpected free afternoon to visit the Crypt of the Capuchin Monks, he noticed an inscription written on the floor at the foot of a pile of bones:

> *What you are, they once were.*
> *What they are, you will be.*

As he read that flowing script of twelve simple words, the past and future burst upon the present. In an instant, the skeletons ceased to be historical curiosities and became fellow travelers on life's fateful journey—our peers. Four hundred years of sunrises and sunsets, fifteen thousand days of feasts, famines, wars, and peace no longer separate us, becoming as inconsequential as the color of the monks' dried skin and ivoried bones, the medieval Latin they spoke, or the style of their robes. The inscription strips us of our well-honed psychological ability to ignore—even to deny—the inevitable: Our time on earth is limited. In the mere blink of the cosmic eye, we will join the billions of our ancestors who have lived, died, and become indistinguishable from the piles of bones in front of us.

The crypt is a solemn reminder to the living of our ultimate destiny. While Rome's other attractions display the life's work of some of the world's greatest artists, this crypt stores remnants of the lives themselves. If the bones could talk, they would tell stories of thousands of aspiring Leonardos, Michelangelos, and Raphaels lying there. Yet the crypt's silent message is not an admonition that we prepare for death but an impassioned plea that we live meaningfully and fully the lives we are living right now.

That is the subject of this book—time and your life: how you can strengthen, deepen, and even reinvent your relationship to it by using the exciting new discoveries we have made in our thirty-plus years of research on time. We want to share with you a new science and psychology of time that we developed based on personal, scholarly, and experimental investigations. Your personal attitudes toward time and those that you share with people around you have a powerful effect on all of human nature, yet their importance is underappreciated by most people, academics and laypeople alike. This is the first paradox of time: Your attitudes toward time have a profound impact on your life and your world, yet you seldom recognize it.

In the course of our work, we have identified six major attitudes toward time, or time perspectives. We will first help you to identify your personal time perspectives and then we will offer exercises designed to expand your time orientation and to help you make the most of your precious time. If our project succeeds, you will learn how to transform negative experiences into positive ones and how to capitalize on the positives in the present and the future without succumbing to blind devotion to either. Therein lies a second key paradox of time: Moderate attitudes toward the past, the present, and the future are indicative of health, while extreme attitudes are indicative of biases that lead predictably to unhealthy patterns of living. Our goal is to help you reclaim yesterday, enjoy today, and master tomorrow. To do so, we'll give you new ways of seeing and working with your past, present, and future.

Over three decades, we have given our questionnaires to more than ten thousand people. Colleagues of ours in more than fifteen countries around the world have used it with several more thousands. It's been rewarding to see individuals take this inventory and realize that they parcel their flow of personal experiences into mental categories or time zones. After we present the broad strokes of our discoveries in Part One, we'll get into how to use these perspectives for better health, more profitable investments, a more successful career and business, and more enjoyment of your personal relationships.

We hope that our discoveries will allow you to find better, different ways of living, freeing you from burdensome, outdated, or tired thoughts and actions to which your old perspective tied you. It's like the classic joke:

A guy from the city is walking down a country road past a farm when he sees a farmer feeding pigs in a highly unusual manner. The farmer is standing under an apple tree, holding up an enormous pig so that the pig can eat as many apples as it wants. The farmer moves the pig from one apple to another until the pig is satisfied, then the farmer starts again with another pig. The city man watches the farmer feed his pigs in this way for some time. Finally, he can't resist asking the farmer, "Excuse me. I can't help notice how hard it is for you to lift and carry and feed these pigs one by one at the apple tree. Wouldn't it save time if you just shook the tree and let the pigs eat what falls on the ground?" The farmer looks at the city guy with a puzzled expression and asks, "But what's time to a pig?"

What pigs are you carrying around that you need to let go of?

Before we get into our new psychology of time, we need to talk about the shared culture of time in which we live, and challenge some popular myths about time. Hopefully, you'll learn to see when you're looking the wrong way at time and when you can drop an old heavy pig of an attitude that simply doesn't serve you anymore.

TIME IS THE MEDIUM IN WHICH YOU LIVE

No man ever steps into the same river twice,
for it's not the same river and he's not the same man.
—Heraclitus

If one of the Capuchin monks awoke from his perpetual slumber and joined us in the twenty-first century, he would not recognize much of the world around him. The world has changed, but our monk may be in a better position than we are to understand the profound impact that time has had on our world. Just as fish may be unaware of the existence of the water in which they swim, most of us are unaware of the ceaselessly flowing time in which we live. Time's power often hits us only after a momentous event, the death of a loved one, a near-death experience, or a massive tragedy such as 9/11. We usually use time almost automatically, to schedule our hours and our days and to mark important life events like births, birthdays, and deaths. Time is the water that moves our stream of consciousness, but despite its centrality in our lives, we seldom reflect upon the ways in which time draws boundaries and gives direction and depth to our lives. For many of us, the time in which we are immersed is murky rather than gin-clean, and it prevents us from seeing up- and downstream. We may not even be aware of time until the stream runs dry, as it did for the monks of Santa Maria della Concezione.

THE ECONOMICS OF TIME

Remember that time is money.
—*Benjamin Franklin*[2]

Time is our most valuable possession. In classical economics, the rarer a resource and the more uses to which it may be put, the greater its value. Gold, for example, has no intrinsic value. It is no more than yellow metal. However, veins of gold on earth are rare, and gold has many uses. People first used gold to make jewelry; more recent, it has become a conductor in electronic components. The relation between scarcity and value is well known, so gold's exorbitant price comes as no surprise.

Most things that can be possessed—diamonds, gold, hundred-dollar bills—can be replenished. New diamond and gold deposits are discovered, and new bills are printed. Such is not the case with time. Nothing that any of us does in this life will allow us to accrue a moment's more time, and nothing will allow us to regain time misspent. Once time has passed, it is gone forever. So, although Ben Franklin was right about many things, he was wrong when he said that time is money. Our scarcest resource, time, is actually much more valuable than money.

We recognize the value of time implicitly in our daily transactions. Typically, the cost of time connotes its value. For example, we are often willing to pay a high price to use other people's time. The higher the price the more valuable the time: a five-hundred-dollar-an-hour lawyer is assumed to be better than a two-hundred-dollar-an-hour lawyer; handmade (translation: slowly made) goods are prized over machine-made goods; and meticulously prepared and eaten food is more valuable than fast food. In the same way, we may be willing to pay more highly for the privilege of conserving our own time. Overnight delivery and dry cleaning, direct flights, and convenience stores all exact premiums because of the inherent value that we place on our time.

In view of the many valuations we assign time, and in view of the fact that time is our most valuable commodity, it is striking to note how little thought we give to how we spend it. If a slightly annoying acquaintance asked you to invest money in her new business, you would probably consider the potential costs and benefits of the proposed transaction. If you judged her project a bad investment, you would have no problem saying no, even at the risk of offending her. After all, who rationally throws money out the window? But suppose the same acquaintance asked you to dinner. Chances are you would not engage in a similar cost-benefit analysis. No matter how little you wanted to go, you would probably take an hour out of your packed schedule to meet for dinner—all the while perhaps feeling resentment because of the time you sacrificed on something you did not want to do.

Why do we often spend our money more wisely than our time? Perhaps it's because we cannot save time; it passes whether we choose to spend it or not. Or perhaps it's because spending time can be intangible. In contrast, financial transactions involve deliberate action with material objects. For instance, you pay for your new alarm clock with a twenty-dollar bill and, in return, gain a material possession. But spending time seems less costly, and it is less closely associated with fungible assets. You can't bottle time and exchange it for an object or event.

On the other hand, perhaps we spend time so easily because we never learned to think about time. For most of history, people didn't have much choice in how to spend their time. They used it to survive, first individually and then collectively. They didn't have much time to "chill" when they needed to hunt and gather, spark fires, seek water, and build shelters. Only during the last few thousand years have people gained the luxury of discretionary time, and only during the last few hundred years have substantial segments of us enjoyed it—or endured it.

In reevaluating how we think about time—since time is more valuable than money—we're led to ask: Are we really putting the right valuations on time? Are people with the biggest bank accounts truly the wealthiest people in our world? How wealthy is someone who spends all of his time making money but doesn't take the time to enjoy life? How do we measure the wealth of people like fly-fishing guru Brent Fox, who chose the lower-paid profession of teaching because it gave him the freedom to build an "invisible mansion of time"? How can we measure the wealth of billionaire developers who spend all their time building mansions of brick and mortar but never enjoy those rooms? A financial planner helps to determine your investment strategy based upon your personal investment goals—if only there were such a person to call upon for investing time. To help figure that out, you'll have to become your own time investment planner and ask yourself these questions: What do *you* want out of life? How can you make your time matter? What is the right use of your time? Ultimately, you must be the arbiter of your personal investment choices, but our research suggests that people are more satisfied with investment in experiences, such as vacations, and in developing meaningful social relationships than with investment in material goods. Our research also suggests that everyone can benefit by looking more closely at time—what it is and what it means to us, and how we can see and use it in new ways that make our lives better.

These questions about time are in fact questions about the meaning of life, and to answer them for yourself, you may need a Bible, Torah, Koran, or quiet mountain stream. Even though we authors cannot offer you universal answers as you journey through this book, we will give you some new advice, strategies, and simple tactics, based upon decades of psychological research, that will allow you to deal more effectively and consciously with time.

Opportunity Cost and Your Time

Another economic principle relevant to our discussion of a new science of time is the concept of opportunity costs, which, in economics, refers to the expense involved in forgoing an opportunity. For example, if you decided to invest a thousand dollars in Google stock, you would lose the opportunity to invest this amount in Yahoo!, or in IBM, or in horse racing, or in just leaving the money in your piggy bank. Whatever you choose to do costs you the opportunity to do something else. The notion of opportunity costs recognizes that your investment resources are scarce and that there are expenses associated with choosing one investment over another. The opportunity costs that you incur with your time and money are omnipresent but always unknown and unknowable. No matter how you choose to invest your time, you face the costs of forgoing another activity—perhaps limitless opportunities—for the one you choose. With money, you have the conservative option of keeping it in the bank, but not so with time. Whether you like it or not, you spend time every moment of your life. It continually seeps out of your pocket. We are "the clocks on which time tells itself" (*Richard II*, Shakespeare).

Once you recognize that your investments of time have opportunity costs, you can become more conscious of how you make your choices about time, and learn to make happier ones. Remember that people are more likely to regret actions *not* taken than actions taken, regardless of outcome. In Shakespeare's words[3] again,

When to the sessions of sweet silent thought
I summon up remembrance of things past,
I sigh the lack of many a thing I sought,
And with old woes new wail my dear time's waste.

For example, a woman who wants to become a Hollywood star is more likely to regret *not* moving to Los Angeles and trying to get a part in a movie than to regret moving to Los Angeles and failing to become a star. So, as you learn in this book to be more proactive in your investments of your time, you will lose fewer opportunities and minimize regrets.[4]

Time matters because we are finite, because time is the medium in which we live our lives, and because there are costs (lost opportunities) associated with not investing time wisely.

THE PSYCHOLOGICAL RELATIVITY OF TIME

Time also matters because it is relative. You're no doubt familiar with this saying and aware of the physics behind it. Einstein's theory of relativity offers both the promise of unlimited energy and the specter of complete annihilation,[5] and it led to a fundamental shift in the way that we view our world and ourselves. But time is relative for more personal reasons than those so elegantly expressed in Einstein's equation. Time is not only subject to the objective laws of physics identified by Einstein and the frame-of-reference effects identified by Newton, but also to more subjective psychological processes. Your emotional state, personal time perspective, and the pace of life of the community in which you live all influence the way in which you experience time.

Scientific investigation of our physical world began in earnest during the Renaissance in the fifteenth and sixteenth centuries, but the scientific investigation of our psychological world began under two centuries ago. One clear finding psychology has made is that time is relative psychologically just as it is physically. Einstein himself is reported to have said:

When a man sits with a pretty girl for an hour, it seems like a minute. But let him sit on a hot stove for a minute and it's longer than any hour. That's relativity.[6]

A fundamental difference between physical laws and psychological principles is that physical laws are unchanging, but psychological principles are elastic: They bend and change according to the situation and frame of reference. You have some control over how these psychological principles bend and when they apply. The psychological term for this process is "construal," which refers to the way that each of us understands and explains the world. Once we understand psychological principles and the world, we can choose to construe the world in the way that is most productive, given our needs and resources.

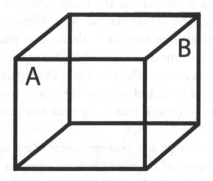

Take the well-known optical illusion above as an example of how people can choose to see the world in different ways. Sometimes people view the bottom Panel A as protruding from the image, and sometimes people view the top Panel B as protruding. Both perspectives are equally valid. But let's imagine for a minute that viewing Panel A as protruding results in a reward, and viewing Panel B as protruding results in punishment. Once you understand the relationship between your perspective and the outcome to which it leads, you quickly learn to view the figure from the most rewarding perspective.

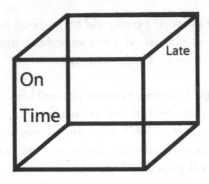

As the psychologist Robert Ornstein pointed out in his classic book *On the Experience of Time*, the perception of time is a cognitive process and is therefore subject to cognitive illusions, such as the Necker cube above.[7] In general, the more cognitive processing you do within a given period, the more time you judge to have passed. For example, researchers at Rice University found that people judge sounds that increase *or* decrease in pitch to be longer than sounds of the same duration and constant pitch. The direction of change does not matter. The amount of change drives the effect.[8] Simple changes in tone and volume can cause temporal illusions that lead people to believe that more time has passed than really has.

As you travel through life, you encounter many optical and temporal illusions, most of them much more complex than these examples. While there may be no "right" way to view the illusions, subjective reasons often make one perspective preferable to another. Viewing the world through one time perspective may result in success, while another may lead to failure. Viewing the world from a future perspective may lead you to be "on time," while viewing the world from a present perspective may lead you to be "late." Again, objectively, there is no difference in validity between the two perspectives, but in the subjective, complex social world in which we live, perspective often makes a difference. Society deems one perspective "right" and dismisses the other. That is, until someone as brilliant as Einstein comes along and reveals a completely new perspective.

We have no control over the laws of physics, but we do have some control over the frames of reference in which we view time. Recognizing how and when these frames of reference are advantageous may allow you to get more out of life and help you to recognize those occasions when time perspectives hinder and impede you. Sometimes perspectives are imposed upon you by society—by your religious upbringing, education, social class, or cultural background—but at other times you do have opportunities to choose them for yourself. Our goals in this book are to help you recognize your particular time perspective and the ways in which it influences your thoughts, feelings, and actions. Finally, we want to help you to develop mental flexibility and agility in choosing the time perspective that is most advantageous for each life puzzle you encounter.

FRAMING TIME IN THE REAL WORLD

Let's join a psychology experiment that was in progress in 1977. Social psychologists John Darley and Dan Batson are investigating how individual Princeton seminary students behave in preparation for giving a speech on the parable of the Good Samaritan.[9] The speech is to be presented in a studio building across campus and is to be evaluated by the seminarians' supervisors. As each student completes his preparation, he is told that: A) He is late for his presentation, that he was expected a few minutes ago, and that he must hurry to the studio; or B) He has plenty of time before his presentation, but he might as well head on over now. The only difference between the two conditions is the subtle manipulation of time pressure. The researchers are curious about how this manipulation of time will or will not affect behavior of these young men preparing for a lifetime of service.

As each student walks alone from the preparation classroom to the presentation studio, he encounters a person slumped and coughing in an alleyway, obviously in need of help. Unknown to the student, this person is an accomplice of the experimenters. With no other people nearby, the seminarians are faced with a choice between helping a stranger in distress—as a Good Samaritan should do—or passing him by to fulfill the obligation to give a speech about the importance of being a Good Samaritan. Would the students in the "late" condition be as likely to help the stranger in distress as the students in the "on time" condition? Doing the right thing for a seminarian ought to take precedence over saying the right thing, right? Not so!

The majority of students who believe that they had plenty of time before their speech—those in the "on time" condition—do stop to help. This behavior is consistent with their choice of vocation. People who have devoted their lives to helping others would be expected to help a stranger in distress. Remarkably, however, 90 percent of the students in the "late" condition fail to stop and help. They pass by the distressed person because they are headed in a future-oriented direction, and their mind-set is focused on not being late for the appointment. They go ahead to give the speech, despite the fact that all seminarians report in a post-study interview that they saw the person in distress.

How do we explain this dramatic difference in likeliness to help? Because the only difference between the two groups was their relation to time, we are forced to conclude that the manipulation of time caused the difference in behavior. A simple, subtle manipulation of time caused good, well-intentioned people to put their immediate concerns ahead of the welfare of someone obviously in need of assistance. Many of the seminarians behaved in ways that they themselves would probably find contemptible.

Darley and Batson's seminal research demonstrates that time perspective changes people's behavior. Nonetheless, the real world is obviously more complicated than a psychology experiment, so another social psychologist, Robert Levine, examined the ways in which time perspective works outside of the psychology lab. Levine calls the attitude toward time that he studies "pace of life,"[10] which emerges from the social behavior of each member of a community. Levine's research teams visit cities and measure walking speeds, clock accuracy, and the tempo of basic business transactions, such as buying stamps at the post office. Using these metrics, Levine has calculated the pace of life in dozens of cities around the world.

Western European countries lead the world in rapid pace of life, with Switzerland at the top of the list. Japan is also high on the index. Second-world countries are found predominantly at the bottom of the list. Of the thirty-one countries measured, Mexico has the slowest pace of life.

Levine has also measured the pace of life in thirty-six American cities by recording walking speed, bank teller speed, talking speed, and the frequency that watches are worn. Boston, New York, and other northeastern cities lead the list as the fastest cities in America, while Southern and Western cities are the slowest. Los Angeles is slowest of all.[11]

Levine's work shows clearly how pace of life, or the "hurry" factor, varies from city to city and from country to country. In addition, Levine investigated "helping behavior" in the same thirty-six American cities. He assessed the likelihood that a city resident would:

- Return a pen that someone "accidentally" dropped without noticing

- Help someone with a large leg brace pick up magazines that he had, again, "accidentally" dropped

- Help a blind person cross the street

- Give change for a quarter

- Mail a "lost" letter

- Donate to the United Way

Consistent with the findings from the Good Samaritan research, Levine found that in general, the cities with the fastest pace of life were the *least* helpful. Rochester, New York, which had a relatively slow pace of life for a northeastern city, was rated the most helpful city in America. New York, New York, ranked third in terms of pace of life, was rated the least helpful city in America. There were notable exceptions, however. California cities typically had slow paces of life but were consistently rated as less helpful than faster cities. This suggests that a slower pace of life may be a necessary but insufficient condition for altruism. Californians may have the time to help others but may be more interested in helping themselves to the good life.

Darley and Batson's work shows how an individual's relationship to time can influence important behaviors such as helping a stranger in distress. Levine's work documents how social relationships with time vary across nations and cities, and he essentially replicates the Darley and Batson findings in the real world.

A NEW PSYCHOLOGY OF TIME

We authors have been working on the psychology of time for about thirty years. We have focused on how aspects of our environment, such as the pace of life within a community, are internalized, become accepted and widespread, and ultimately influence an individual's thoughts, feelings, and behaviors. We believe that your individual attitude toward time is largely learned, and that you generally relate to time in an unconscious, subjective manner—and that, as you become more conscious of your attitude on time, you can change your perspective for the better. Each of us, in fact, has a time perspective that is largely unconscious and subjective. We all divide the continual flow of our experiences into time frames that help to give order, coherence, and meaning to events. These time frames may reflect cyclical patterns, such as the changing seasons, your monthly cycle, your children's birthdays, or they can reflect unique and singular linear events, like the death of a parent, the day of an accident, the start of a war. You use time perspectives in encoding, storing, and recalling your experiences; in feeling and being; in shaping expectations, goals, contingency plans; and in imagining scenarios.

In our work, we have consistently found that time perspective plays a fundamental role in the way people live. People tend to develop and overuse a particular time perspective—for example, focusing on the future, the present, or the past. Future-oriented people tend to be more successful professionally and academically, to eat well, to exercise regularly, and to schedule preventive doctor's exams. The "late" seminarians and other individuals who live in fast-paced communities are likely future-oriented and so are less willing to devote their time to altruistic pursuits.

In contrast, people who are predominantly present-oriented tend to be willing to help others but appear less willing or able to help themselves. In general, present-oriented people are more likely to engage in risky sexual behavior, to gamble, and to use drugs and alcohol than future-oriented people are. They are also less likely to exercise, to eat well, and to engage in preventive health practices such as flossing their teeth and getting regular doctor exams.

Consequently, future-oriented people are the most likely to be successful and the least likely to help others in need. Ironically, the people who are best able to help are the least likely to do so. In contrast, present-oriented people are less likely to be successful but are more likely to help others. Again ironically, individuals who are most likely to help others may be those least likely to help themselves. The situation is more complicated when we consider people whose primary time perspective is the past. For some, the past is filled with positive memories of family rituals, successes, and pleasures. For others, the past is filled with negative memories, a museum of torments, failures, and regrets. These divergent attitudes toward the past play dramatic roles in daily decisions because they become binding frames of reference that are carried in the minds of those with positive or negative past views.

How You Spend Today Ultimately Determines Both Your Past and Your Future

> *Who controls the past controls the future.*
> *Who controls the present controls the past.*
> *—George Orwell (party slogan from*
> *the Ministry of Truth, 1984)*[12]

The famous saying above from Orwell's novel *1984* is typically understood in the context of societal and governmental control. The segment of society that controls the present can rewrite the past and thereby control the future. The main character in *1984*, Winston, is employed in the Ministry of Truth, where he actively rewrites history as propaganda destined to appear in textbooks.

In spite of the negative context from which the above quote came, controlling the past, present, and future is equally important to everybody, including you, and your ability to cast your time consciously in a positive light is a good indicator of psychological and emotional health. We don't mean for you to be Pollyanna-ish in your optimism, but when you have control over your present, you can control your past and your future. In fact, you can reinterpret and rewrite your personal past, which can give you a greater sense of control over the future. In fact, all of psychotherapy can be seen as an attempt to work through the present to gain control over the past and thereby the future. Different psychological schools stress the importance of different temporal dimensions, although all of them work from the present. For example, psychoanalysis stresses the importance of the past; existential psychotherapy stresses the importance of the present; and humanistic psychotherapy stresses the importance of the future.

The present is more than the means through which you can *rewrite* the past. The present is also the medium through which you initially write into memory thoughts, feelings, and actions. Each decision and action in the present quickly becomes part of your past. Control of the present therefore allows you to determine what constitutes part of your past so that you can minimize the need to rewrite retrospectively. In the course of a typical day, you make hundreds of decisions, such as what to wear, what to eat, what to do with your free time, with whom to associate, and whom to avoid. On any given day, these decisions appear trivial, even inconsequential. Taken as a whole, they define who you were, who you are, and who you will become.

WHY THIS BOOK IS WORTH YOUR TIME

This book respects your time. Ernest Becker won a Pulitzer Prize for arguing that a universal fear of death is at the heart of the human condition. From Becker's perspective, the reality of death is psychologically unbearable, so we refuse to accept it. We universally deny death. Most important, we deny our own death. The Capuchin Crypt touches us precisely because it short-circuits a well-refined ability. Becker wrote:

> The idea of death, the fear of it, haunts the human animal like nothing else; it is a mainspring of human activity—activity designed largely to avoid the fatality of death, to overcome it by denying in some way that it is the final destiny for man.[13]

Death is the end of a lifetime. Denial of death is a denial that time will end. If you deny that time will end, you are likely to treat time much differently than you would if you felt time to be scarce and of limited duration. If you imagine your life as infinite, you are unlikely to value time as more precious than gold and more likely to treat it as ordinary grains of sand on a beach. Ironically, denying death relieves anxiety and psychological stress, but it may also lead you to devalue life, so you may live less fully.

This book is about living life fully, about squeezing life from every year, month, hour, minute, and second that you are allotted. We two authors have spent our lives observing how people spend time, and we want to help you get the most out of yours.

A TIMELY PERSONAL NOTE

As we are about to embark on this exciting journey into new time zones, your travel guides, Phil Zimbardo and John Boyd, would like to give you some background on why and how we got interested in studying time and how our discoveries have come to influence much of what we do in our lives.

For Phil, five experiences contributed to shaping a deep interest in time in general: being ill for a long time as a child; growing up in poverty; living in an Italian family; being blessed by dedicated elementary school teachers; and the Stanford prison experiment that he supervised. Later in the book, he'll go more into his illness, but here are his other recollections.

Growing up in the South Bronx, New York ghetto in the 1930s, we kids did not have things—toys, games, or books. But we did have people: our families as well as other kids with whom we would play in the streets every moment we were not in school or at home. We invented games and modified traditional games to keep them interesting. We could play stickball or softball for hours on end and never get tired. I developed a full appreciation of living totally in the present moment, but I gradually became aware of the dangers of impulsivity and being a daredevil. Some of my friends got hurt badly, and some died.

My Sicilian family encouraged a regard for our rich historical tradition, as well as a love of good food, wine, and music. I loved being allowed to stay up late to listen to family get-togethers when my father played the mandolin and Grandpa the guitar, backed by an uncle and cousin on guitar or another instrument. They would play and sing the familiar old songs until their fingers got numb or bloody from the strings. The songs would trigger memories of good times and loved family members now departed but still with us in vividly detailed memories.

Even though we were close, my family was relatively uneducated and did not value formal education, like many Italians from southern Italy in those days. They went to school only because it was required by law to do so, and then they went to work as soon as they could. But with limited marketable skills and no degrees, they all had menial dead-end jobs that kept them poor.

Thankfully, the dedicated teachers of my elementary school taught me to look beyond this powerful family and community example of living each day for whatever pleasure we could extract from it. They made it clear that hard work now was the only way to make it in the future, to be successful in the world. I actually loved school because it was clean, orderly, and predictable. You got out of it what you put into it. You just had to do what the teachers expected you to do, and you got gold stars, pencil rewards, and an honored place sitting in the first-row seat. Those dedicated teachers made me turn away from immediate gratification for the bigger rewards that came with delayed gratification, making me put schoolwork and homework before play and fooling around. In a sense, they were more like missionaries than ordinary teachers because they gave us lessons in living and surviving.

I carry those past lessons deep within me to this day.

In 1971 I conducted a now-infamous experiment, the Stanford prison experiment, on the Stanford University campus in order to investigate the power that social situations have to influence the behavior of ordinary people—in particular, how good people can be led to treat others badly. I divided the students into "prisoners" and "guards" and made one of the basements in a classroom building the location of this "prison." As superintendent of this Stanford prison, I learned another valuable lesson about time.

Even though the student-prisoners knew they would be part of this experiment for only a limited time, they didn't behave that way. They behaved as if they were trapped. Although the prisoners could have escaped their dismal daily grind by sharing with other prisoners their past identities and future hopes for when the experiment would be over, they rarely did so. Instead, the tape recordings we psychologists made of their conversations in their (bugged) cells revealed that the majority of their discussions were about the negative immediate aspects of their current situation: bad food, bad guards, bad work assignments, being put into solitary, and so on. Because they did not share who they were, or their future aspirations, before they were randomly assigned to the prisoner role, they knew little about one another except their humiliating, degrading identities as prisoners. I was struck that their experience was so much the opposite of my childhood experience, when I was hemmed in by circumstance and poverty but projected a future that was more positive. I also extracted whatever enjoyment I could from whatever current situation I found myself in order to survive. These mock prisoners had quickly imprisoned themselves in despair by focusing on very recent negative experiences of only days in a mock prison.

How can our long-held identities be changed so quickly? What is it that makes different people react to situations differently? Searching for answers, I began my research into time perspectives. My early research on time perspective got a big boost when John Boyd joined my research team at Stanford University back in 1994. Together, we developed a reliable, valid measure of time perspective. After three decades of research, John's and my ideas have influenced researchers around the world, and I am more convinced than ever that time perspective is one of the most powerful influences on human thought, feeling, and action—and the least recognized or appreciated.

Let's hear John's personal side of this time tale:

A unique combination of nature and nurture led me through—and to—time. Naturally shy and introverted as a child, I spent my early years in the forests of South Lake Tahoe, California, with imaginary cowboys and Indians as my friends. As I entered kindergarten, my dad took a job at the UCLA University Elementary School, and my family moved to Los Angeles, California. This urban environment contrasted dramatically with the remoteness of Tahoe that I was used to, and it took me a while to adjust to the hustle and bustle of the big city—and all the real people.

One day when my mother arrived at my kindergarten class to pick me up for an appointment, class was at recess, but when she searched the playground, she couldn't find me. Somewhat alarmed, she retreated to the classroom and asked my teacher where I was. "Did you check in the tree in the middle of the playground?" my teacher replied. "He spends most recesses there, watching the other kids play." There she found me, perched high atop that lone tree in the middle of the blacktop. I spend less time in trees today, but continue to be fascinated by people's behavior, questioning why they do what they do and why they view life as they do.

As with Phil, public education played a large role in the development of my time perspective. I felt its influence in the classroom and at home. Both of my parents had successful careers as public educators. In addition, my mother has her doctorate in education, my father his master's degree. They started their careers as public school teachers and will end them as principals and superintendents. As a result of their influence and my own academic interests, I developed a future orientation that nearly matches Phil's.

Then I turned eighteen, and my parents divorced after nearly twenty years of marriage. I was shocked and confused. I had expected to spend the next twenty years of my life working to obtain the life that my father was giving up. The fact that he suddenly seemed to want something different didn't make sense. During a very memorable conversation, I asked my dad what had changed in his life from the time when he was my age to his current age of forty. He answered as honestly as he could, but people don't always know why they change. Sometimes they just do. The best answer that he and I could come up with was that he had been resisting change for some time but could no longer do so and stay true to himself. That very day I resolved not to save all of my change until I turned forty. I resolved to have what I termed a *little midlife crisis* each day of my life in the hope of avoiding a larger one once I reached forty.

I turned forty recently, and my strategy appears to have worked, to some extent. I have not avoided the changes that naturally accompany aging, but I have been better able to embrace the changes that occurred between eighteen and forty. I learned not to fight time but to surrender myself to it. I married later in life and have worked to welcome change in my marriage and myself. Although I've avoided the desire for sudden dramatic change, I continue to work on listening to my own advice in other areas. While I love fly-fishing, woodworking, traveling, and spending time with family and friends, sometimes my future time perspective still gets in the way.

Professionally, I have pursued my passions, which include psychology, time, technology, and the interaction of the three. My initial psychological research at Stanford, in fact, attempted to explain why people do things that are often considered crazy—for instance, sui-

cide bombing. I speculated that the answers are not cut-and-dried
nor simplistic, that they must unfold according to a highly personal
view of time and a person's place within it. I found that much of the
field of psychology had intentionally blinded itself to the effect of
beliefs about the distant future, because such beliefs are strongly
associated with religiosity, which approaches the level of a taboo
subject within mainstream psychology. Ultimately, my work validated
Phil's early work and extended it further into the future, as you will
see in Chapter Six. We have been collaborating on research for the
last fourteen years. Between us, we have lived fifty-two years since
we began research in earnest. During that time, we have interviewed
and worked with tens of thousands of students and thousands of
human experimental participants to develop the insights we'll now
share with you.

This book is an investment guide for your future. Time matters,
no matter who you are, where you live, how old you are, or what
you do. Whether you drink alone or are a leader of nations, time
matters. Whether you are a single mom, an executive, a teacher,
student, or prisoner, time matters. Whether you are a laid-back hedonist or a vigorously aspiring Type A workaholic, time matters.
Your time is precious. You pass through this life only once, so it is
vital that you make the most of the journey.

The ideal we want you to develop is a balanced time perspective
in place of a narrowly focused single time zone. A balanced time
perspective will allow you to flexibly shift from past to present to
future in response to the demands of the situation facing you so
that you can make optimal decisions. However, while we advise,
you must consent. You will have to make a commitment to learn
and to change in order to get the best return on your investment.
You are the only one who can make your time matter. If not you,
who? If not *now*, when?

Time-out One: Match the quote to the author and era

Quote		Author
1. Dost thou love life? Then do not squander time, for that is the stuff life is made of.		A. Elizabeth I (1533–1603)
2. All my possessions for a moment of time.		B. Theophrastus (371–287 B.C.)
3. Time is the most valuable thing a man can spend.		C. Benjamin Franklin (1706–1790)
4. Your time is limited, so don't waste it living someone else's life. . . . Everything else is secondary.		D. Charles Darwin (1809–1882)
5. Time is the coin of your life. It is the only coin you have, and only you can determine how it will be spent. Be careful lest you let other people spend it for you.		E. François Rabelais (1494–1553)
6. Nothing is so dear and precious as time.		F. Carl Sandburg (1878–1967)
7. A man who dares to waste one hour of time has not discovered the value of life.		G. Plutarch (~46 A.D.–c. 120)
8. Time is the measuring by the soul of its expectation, its attention and its memory.		H. Saint Augustine (354–430)
9. Pythagoras, when he was asked what time was, answered that it was the soul of this world.		I. Baltasar Gracian (1601–1658)
10. All that really belongs to us is time; even he who has nothing else has that.		J. John Randolph (1773–1833)
11. Time is at once the most valuable and the most perishable of all our possessions.		K. Steve Jobs (2005)
12. You can ask me for anything you like, except time.		L. Napoleon (1769–1821)

Answers: 1. C; 2. A; 3. B; 4. K; 5. F; 6. E; 7. D; 8. H; 9. G; 10. I; 11. J; 12. L.

two

TIME

A Retrospective on
Time Perspectives

Change alone is unchanging.
—Heraclitus

According to Carl Sagan's famous Cosmic Calendar, the earth formed in September of the first year in the life of the cosmos.[1] Dinosaurs emerged on Christmas Eve, and apes appeared at 10:15 P.M. on December 30. Our first human ancestors walked upright at 9:42 P.M. on December 31, and the first anatomically modern humans appeared at 10:30 P.M. Today is the first second of the cosmic year number two. The 364 days, 10 hours, and 30 minutes of the first year before humans appeared were eventful. Galaxies formed, solar systems balanced their delicately synchronized orbits, and planets filled them. For Sagan, a cosmologist, this vast universe is the backdrop against which time is measured:

> The world is very old, and human beings are very young. Significant events in our personal lives are measured in years or less; our lifetimes in decades; our family genealogies in centuries; and all of recorded history in millennia. But we have been preceded by an awesome vista of time, extending for prodigious periods into the past, about which we know little—both because there were no written records and because we

have real difficulty in grasping the immensity of the intervals involved.

—Carl Sagan, The Dragons of Eden

Sagan measured distance in light-years and time in millennia. Most of us measure time against the linear chart of our lives. These lives may be but brief flickers in the grand vastness of the cosmos, but they are all we have. They matter to us. From this life-bound perspective, birthdays and deaths mark the beginning, passing, and end of our personal time. To us, a hundred years is a long lifetime, and a thousand years seems an eternity. We view each birth as the arrival and each death as the departure from life. At birth, each of us is a completely new instance of life, but each of us is cast from a mold that is as old as the cosmos. Those first 364 days on Sagan's calendar were not spent idly. They were spent creating us.

YOU ARE A LIVING ANACHRONISM

Because of the rapid change in the world around us since our birth, we humans are living anachronisms. Our world has changed dramatically in the past 150 years. Human physiology, in contrast, took millions of years to create and has not changed much in 150,000 years. Your body—even if it is in mint condition—is designed for success in the *past.* It is an antique biological machine that evolved in response to a world that no longer exists. Although we live in a world in which computer processing speed doubles roughly every twenty-four months,[2] human information processing has not expanded substantially over the past 150,000 years. Our physiology is clearly behind the times.

We are hertz machines in a megahertz world. For an average human, simple reaction time is about 250 milliseconds. Simple reaction time is the time that it takes to react to a stimulus, such as pushing a button when a light goes on. Therefore, each "cycle" of light input and button depression response takes a quarter second. Four complete cycles can take place each second. Thus, a typical human has a processing speed of about four hertz. In comparison, modern desktop computers have central processing unit (the "brain" of a computer) clock speeds of over three gigahertz; they are roughly 750,000,000 times faster than we are.[3]

This relatively slow processing speed has two important implications. First, it means that all of us live more than 250 milliseconds in the past.[4] Our bodies take approximately that long to register things going on around us, such as a light turning on. We take even longer to perceive sound, because the speed of sound is much slower than the speed of light.

Second, because our mental CPU runs slowly, we humans have to be careful about how much time we spend thinking about any one thing. We protect our mental cycles, much as a miser guards his money. Psychologists have actually coined a term for this tendency, calling humans "cognitive misers."[5] In daily life, when faced with routine decisions, people conserve their thought cycles and rely instead on mental heuristics[6]—simple, practical rules of thumb that we learn through trial and error. We save our judgment and decision-making skills for thinking about the novel, unpredictable, and dangerous forces in our lives: indeed, for predicting the future. Unfortunately, what has worked in the past may not work well in the immediate present, especially if now differs from then. Furthermore, our past successes are not automatically reproduced in the future, as much as we wish they were.

THE STATE OF NATURE AND EVENT TIME

Since time immemorial mankind has been undergoing a process of cultural development. . . . To this process we owe the best that we have become, and a good part of that from which we suffer.
—Sigmund Freud, from "Why War?,"
an open letter to Albert Einstein[7]

If human physiology has not changed in 150,000 years, what has? Let's drift back in time to 10:30 P.M. on December 31 on Sagan's cosmic calendar and meet a common distant relative, Tag, at twenty-one years old, an elder clansman in his social circle. He's in East Africa with his mate, Eve, two children, and a clan of approximately forty other nascent humans. His 'hood covers about a hundred square miles of rolling grasslands, mantled in thick rain forests. Trees provide a nearly constant source of food that Tag supplements with monkey and rodent meat.

In many ways, Tag has it good. There is no harsh winter to endure—as there is at more northern and southern latitudes—and the land provides all that he needs. Tag's clan lives, loves, and works together before the advent of modern scourges such as drugs, gang violence, the impending collapse of the retirement system, and the humiliation of not having his children selected to attend the most prestigious day-care center in town. But Tag, too, has vital concerns. Foremost among them is the fear that he and his family will be killed and eaten by wild beasts, a real possibility. Tag also worries about slightly less wild beasts—namely, men from a nearby clan. Tag saw the way the men looked at the lovely Eve when the clans met on opposite sides of the river, and he fears that one of these men will drop a rock on his head as he sleeps. Whenever his fears of immediate death are assuaged, Tag turns his thoughts toward another of the notorious F's (Fighting, Fleeing, Feeding, and Sex), and the procurement and satisfaction of one of these occupies much of his time: Food. Eating means finding food in a location where he and his clan are more likely to eat than be eaten. After eating, if time is left in his day, he turns his attention to other F's.

Thomas Hobbes famously characterized the lives of Tag and his contemporaries in the state of nature as "solitary, poor, nasty, brutish, and short."[8] While Tag's life is not solitary, it is no doubt poor, nasty, and brutish, which he accepts. Nevertheless, the fact that Tag's life could be short keeps him up at night. In fact, Tag spends many cognitive cycles thinking about the many ways that he might meet his end and how to protect against them.

Because of his healthy obsession with avoiding his own death, Tag's conception of time is almost completely present-oriented. He focuses on avoiding things that could kill him today and ignores things that might kill him tomorrow. He has no need for a calendar that marks the passing of days, weeks, months, and years. If he lives long enough, Tag will be susceptible to the very same chronic maladies of aging that he will pass on to us—cancer and heart disease. Instead, he focuses on more pressing threats and lives by this mantra: Keep your eyes, ears, and attention on the present, or it will kill you. Tag worries little about saving for a rainy day, instead spending rainy days as he does the others—trying to save himself. If someone were to give Tag a sunflower seed, he would not plant it but eat it.

If we could ask Tag what he thinks about time, he would not understand the question. His present-oriented life does not require conceptions of the past or the future, so he has no vocabulary for describing time. Like the Pirahã, a happy and harmonious tribe of 350 people who live along the Maici River in Southwest Brazil today, Tag's present orientation is so complete that he and his people have no words to describe a time beyond the time of a single day.[9] The Pirahã have no words for the past or future. They live today in an expanded present, much the way that Tag lives at 10:30 P.M. on December 31 on the cosmic calendar. They enjoy today and don't worry about tomorrow.

The lives of the Pirahã and Tag are organized and governed by "event" time—the time when events occur in the environment—for example, when the sun is high in the sky, when a species of birds sings, or when the tide comes in. The process and progress of events give order and structure to their lives. Meals, dances, and musical performances start when the time feels right, not when the hands of a clock say the events should start.[10] This detachment of event time from clock time can be extremely unnerving for those of us who are accustomed to organizing our lives around clock time.

Years ago, while vacationing in Bali, our colleague Patricia wanted to attend a dance performance by a local group. People who had seen the show raved about it. A drama teacher at Stanford University, Patricia eagerly awaited the performance.[11] However, after looking in all of the logical places—newspapers, bulletin boards, and printed signs, she could not figure out when the performance started, so she approached a local man to get the right time.

Time-out One: The Vocabulary of the Expanded Present

Pirahã Word	Meaning	Literal Translation
ʼahoapió	another day	other at fire
soʼóá	already	time-wear
ahoái	night	be at fire
ʼahoakohoaihio	early morning, before sunrise	at fire inside eat go
piʼi	now	now
kahaiʼaiiʼogiiso	full moon	moon big temporal
piiáiso	low water	water skinny temporal
hibigibagáʼáiso	sunset/sunrise	he touch come be temporal
hisó	during the day	in sun
hisóogiái	noon	in sun big be
hoa	day	fire
piibigaiso	high water	water thick temporal

Pat: Excuse me, please. What time does the dance performance start tonight?

Local: After dinner, when it gets dark.

Pat: Okay, right after dinner?

Local: Sometimes, but not usually.

Pat [mildly frustrated]: So, later. Like nine P.M.?

Local [casually]: Sometimes, but usually before.

Pat [exasperated]: So, like, seven P.M.?

Local: Sometimes, but sometimes there is no show.

Pat [irate]: What do you mean, sometimes there is no show?

Local: If the time is not right or the dancers don't feel like dancing, then they don't dance.

Pat [calming herself and trying a new tactic]: So when do people start showing up to see the show?

Local: They start coming before dinner, but some come after the show starts.

For the sake of brevity, we will end the dialogue here, but it took a lot more questions before our flustered friend realized that she and the local man were speaking different languages—figuratively. Even though they both spoke English, Pat was speaking the language of clock time, while the local was speaking the language of event time. For the local, the dancers and the audience together unconsciously negotiated the starting time of the performance. Social consensus determined when the performance started, when the time was right. For Pat, as most likely for you, clocks determine when special events should and do start. In the end, Pat and her friends learned to understand the language of event time and acquired a new sensitivity to the influence that culture has on time.

Tag's Temporal Legacy

Alas, Tag's life ended at the ripe old age of twenty-five, but not before he fathered eight children, two of whom survived their tenth birthday, and one of whom is a direct ancestor of ours. Between Tag, Eve, and us stretches a long line of brave people who progressively left behind their present-oriented lives for a new perspective that embraces the future. Our prescient relatives began to look beyond a single day/night cycle to lunar cycles and then to seasons. They noticed consistencies in nature, that cold winters regularly gave way to bountiful springs, that hot summers lasted a predictable number of days, that cool fall mornings portended the return of winter, and that the cycle was repeated each year. To take advantage of this seminal insight, they began to plant crops in the spring and harvest them in the late summer and fall. They also noticed that animals give birth when the weather is good and food is plentiful.

First, their observations allowed them merely to subsist. Nevertheless, as time passed, their skill as farmers allowed their society to develop other pursuits and vocations. A fortunate few were free to devote their time to new endeavors and even enjoy discretionary time.

Nearly all of these new activities related to that most troubling aspect of life, the point on which Hobbes had hit—that life was short. People worked to eliminate the things that were most likely to kill them, the most pressing threats to their survival. Wild animals were killed and separated from people. Shelters were erected to protect families from the elements. Foodstuffs were stored to prepare for hard times. As our ancestors succeeded in eliminating threats, they were free to look further into the future without the fear that they would be killed if they took their eyes off the present. So began our incessant march into the future.

Abdul's Time

Abdul, a descendent of Tag's and an ancestor of yours, lived at about 11:59:52 P.M. on December 31st on the cosmic calendar—about 2,500 years ago. A cobbler, Abdul sold shoes from his small shop near the center of a town in what is now Egypt. Most of his customers were locals, but he also did a brisk trade with travelers and merchants who were passing through. Earlier in life, Abdul imagined joining the travelers to seek adventures to the east, but now his place was with his family, wife, four children, and six grandchildren. Recent talk of war troubled him—his son had been conscripted into the army—and his youngest daughter would reach marrying age soon and need a dowry. She had dreamed of a large traditional wedding from the time she was little, and he did not want to disappoint her, even if it meant adding more calluses to his worn hands as he made more shoes.

Unlike Tag, Abdul seldom worried about the present, although his clients often regaled him with tales of their encounters with exotic beasts in the East. He talked about time and what the future held and organized his day according to the shadows the sun cast around the obelisk in the town square. The then-new Egyptian calendar, like our modern calendar, had 12 months and 365 days. Months, however, had only three weeks, each consisting of ten days. Twelve months of 30 days each accounted for 360 days, but the Egyptians pragmatically added 5 "extra" days at the end of the year to more closely match the 365-day solar year. Despite its shortcomings, this calendar was an improvement over their previous reckoning of time, which was based on the seasonal flooding of the Nile.

Abdul usually opened his shop as the first rays of sunlight touched the tip of the obelisk, since the travelers he planned to greet began their journeys during the cool morning hours. Abdul closed his shop when the last sliver of sunlight slipped off the obelisk at the end of the day. Customers were often waiting for him when he opened his shop for business in the morning, but his shop opened when it opened, and if they needed shoes, they waited and passed time talking with others. Abdul lived between event time and clock time, a time that was yet to come. If someone gave a sunflower seed to Abdul or a contemporary, he might eat it, or he might plant it, depending upon how hungry he was.

THE TRANSITION TO CLOCK TIME

After Abdul's life, time continued to change. Julius Caesar's Julian calendar, which replaced the Roman calendar in 45 B.C., eliminated the need for extra days—and occasionally extra months. The Gregorian calendar in turn replaced the Julian calendar in 1582. After 1854, timekeeping became more precise and timepieces more compact.[12] Train conductors and wealthy people began to wear pocket watches, products of the Industrial Revolution; the watches quickly became status symbols. In 1884 Britain adopted the standard Greenwich Mean Time, which did away with the confusion that arose from the different time standards that each town observed. A universal "standard" time allowed trains to be scheduled with much greater precision and safety. Before then, trains ran according to the

clock in the town where the train company headquarters was located.[13]

Edward, a descendent of Abdul's, lived at 11:59:59 P.M. on Sagan's calendar, or about 150 years ago in England. Like Abdul,
Edward was a cobbler but closed his shop in a small English village
because he could not compete with the lower-priced shoes produced
by a new factory. On a good day, working for himself, Edward
could make five pairs of shoes by hand, but on any day, relatively
unskilled factory workers could make five pairs of shoes an hour.
He could not beat them, so he joined them and moved to Birming-
ham to work in the factory.

Edward's change in job location also required him to change how
he thought about time, which, in many ways, was no longer his
own. The sound of the factory whistle and the cadence of the machines now ruled Edward's life. The whistle told him when to get
up, when to report for work, and when to leave for home. When he
was out of reach of the factory whistle, church bells and his new
pocket watch kept Edward firmly tethered to the rhythms of the
industrial city. By the nineteenth century, a simple fear of a short life
had transformed the world so profoundly that time was no longer
measured solely against the rhythms of the natural world. Time had
become the currency—the very foundation—of social life. Stores
opened on it, people worshipped according to it, train schedules
were built upon it, and theatrical performances began on it. Even
mundane events such as afternoon tea had a prescribed time. If
someone gave Edward or a contemporary of his a sunflower seed,
one man would plant it, another would tend it and watch it grow,
and another would sell the flower.

The transition from event time to clock time profoundly changed
society, especially economic relations. For example, when Abdul
needed money for his daughter's dowry, he simply made and sold
more shoes. Edward had a daughter as well, but making and selling
more shoes would not make Edward any more money. To make
more money, Edward had to devote more time to making shoes,
which meant that he had to work overtime. Abdul sold his shoes,
but Edward—and most of us today—sold his time. If Edward

Time-out Two: The Vocabulary of the Expanded Present

Keeping Watch

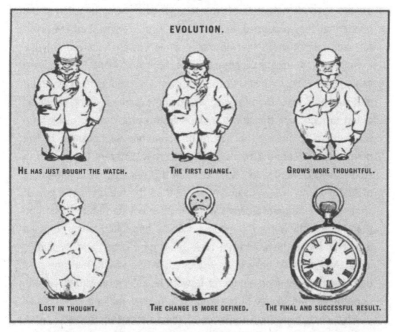

EVOLUTION.

HE HAS JUST BOUGHT THE WATCH.   THE FIRST CHANGE.   GROWS MORE THOUGHTFUL.

LOST IN THOUGHT.   THE CHANGE IS MORE DEFINED.   THE FINAL AND SUCCESSFUL RESULT.

This little man had trouble with every watch he ever bought, until he found one that so pleased him that he could not stop looking at it, and from constant attention he underwent the following series of changes. *Based on an 1888 illustration from* The Waterbury, *an advertising almanac published from about 1887 to 1895.*

made fifty or a hundred pairs of shoes during a day, his wages remained the same. Usually, Edward had only a fixed amount of his time to sell, whether he used the time efficiently or not. On some days, when factory orders were down, Edward was assigned a fixed number of shoes to make. In these cases, Edward's reward for finishing his work in half a day was half a day's pay. It was therefore in Edward's financial interest to ensure that his assigned task filled the time that he was willing to sell to the factory. Efficiency was not Edward's priority. Filling the time that he had to sell was. For Edward, time was money.

Time-out Three: Marx, Power, Labor, and Time

Karl Marx believed that workers in the industrialized world were exploited because they did not receive payment for the full value of the goods that they produced. For example, Abdul received all the profit for each pair of shoes that he made, while Edward received only his hourly wage. From Marx's point of view, both Abdul and Edward were selling their labor. It followed that if Edward worked as hard as Abdul and was paid less, then Edward was being exploited. Marx, however, failed to recognize that the transition from event time to clock time fundamentally altered the nature of economic relationships to the point that Abdul and Edward sold completely different things. Abdul sold shoes; Edward sold his time. From this perspective, exploitation of Abdul would involve paying him less than the full price of a pair of shoes. Exploitation of Edward would involve paying him for less time than he actually worked. Similarly, if Abdul had taken longer to make a pair of shoes, he would not have been paid more, and by Marx's logic, Abdul would have been exploited. While selling his time may not have been as good a deal for Edward as selling his shoes, he was nonetheless fully aware of the trade that he was making.

Physicists have long understood the relationship between work and time and actually define Work as Power x Time. Like Marx, physicists are also interested in Power, and physicists define Power as Force x Distance / Time. While the laws of physics did not change during the Industrial Revolution, the human relationship to time did. We transitioned from an event-based and product-based economy to a time-based economy in which we are paid per unit sold, if hourly, or lump sum, if salaried.

Factory owners had great incentive to get as much value as possible out of the time that they purchased from their employees. Enter a man named Frederick Winslow Taylor, the father of scientific management.[14] Taylor felt that there was a right way and a wrong way to do everything, including basic tasks such as shoveling coal, stamping parts, and making shoes. The "right" way was the way that completed a desired task in as little time as possible. The "wrong" way was any way that wasted time or money. Taylor conducted time and motion studies that timed workers as they performed their jobs; then he identified techniques that would allow workers to complete their jobs in as little time as possible. The most efficient techniques could be propagated throughout a factory. For Taylor, time really was money, and he worked to ensure that companies received the best value for the time that they purchased from their employees. Time became a commodity that could be saved, spent, wasted, earned, and even lost. To his credit, Taylor felt that employees should be compensated for adopting time-efficient methods. Not surprising, many employees saw his efforts as a management ploy to get them to work harder for the same amount of pay. This contentious issue continues to occupy labor/management negotiations today.

TIME TODAY

The relentless striving to lengthen our individual and collective futures shaped the course of human history, and today we continue to push most threats to our survival further into the future. Life expectancy has increased by 300 percent over the last few thousand years, from about twenty-five to over seventy-five years. The general quality of our lives has improved as well. Two hundred years ago, 90 percent of the population farmed. Today under 4 percent do.[15] A century ago in the United States, 80 percent of an average family of five's income went toward housing, food, and clothing. Ten percent of this income came from the children.[16] By 2002, under 1 percent of an average family of 2.5's income came from children, and only 50 percent of the family's total income went to housing, food, and clothing. Much more time now is spent on entertainment, travel, hobbies, and having fun. Clearly, the allegedly "good old days" were not all that good for everyone.

Time-out Four: Average Minutes Spent in Waking Life Activities* [17]

Life Activity*	Type of Media	Average Minutes/Person
Media use (not combined with other activity)		226
Media use (combined with other activity)		296
	Television	266
	Radio	109
	Internet	137
	Computer (non-Internet)	143
	Phone	45
	Music	109
	Books, newspapers, and magazines	52
	Video	101
	Game console	75
	Other	52
Work[†]		157
Social activity		62
Meal eating		49
Housework		41
Personal needs (grooming)		28
Meal preparation		24
Child care		22
Shopping/services		17
Education		12
Sports/hobbies		8
Exercise		6
Religion		5
Events		3
Organizations		2
Other or unknown		95

* Based on an observed day of 757 minutes.
† Not all participants worked, and observations were spread across all seven days of the week.

Time-out Five:
The Most Common
English Nouns[19]

1. **Time**
2. Person
3. **Year**
4. Way
5. **Day**
6. Thing
7. Man
8. World
9. Life
10. Hand

We now find ourselves obsessed with Internet time, daily news, monthly reports, financial quarters, and school years. We have created and so completely adapted to clock time that many of us feel naked without a wristwatch. Curiously, time has permeated our lives so completely that wristwatch sales in 2007 were down. Although time has not become less important—because cell phones, PDAs, laptops, and iPods all display the time—watches have become redundant.[18]

Our lives, years, months, days, hours, minutes, and even seconds are scheduled. For example, our use of electronic media—use of televisions, radios, computers, phones, iPods and MP3s, videos, and game players—now accounts for an average of slightly under eight hours (470 minutes) in an average American's typical twelve-and-a-half-hour day. Over three hours of this time (202 minutes) is spent entirely focused on electronic media. Only fifty-two minutes—or 7 percent of the day—is spent reading books and other printed media. The remaining four-plus hours are spent using media and performing other nonmedia activities concurrently. None of these media innovations—except print—existed 150 years ago. It's easy to see why we don't have time to be eaten by lions anymore.

Time Trumps Sex

Our preoccupation with time is so complete that the word "time" has become the most popular noun in the English language.[20] In fact, time-related words occupy three of the top ten spots. A search on Yahoo.com for "time" results in more than 7 billion hits. In contrast, there are fewer than 3 billion hits for "money" and less than a billion hits for "sex." Time-related words are also woven into works of art that express our complicated relationship with time or seek to inculcate the audience with socially sanctioned attitudes toward time. For example, the fairy tale "The Three Little Pigs" encourages children to prepare for the future and protect themselves. The idea that a wild beast can kill you is not new. Ancient Tag could have told us that. What is relatively new is the recognition that the threat exists in the future and that we can avoid it through wise preparation. Time is also a consistent theme in song and literature. Some artists lament its passing, while others lament that it is not passing more quickly. Time even influenced postmodern artists such as Picasso, Braque, and Dalí. Picasso and Braque's cubist style, for instance, depicts people and objects as they exist from all perspectives simultaneously, while Salvador Dalí's *Persistence of Memory* depicts the malleability and relativity of time.

Today we look further into the future than ever before. We need to, for our actions today will affect the world that our

Time-out Six:
Fairy Tales About Time

"The Three Little Pigs" (1843)

"The Three Little Pigs" is a story about the need to prepare for the future. The first little pig builds a house of straw. The big bad wolf huffs and puffs and blows the house down. He then eats the first little pig. The second little pig builds a house of sticks. Its construction takes more planning and work than the first pig's house of straw, but the wolf still manages to blow the house down. The wolf then eats the second pig. The third little pig, however, has more foresight and is more assiduous than his brothers. He builds a house of brick. The wolf can't blow the house down. In more recent versions, the first two pigs are not eaten but instead move in with the third pig. In a commercial version, they kill the wolf and sell his fur.

"The Ugly Duckling" (1843)

"The Ugly Duckling" is a story about patience and the transformational power of time. The ugly duckling is hatched in a barnyard with ducks and believes that he, too, is a duck. The ugly duckling never fits in and ultimately leaves the barnyard feeling ashamed and worthless. After nearly dying during a harsh winter, the ugly duckling encounters a flock of swans that he finds breathtakingly beautiful. Although the ducks in the barnyard had been cruel, the swans treat the ugly duckling with warmth, love, and respect. At first he questions why the swans treat him so well. Then one day the ugly duckling looks into the water and sees his reflection. He is thrilled and surprised to see that time has transformed him into a beautiful swan.

Peter Pan *(1902)*

Peter Pan is a story about the magic of the present and a boy who refuses to grow up. By not growing up, Peter avoids the future orientation that is necessary to cope with the demands and responsibilities of adulthood. In the novel, the love of Peter's life, Wendy, returns to the real world from Neverland. Twenty years pass, and Peter—still a boy—returns to the real

descendents will inherit millennia from now. Nuclear waste, nuclear winter, and nuclear war all have the potential to end our future completely. Global warming is a proved scientific reality. Unless all nations immediately begin to reduce carbon emissions and induce fundamental changes in energy conservation and waste reduction, global catastrophes await us in the near future.

As we look further into the future, we are forced to do more in the present. Cell phones ring incessantly; e-mails pile up in our in-boxes; TV shows, movies, and books all cry for our attention. Many people in modern societies report feeling a time crunch, a sense of being continually hurried and pressed for time. Today more people are looking to balance the demands on their time. If we each balance our time, we may be able to extend our streak of evolutionary good fortune to something that approaches the periods contemplated by Carl Sagan.[21] However, individuals no longer live in contained, isolated villages. For better or for worse, we are all part of a common global village, and the outcome will depend on our and many other nations' actions, as well as our perception of the threat to our time on earth.

REACTIONS AGAINST CHANGE

Change has always been challenging, largely unwelcome, and ever present. As Heraclitus said 2,500 years ago, "Change alone is unchanging." He could have added "no matter how much we prefer otherwise." Contemporary thinkers agree and have identified the *rate* of this change as especially problematic. For example, over forty years ago, organizational psychologists Warren Bennis and Philip Slater argued that the world was changing so rapidly that everything—careers, homes, roles, and responsibilities— would soon be temporary.[22] More recent, James Gleick documented the acceleration of everything in his tour de force, *Faster*.[23] Fortunately, if everything accelerates at the same pace, the relative position between things will remain constant. Gleick's arguments echo those of Bennis, Slater, and

world to find that Wendy has aged while Peter has not. Peter weeps when he learns that Wendy has gotten married and had children, while he refused to grow up. In the end, Peter's refusal to grow up prevents him from leading a normal life. Most theatrical versions focus on the magic of the present, which continues to captivate children and adults alike.

Cinderella (*860 A.D. in China, 1697 in France, 1950 in U.S.A.*)
Cinderella has been told for centuries around the world. The 1950 Walt Disney version stresses the need for punctuality. Cinderella stays out past her midnight curfew, and as a result, her beautiful gown turns to rags, her attendants turn into mice, and her coach turns into a pumpkin. The moral of *Cinderella* is that punctuality can lift the peasants among us to become equals of royalty. Another moral is that you must always be guided by your awareness of time because you can lose everything by getting too caught up in fleeting momentary pleasures.

Rip Van Winkle (1819)

Rip Van Winkle is about the need to use time wisely, lest it be lost forever. One day, after escaping from his nagging wife, Rip decides to take a nap under a tree. He sleeps for twenty years and awakes to find his wife dead and his friends gone. The message is clear: Don't sleep your life away, or you'll be sorry. Use your time wisely and well and work out your problems as they arise, rather than ignoring or dreaming them away.

Alvin Toffler, who felt that pace of life was accelerating and that packing too much change into too little time could actually make us sick. Indeed, the health scourges of modern life—some cancers, heart disease, and hypertension—are diseases on which stress has a great influence. Toffler argued that the rate of change in the future would lead to a condition that he called "future shock." In the simplest terms, future shock results from too much change in too little time. Individuals experience future shock as stress, anxiety, and disorientation, all of which affect personal relationships and social institutions.[24]

Yet change is not new. People and societies have been dealing with it in one way or another since the dawn of consciousness. For example, the ancient Egyptian empire dealt with change by avoiding it. Charles Van Doren writes:

> The Egyptians had a great secret, which they did not forget for thirty centuries. They feared and hated change, and they avoided it wherever possible.[25]

The currents of change that the Egyptians held at bay for three thousand years were a mere trickle compared to the raging seas of change that buffet us today. But sounding alarms that we are about to be overcome by the future is not new, either. While we often view the future with apprehension, we are typically much more charitable toward the past. Neither our apprehensive views toward the future nor our nostalgic views of the past appear well justified.

Those who compare the age in which their lot has fallen with a golden age which exists only in imagination, may talk of degeneracy and decay; but no man who is correctly informed as to the past, will be disposed to take a morose or desponding view of the present.[26]

Although these words could have been written by a contemporary of yours, they were actually penned over 150 years ago by Lord Thomas Babington Macaulay.

While ancient Egyptians tried to stop time, modern youth in the 1960s rebelled against the conventional time perspective of the 1950s. The slogan of the sixties generation, "Turn on, tune in, and drop out," was adopted from a speech by Timothy Leary in which he defined the present-time goals of the 1960s counterculture revolution:

Like every great religion of the past we seek to find the divinity within and to express this revelation in a life of glorification and the worship of God. These ancient goals we define in the metaphor of the present—turn on, tune in, drop out.[27]

The free spirits practicing Leary's euphoric "live in the moment" attitude toward time were soon assimilated into the dominant conventional future orientation. This is the same attitude espoused by business leaders since the Industrial Revolution. It values using the present to plan for the future, which is the heart of a capitalist economy.

Given that our pace of life is likely to continue to accelerate and that we humans are stuck with an antique physiology, how can we possibly cope? Are we doomed to die from the effects of future shock, the constantly accelerating culture of speed? Fortunately, the answer is no, for in the legacy that Tag bequeathed us is a most remarkable piece of technology: the human brain, which remains state-of-the-art. When the human brain evolved 150,000 years ago, no one could have imagined the need to plan for retirement; the proliferation of information through media such as the Internet; or

Time-out Seven: Songs About Time

Title	Artist
100 Years	Five for Fighting
3am	Matchbox 20
A Little Night Music	Mozart
All This Time	Sting
Always on My Mind	Willie Nelson
A Memory of a Happy Moment	Aspects of Love
April in Paris	Louis Armstrong
As Time Goes By	Jimmy Durante
At the End of the Day	*Les Misérables*
Don't Stop (Thinking about Tomorrow)	Fleetwood Mac
Glory Days	Bruce Springsteen
Good Riddance (Time of Your Life)	Green Day
Haven't Got Time for the Pain	Carly Simon
I Am Sixteen	*The Sound of Music*
It's Now or Never	Elvis Presley
It's Too Late	Carole King
Let the Good Times Roll	B. B. King and the Cars
Let's Live for Today	The Grass Roots
Manic Monday	The Bangles
Maybe I'm Amazed (At the Way You Pull Me Out of Time)	Paul McCartney
Memory	*Cats*
Oh, What a Night	The Four Seasons
Con Te Partiro (Time to Say Goodbye)	Andrea Bocelli
Rainy Days and Mondays	The Carpenters
Ruby Tuesday	The Rolling Stones
Saturday Night	Bay City Rollers
Sign o' the Times	Prince
Summer of '69	Brian Adams
Summertime	Louis Armstrong
Sunrise, Sunset	*Fiddler on the Roof*
The Best of Times	Styx
The Four Seasons	Vivaldi
The Times They Are a-Changin'	Bob Dylan
Time	Hootie and the Blowfish
Time After Time	Frank Sinatra
Time in a Bottle	Jim Croce
Time Is on My Side	The Rolling Stones
Tomorrow	*Annie*
Too Much Time on My Hands	Styx
Urgent	Foreigner
Wishing You Were Somehow Here Again	*The Phantom of the Opera*
When I'm Sixty-four	The Beatles
Lament	*Evita*
Yesterday	The Beatles

the speed of transportation and communication in temporary society. Fortunately, our brains can stretch into the future to predict the outcome of present behavior and can contract into the past to learn from previous experience. To some degree, we have conscious control over how we predict or learn. Not only can we avoid future shock, we can use our capacity for psychological change to harness control of the time of our lives.

THE SCIENTIFIC STUDY OF PSYCHOLOGICAL TIME

Time travels in divers paces with divers persons. I'll tell you who
Time ambles withal, who Time trots withal, who Time gallops
withal, and who he stands still withal.
                        —*William Shakespeare*
                  As You Like It, *Act III, Scene II*[28]

Your authors were not the first psychologists to be interested in time. Wilhelm Wundt, the father of psychology; William James, the father of American psychology;[29] and Kurt Lewin, the father of social psychology[30] all recognized time's importance. Each wrote about or conducted simple experiments on time. Lewin even commented favorably on Fredrick Winslow Taylor's application of scientific principles to time and management.[31] Few psychologists, however, made the study of time the central focus of their work.[32] But those who did were hampered by their intellectual independence. Each researcher defined, measured, and talked about time in his unique way and did not attempt to collaborate or reach a consensus with colleagues.

Over the last twenty years, your authors have interviewed, surveyed, analyzed, talked with, and observed thousands of people from childhood to age ninety-four. One of our striking findings is that no two people's attitudes toward time are identical. If we looked in the right places today, we would undoubtedly find people who hold attitudes similar to those of Tag, Abdul, and Edward.

For us scientists used to organizing, counting, classifying, and tagging phenomena, this diversity in attitudes toward time is dis-

Time-out Eight: Traditional Definitions of Time Perspective

William James
(the father of American Psychology and Henry James's brother)

Time perspective is the knowledge of some other part of the stream, past or future, near or remote, that is always mixed in with our knowledge of the present thing.

Kurt Lewin (the father of social psychology)

Time perspective is the totality of the individual's views of his psychological future and his psychological past that exist at a given time.

Paul Fraisse (the father of the psychological study of time)

Our actions at any given moment do not depend only on the situation in which we find ourselves at that instant, but also on everything we have already experienced and on all our future expectations. Every one of our actions takes these into account, sometimes explicitly, always implicitly. . . . We might say that each of our actions takes place in a temporal perspective; it depends on our temporal horizon at the precise moment of its occurrence.

Zimbardo and Boyd

Time perspective is the often nonconscious personal attitude that each of us holds toward time and the process whereby the continual flow of existence is bundled into time categories that help to give order, coherence, and meaning to our lives.

concerting and makes it difficult to identify similarities that people share. Psychology needs a consistent measure and vocabulary to discuss time. So, two decades ago we set out to develop a yardstick for attitudes toward time and in 1997 and 1999 published the Zimbardo Time Perspective Inventory (ZTPI) and the Transcendental-future Time Perspective Inventory (TFTPI).[33] As we had hoped, these scales have been adopted and validated extensively in the

United States, France, Spain, Brazil, Italy, Russia, Lithuania, South Africa, and other countries.[34]

Your time perspective reflects attitudes, beliefs, and values related to time. For example, do you spend more time thinking about the past, present, or future? When you think about the past, the present, and the future, are your thoughts positive or negative, happy or sad, hopeful or fearful? Your time perspective helps determine your answers to these types of questions and reflects your thoughts, feelings, and behaviors—in fact, all aspects of your life.

Our research reveals that there are multiple dimensions of time perspective. Just as you cannot capture all the dimensions of a wooden box with a single number—you need to measure width, height, and depth—you cannot capture the multiple dimensions of time perspective with a single number. While time perspectives will continue to emerge, change, and evolve, for the Western world, we have identified six time perspectives: two past, two present, and two future. These time perspectives are called the:

- Past-negative

- Past-positive

- Present-fatalistic

- Present-hedonistic

- Future

- Transcendental-future

These time perspectives are theoretically unrelated. Your score on one dimension is unrelated to your score on others. In practice, however, we find consistent patterns in individual time perspective profiles.

We recommend that you complete the ZTPI and the TFTPI before reading about the individual time perspectives below. You can complete them online at www.thetimeparadox.com, or you can complete the versions included in this book and look up comparisons for your scores online. Don't worry. There are no right or wrong answers, and only you will know your results. There is a penalty for cheating—it robs you of a unique opportunity to understand yourself and your place in the world.

Subsequent chapters will explore each of these categories in detail, to help you determine the time perspective—the lens through which you see the world—that is most beneficial to your life situation.

Another present-oriented time zone can be called the Holistic Present. It involves training to live one's life in the present moment and to include past and future in an expanded state of focus on the present. Such a time sense is central to Zen Buddhism, and Zen meditative practices are one means of achieving this unique state of consciousness. Because it is less common in western than eastern cultures and is rather vague in its components, we did not include it in our ZTPI assessment. Nevertheless, it is an important time zone and one very different from the two present zones we have studied—hedonism and fatalism. For now let's see how your time perspective compares with that of other people who have taken our inventories. The people described below are composites, but their characteristics are based upon years of research and thousands of data points.

The Zimbardo Time Perspective Inventory (ZTPI)

Read each item and, as honestly as you can, answer the question: "How characteristic or true is this of me?" Check the appropriate box under the scale at the right. Please answer *all* of the following questions.

	Very Untrue	Neutral			Very True
	1	2	3	4	5
1. I believe that getting together with one's friends to party is one of life's important pleasures.					
2. Familiar childhood sights, sounds, and smells often bring back a flood of wonderful memories.					
3. Fate determines much in my life.					
4. I often think of what I should have done differently in my life.					

		Very Untrue	Neutral		Very True	
		1	2	3	4	5
5.	My decisions are mostly influenced by people and things around me.					
6.	I believe that a person's day should be planned ahead each morning.					
7.	It gives me pleasure to think of my past.					
8.	I do things impulsively.					
9.	If things don't get done on time, I don't worry about it.					
10.	When I want to achieve something, I set goals and consider specific means for reaching those goals.					
11.	On balance, there is much more good to recall than bad in my past.					
12.	When listening to my favorite music, I often lose all track of time.					
13.	Meeting tomorrow's deadlines and doing other necessary work come before tonight's play.					
14.	Since whatever will be will be, it doesn't really matter what I do.					
15.	I enjoy stories about how things used to be in the "good old times."					
16.	Painful past experiences keep being replayed in my mind.					
17.	I try to live my life as fully as possible, one day at a time.					
18.	It upsets me to be late for appointments.					
19.	Ideally, I would live each day as if it were my last.					
20.	Happy memories of good times spring readily to mind.					
21.	I meet my obligations to friends and authorities on time.					
22.	I've taken my share of abuse and rejection in the past.					
23.	I make decisions on the spur of the moment.					
24.	I take each day as it is rather than try to plan it out.					
25.	The past has too many unpleasant memories that I prefer not to think about.					
26.	It is important to put excitement in my life.					
27.	I've made mistakes in the past that I wish I could undo.					
28.	I feel that it's more important to enjoy what you're doing than to get work done on time.					
29.	I get nostalgic about my childhood.					
30.	Before making a decision, I weigh the costs against the benefits.					
31.	Taking risks keeps my life from becoming boring.					
32.	It is more important for me to enjoy life's journey than to focus only on the destination.					
33.	Things rarely work out as I expected.					
34.	It's hard for me to forget unpleasant images of my youth.					
35.	It takes joy out of the process and flow of my activities if I have to think about goals, outcomes, and products.					
36.	Even when I am enjoying the present, I am drawn back to comparisons with similar past experiences.					

		Very Untrue		Neutral		Very True
		1	2	3	4	5
37.	You can't really plan for the future because things change so much.					
38.	My life path is controlled by forces I cannot influence.					
39.	It doesn't make sense to worry about the future, since there is nothing that I can do about it anyway.					
40	I complete projects on time by making steady progress.					
41.	I find myself tuning out when family members talk about the way things used to be.					
42.	I take risks to put excitement in my life.					
43.	I make lists of things to do.					
44.	I often follow my heart more than my head.					
45.	I am able to resist temptations when I know that there is work to be done.					
46.	I find myself getting swept up in the excitement of the moment.					
47.	Life today is too complicated; I would prefer the simpler life of the past.					
48.	I prefer friends who are spontaneous rather than predictable.					
49.	I like family rituals and traditions that are regularly repeated.					
50.	I think about the bad things that have happened to me in the past.					
51.	I keep working at difficult, uninteresting tasks if they will help me get ahead.					
52.	Spending what I earn on pleasures today is better than saving for tomorrow's security.					
53.	Often luck pays off better than hard work.					
54.	I think about the good things that I have missed out on in my life.					
55.	I like my close relationships to be passionate.					
56.	There will always be time to catch up on my work.					

THE ZIMBARDO TIME PERSPECTIVE INVENTORY (ZTPI)

SCORING KEY

Scoring Instructions

Before scoring the ZTPI, you have to reverse the answers for questions 9, 24, 25, 41, and 56. This means a:

1 becomes a 5
2 becomes a 4
3 becomes a 3
4 becomes a 2
5 becomes a 1

After reversing these answers, add your scores for the questions that comprise each factor. After adding your scores for each factor, divide the total score by the number of questions that comprise each factor. This results in an average score for each of the five factors.

The Past-negative Time Perspective

Add your scores on questions 4, 5, 16, 22, 27, 33, 34, 36, 50, and 54. Then divide this number by 10.

Question

4. I often think of what I should have done differently in my life.
5. My decisions are mostly influenced by people and things around me.
16. Painful past experiences keep being replayed in my mind.
22. I've taken my share of abuse and rejection in the past.
27. I've made mistakes in the past that I wish I could undo.
33. Things rarely work out as I expected.
34. It's hard for me to forget unpleasant images of my youth.
36. Even when I am enjoying the present, I am drawn back to comparisons with similar past experiences.
50. I think about the bad things that have happened to me in the past.

54. I think about the good things that I have missed out on in my life.
Score:

The Present-hedonistic Time Perspective

Add your scores on questions 1, 8, 12, 17, 19, 23, 26, 28, 31, 32, 42, 44, 46, 48, and 55. Then divide this number by 15.
Question
1. I believe that getting together with one's friends to party is one of life's important pleasures.
8. I do things impulsively.
12. When listening to my favorite music, I often lose all track of time.
17. I try to live my life as fully as possible, one day at a time.
19. Ideally, I would live each day as if it were my last.
23. I make decisions on the spur of the moment.
26. It is important to put excitement in my life.
28. I feel that it's more important to enjoy what you are doing than to get work done on time.
31. Taking risks keeps my life from becoming boring.
32. It is more important for me to enjoy life's journey than to focus only on the destination.
42. I take risks to put excitement in my life.
44. I often follow my heart more than my head.
46. I find myself getting swept up in the excitement of the moment.
48. I prefer friends who are spontaneous rather than predictable.
55. I like my close relationships to be passionate.
Score:

The Future Time Perspective

Add your scores on questions 6, 9 (reversed), 10, 13, 18, 21, 24 (reversed), 30, 40, 43, 45, 51, and 56 (reversed). Then divide this number by 13.

Question

6. I believe that a person's day should be planned ahead each morning.
9. If things don't get done on time, I don't worry about it.
10. When I want to achieve something, I set goals and consider specific means for reaching those goals.
13. Meeting tomorrow's deadlines and doing other necessary work come before tonight's play.
18. It upsets me to be late for appointments.
21. I meet my obligations to friends and authorities on time.
24. I take each day as it is rather than try to plan it out.
30. Before making a decision, I weigh the costs against the benefits.
40. I complete projects on time by making steady progress.
43. I make lists of things to do.
45. I am able to resist temptations when I know that there is work to be done.
51. I keep working at difficult, uninteresting tasks if they will help me get ahead.
56. There will always be time to catch up on my work.

Score:

The Past-positive Time Perspective

Add your scores on questions 2, 7, 11, 15, 20, 25 (reversed), 29, 41 (reversed), and 49. Then divide this number by 9.

Question

2. Familiar childhood sights, sounds, and smells often bring back a flood of wonderful memories.
7. It gives me pleasure to think about my past.
11. On balance, there is much more good to recall than bad in my past.
15. I enjoy stories about how things used to be in the "good old times."
20. Happy memories of good times spring readily to mind.

25. The past has too many unpleasant memories that I prefer not to think about.
29. I get nostalgic about my childhood.
41. I find myself tuning out when family members talk about the way things used to be.
49. I like family rituals and traditions that are regularly repeated.
Score:

The Present-fatalistic Time Perspective

Add your scores on questions 3, 14, 35, 37, 38, 39, 47, 52, and 53. Then divide this number by 9.

Question

3. Fate determines much in my life.
14. Since whatever will be will be, it doesn't really matter what I do.
35. It takes joy out of the process and flow of my activities if I have to think about goals, outcomes, and products.
37. You can't really plan for the future because things change so much.
38. My life path is controlled by forces I cannot influence.
39. It doesn't make sense to worry about the future, since there is nothing that I can do about it anyway.
47. Life today is too complicated; I would prefer the simpler life of the past.
52. Spending what I earn on pleasures today is better than saving for tomorrow's security.
53. Often luck pays off better than hard work.
Score:

The Transcendental-future Time Perspective Inventory

Read each item and, as honestly as you can, answer the question: "How characteristic or true is this of you?" Check the appropriate box using the scale. Please answer *all* of the following questions.

	Very Untrue	Neutral			Very True
	1	2	3	4	5
1. Only my physical body will ever die.					
2. My body is just a temporary home for the real me.					
3. Death is just a new beginning.					
4. I believe in miracles.					
5. The theory of evolution adequately explains how humans came to be.					
6. Humans possess a soul.					
7. Scientific laws cannot explain everything.					
8. I will be held accountable for my actions on earth after I die.					
9. There are divine laws by which humans should live.					
10. I believe in spirits.					

Scoring Instructions

To calculate your score on the Transcendental-future Time Perspective, reverse code your response to question 5. This means a:

    1 becomes a 5
    2 becomes a 4
    3 becomes a 3
    4 becomes a 2
    5 becomes a 1

The Transcendental-future Time Perspective

After reverse coding question 5, add your scores on all of the questions, then divide by 10.

Score:

THE SIX MOST COMMON TIME PERSPECTIVES IN THE WESTERN WORLD

The Past-positive Time Perspective: Past-positive Polly

Polly is thirty-five years old. When she took our tests, Polly strongly agreed with statements like "Familiar childhood sights, sounds, and smells often bring back a flood of wonderful memories" and "It gives me pleasure to think about my past." For Polly, the past is half full. She lives in an old Victorian house with her husband and two children. Polly and her husband have been "going steady" since their junior year in school. A stay-at-home mom, she hopes that her children can enjoy many of the same life experiences that she's had. Her numerous friends describe her as warm, sentimental, friendly, happy, and self-confident. She is very seldom anxious, depressed, or aggressive. Most evenings Polly cooks dinner for her family, which they then eat around their large kitchen table. For fun, Polly listens to "oldies" music and watches classic movies. She also likes hosting family reunions and quilting club meetings. Polly manages the family finances and is careful with money, most of which is in a bank savings account. Polly wears a mechanical wristwatch handed down from her grandmother.

The past-positive time perspective captures attitudes toward the past, not an objective record of good and bad events. Positive attitudes toward the past may reflect positive events that people actually experienced, or a positive mindset that allows individuals to make the best of very difficult situations. Psychologically, what individuals *believe* happened in the past influences their present thoughts, feelings, and behavior more than what did happen. Nietzsche's famous saying "That which does not kill me makes me stronger" captures this attitude well. People who experience aversive events but recall them in positive ways may become resilient and optimistic.

If you scored high on the past-positive time perspective, congratulations! If you did not, you have an opportunity for self-discovery and growth ahead of you. Chapter Three will show how many of our views about the past are imperfect and changeable.

The Past-negative Time Perspective: Past-negative Ned

Ned is forty years old. When he took our tests, he strongly agreed with statements like "I often think of what I should have done differently in my life" and "Painful past experiences keep replaying in my mind." For Ned, the past is half empty. Ned hopes that his four children can avoid the painful experiences that he's endured. He does not have many close friends, and his few acquaintances describe him as unhappy, depressed, anxious, and shy. Occasionally, Ned becomes so frustrated that he loses his temper and throws things. He seldom exercises or does anything fun, has poor impulse control, and is fond of gambling. Although he does not have a lot of energy, Ned tries to stay busy so that painful memories do not replay in his mind.

Like the past-positive, the past-negative time perspective assesses your attitude about events that occurred in the past. Negative attitudes may be due to the actual experience of negative events or to the current negative reconstruction of earlier events that may have been benign. While no one can change events that occurred in the past, everyone can change attitudes and beliefs about them. Changing your mind and attitudes is not easy, but you have undoubtedly done it.

You can approach changing your attitudes toward time as you would approach changing the course of a river. In both cases, small changes over time can have a dramatic effect. Think of time as a river, a very large and powerful one, say, the Mississippi. In the nineteenth century, people who owned land along the banks of the Mississippi often hired men to shoot on sight anyone caught on their property with a shovel.[35] This immediate justice sounds severe unless you appreciate the power of small, incremental actions. During the nineteenth century, ambitious landowners would buy property on one side of the Mississippi and, afterward, trespass on their neighbor's property on the opposite bank, where they would covertly shovel away key areas and dramatically change the course of the river. Consequently, the ambitious landowner's holdings increased, and the landowner on the opposite bank saw his holdings washed away by the river. The moral of this story is threefold: First, small changes can have large consequences. Second, your goal is not to cause change but to shape the change that you know will occur. Change is inevitable, so your real task is to shape the direction of this inevitable change in positive ways. Third, leave your shovel at home when you make your next trip to the banks of the Mississippi.

The Present-hedonistic Time Perspective: Hedonistic Hedley

Hedley is twenty-five years old. When he took our inventories, Hedley strongly agreed with statements like "I believe that getting together with one's friends to party is one of life's important pleasures" and "I do things impulsively." Very creative, Hedley has many friends and tons of energy. He is adventurous, can make anyone laugh, and always has a good time. He is the life of the party, governed by the situational pressure of his immediate environment, or by what Freud referred to as the "pleasure principle." [36] His motto is "If it feels good, do it." Some of the things that feel good to Hedley are masturbation, unsafe sex, alcohol and drug use, and driving fast. He engages in all of them frequently. [37,38,39] Hedley's parents are divorced, he doesn't wear a wristwatch, and he wears new, hot clothes when he has the money to buy them. Hedley loves jazz, plays pickup basketball games, and lives on fast food. Although he's never held a job for larger than six months, he drives a fancy new sports car. His credit cards are maxed, which doesn't faze him, because he counts on winning the lottery.

The Present-fatalistic Time Perspective: Fatalistic Fred

Fred is twenty years old. When Fred took our inventories, he strongly agreed with statements like "Fate determines much in my life" and "Since whatever will be will be, it doesn't really matter what I do." This absence of personal efficacy may be partially responsible for Fred's anxiety and depression. His roommate describes him as "a hard sell" when introducing him to girls or buddies, because he is such a downer. Fred is unhappy, not conscientious, and apathetic; he lacks Hedley's pleasure-seeking. Although Fred uses drugs and practices unsafe sex, it's not because they make him feel good but because he doesn't believe that practicing safe sex or refraining from drug use will make any real difference in future consequences—whatever will be, will be. It just doesn't matter. In fact, drug users who are high in present-fatalism are more likely to share needles than individuals low in present-fatalism.[40]

The Future Time Perspective: Future Felicia

Felicia is thirty-two years old. When she completed our inventories, Felicia strongly agreed with statements like "I believe that a person's day should be planned ahead each morning" and "When I want to achieve something, I set goals and consider specific means for reaching those goals." Felicia is governed by what Freud referred to as the "reality principle"; part of her wants immediate gratification, just like Hedley, but she carefully weighs the benefits of immediate gratification against future costs. Often she forgoes immediate gratification, because she believes that she will receive a greater reward in the future. Felicia has many acquaintances but not many close friends. Her acquaintances describe Felicia as extremely conscientious, consistent, and concerned about future consequences. At work, she meets deadlines on time and is a top performer. She does not like novelty or excitement; she balances her checkbook, uses a day planner, and makes to-do lists. She always wears a watch and reports having little free time. Mindful of her annual checkups, she flosses her teeth regularly and watches what she eats,[41] because she has high blood pressure and irritable bowel syndrome. Felicia believes that risk-taking, alcohol, drugs, and unsafe sex will just get in the way of reaching her dreams.[42]

The Transcendental-future Time Perspective: Transcendental Tiffany

Tiffany is fifty years old. When she completed our inventories, Tiffany strongly agreed with statements like "Death is just a new beginning" and "Only my physical body will ever die." A born-again Christian, Tiffany believes that she will go to heaven when she dies. Tiffany regularly attends religious services and performs rituals at home. Tiffany has good impulse control, is not aggressive, and is concerned with future consequences.

While these descriptions give a sense of the six individual time perspectives, such orientations are most evident in the way that people interact with the world around them. To illustrate how time perspectives color people's thoughts, feelings, and behaviors, let's imagine that Polly, Ned, Hedley, Fred, Felicia, and Tiffany were high school classmates gathered for the wake of another classmate, Bob. In high school, the group was inseparable. Bob had a heart attack recently and was on life support for a short time before passing away. Let's listen in to our imaginary circle of old friends as they interact at Bob's wake in one of their favorite restaurants.

[Future Felicia arrived ten minutes early. She did not want to be late and impatiently waits for the others. The rest—except for Hedley, who is late as usual—arrive on time.]

> Past-positive Polly: It's so good to see you all! When I heard the
> news about Bob, I was so sad. Then I looked through our old
> yearbooks. It cheered me up some. We had some great times.
> Past-negative Ned: We had our tough times, too. But it is good
> to see everyone. I just wish it were under better circumstances.
> Fatalistic Fred: Yeah, but it's going to happen to the rest of us.
> We better get used to it.

Future Felicia: We need to take better care of ourselves. We have lots of exciting things still to do in life.

Fatalistic Fred: When your number's up, there's nothing you can do about it.

Past-positive Polly: You can have your cholesterol checked. Doesn't heart disease run in your family, Fred?

Fatalistic Fred: Yeah, but that's just a waste of time. I could eat lousy-tasting organic food for twenty years and then get hit by a bus one day walking home from the health food store.

[Hedonistic Hedley arrives late.]

Hedonistic Hedley: Hey, guys! How's it going?

Future Felicia [sarcastically]: Don't tell me you had to work late.

Hedonistic Hedley: Work? Naw, I was playing Halo V. I kept getting to the last level and getting wasted. . . . Hey, there's a buffet. Far out! I'm starved.

Past-positive Polly: I've been thinking a lot about how Bob would want us to remember him. Maybe we should donate a bench in his name to the high school.

Past-negative Ned: So the students can carve their initials in it?

Past-positive Polly: No, I just know how much fun Bob had in high school. It would be a meaningful way to remember him.

Past-negative Ned: It's going to take a long time before I get the pictures of him hooked up to those terrifying machines out of my mind.

Transcendental Tiffany: He's in a better place now. He will be waiting for us to join him in heaven.

Future Felicia: What about funding a scholarship? Bob was a good student. We could do it in his name. [She checks her watch. She told her husband she'd be home by nine P.M.]

[Hedley returns from the buffet.]

Hedonistic Hedley: Oh, man. You've got to try the buffalo wings. They're awesome, the best I've ever had!

Past-positive Polly: I thought that mine were the best you ever had.

Hedonistic Hedley: They were. Till now.

Past-positive Polly: We were just talking about donating a bench to the high school in Bob's name.

Future Felicia: Or starting a scholarship in his name.

Hedonistic Hedley: How about we buy an old car, paint Bob's name on the doors, and park it at lovers' lane as a service to today's youth. Who knows, we might even save a marriage or two.

Future Felicia [sarcastically]: Or we could put a free condom dispenser in the boys' restroom!

Fatalistic Fred: His number was up. Give me one of those buffalo wings.

Transcendental Tiffany: Bob was just called home before we wanted him to leave us.

Future Felicia: If we start a scholarship, we could help students whom Bob won't be able to help himself. It would make the world a better place.

Past-negative Ned: I don't know. When we were in school, all the scholarships went to rich kids or nerds who didn't need them.

Future Felicia: Well, I have to go. Think about our options. I'll call the school to see how we could set something up, and plan a time for us to get together again soon. Polly, can we meet at your house?

Past-positive Polly: Sure, I'll even make that dessert Hedley loves. Seeing everyone was just like old times!

Transcendental Tiffany: Knowing that Bob is in a better place makes it easier for me.

Hedonistic Hedley [to Fred]: Hey, buddy, you're not bailing on me, are you?

Fatalistic Fred: No, I don't have anything better to do. Let's hit the bar.

Hedonistic Hedley: Now you're talking! Let's knock a couple back for the Bobster!

All six people participated in the conversation, contributing through the lens of their particular time perspective, interpreting one another's comments and adding comments in ways that reveal underlying attitudes about time. They all loved Bob and love one another but see the world through different lenses and different time perspectives. Past-positive Polly remembers good times. Past-negative Ned remembers bad times. Fatalistic Fred believes that he is powerless and that fate rules his life. Hedonistic Hedley enjoys life today. Future Felicia plans for tomorrow. Transcendental Tiffany takes comfort in the belief that Bob is gone physically but lives on spiritually. None of their interpretations or comments was wrong or crazy, just different. Of course, few people are as one-dimensional as our characters. Nonetheless, you probably see some of yourself and some of the people whom you are close to in our example.

Throughout the rest of the book, we will refer back to these six time perspectives. When doing so, we will often use shorthand that simplifies discussion of a complex matter. When we describe the thoughts, feelings, and behaviors of a specific time perspective, we are referring to a person who is high on that particular time perspective and relatively low on all others. In the real world, people can be high on multiple time perspectives, all of which interact. We will talk as if individuals were characterized by a particular type, like Hedonists, Fatalists, and Transcendentals—but we ask you to remember that each person has a profile of six time perspective scores, each of which varies across a continuum from low to high.

LIKELY FUTURE DEVELOPMENTS

We are confident that as you've read this chapter, you have already begun to identify the effects of time on your own life. It is not difficult to do. Examples are all around us. You may place mementos around your home to remind you of the past. You may decorate with only abstract art and no pictures of people, in order to avoid the past. You may always be late. You may hate to wait. As Carl Sagan so vividly illustrated with his cosmic calendar, time is the backdrop of our lives and the very fabric of the cosmos.[43] You have seen how time perspective affects the thoughts, feelings, and behavior of our imaginary classmates. In the following chapters, we will explore the roles that each of us plays on the stage of life, and how you can have a hand in shaping—or writing—the script that is your life.

All the world's [and all of time's] a stage
And all the men and women merely players.
They have their exits and their entrances;
And one man in his time plays many parts
                    —William Shakespeare
                As You Like It, *II, vii*

three

THE PAST

How You See Yesterday
Through the Lens of Today

Those who cannot remember the past are condemned to repeat it.
—George Santayana[1]

Events in the past may be roughly divided into those which
probably never happened and those which do not matter.
—William Ralph Inge[2]

A MEMORY OF PHIL ZIMBARDO'S

When I was five years old, I developed a severe case of whooping cough and double pneumonia. At the time, in 1939, before the wonder drugs of penicillin and sulfa, there were no effective treatments. I was quarantined alongside hundreds of other poor children in New York City who had these and other contagious diseases, such as polio, tuberculosis, and scarlet fever, in the charity ward of the Willard Parker Hospital for Children with Contagious Diseases. Visitors—including parents—were limited to two hours on Sundays and were required to interact from behind a glass window designed to contain the infections. Nurses wore surgical masks as they administered to children who lay in cots arranged in neat rows. There was no radio, TV, video games, or anything else to do for amusement, except to read worn-out comic books. Consequently, I quickly developed close friendships with the children assigned to nearby cots. These friendships would not last.

Some mornings I would awaken to find the cots next to me empty and stripped of bedding. When I asked about the friends who had occupied the cots the night before, I was told that this or that friend had "gone home" during the night. In reality, my friends had died, and their bodies had been quickly removed so the other children would not be alarmed. Nurses and we kids conspired to deny the obvious: The missing children had died. My initial envy of departed friends going home soon gave way to the realization that they had been robbed of their lives, of their futures.

Somehow I survived this five-month ordeal with a direct blood transfusion from my father's arm into mine. I was in an oxygen tent for a long time, and some family visited occasionally on Sundays when winter weather permitted them to travel the long distance from home to the hospital. Part of my survival consisted of inventing games and play activities that involved all the kids in nearby beds, such as rafting down the Nile to capture the huge white alligator. Another survival strategy involved praying hard and long twice a day: in the morning to God, in thanks for surviving the night and toward giving me the strength to endure another day. In the night I also prayed to the devil to spare me when his shadowy presence loomed large in that dark hospital chamber. The double dose of prayer proved its worth.

It was a horrendous time, with children always crying and coughing and wheezing and dying. But I survived in part by praying for a better future that I filled with vivid images of playing with my kid brothers and friends and of being big and strong and healthy. I began to develop a focus on a possible future self that transcended the nightmare I was forced to live each day and night.

Amazingly, when the ordeal was over, I had transformed my negative experience into a positive one by reframing it as the time and place where I learned to read and write before going to school, learned to ingratiate myself to nurses with flattery, and learned to entertain other kids with imaginative group games. As a survivor, I had learned to be self-reliant. In 1939, when I arrived in that hospital with double pneumonia and whooping cough, fully half of all deaths of kids up to age ten were from pneumonia, influenza, and diarrhea/enteritis, while TB, diphtheria, dysentery, and whooping cough contributed an additional 13 percent of deaths to children under ten. So 63 percent of the kids in my age bracket who died (approximately two hundred males ages one to ten per one hundred thousand population) had my contagious diseases or their close cousins. Plus, I was "quarantined" in a hospital that specialized in infectious diseases where I was exposed to everything else, including polio. It is amazing and blessed that I was one of the rare survivors.

From this experience, I also learned that the past can be psychologically remodeled to make a heaven of hell. Other people learn the opposite lesson, storing and recalling only the worst of times. While I made the most of a bad situation psychologically, some people create Smithsonians to store their past traumas. The horrors and sheer ugliness of the past they have experienced become a permanent filter through which they view all their current experiences.

Human memory is fallible, and I have to admit that my recall of these childhood events may be imperfect, incomplete, and somewhat distorted—but not by much. Sufficient independent evidence about the terrible conditions of that hospital leads me to believe that the events happened as I etched them in my memory. These beliefs have shaped my life. I have taken the good out of my past and have found much for which to be grateful.

YOUR PAST AND YOUR FIRST MEMORY

What really happened matters, and so do the ways that you interpret, code, and give emotional meaning to events. What memories shape your life? To help you narrow your search, focus on your very first memory. This isn't just a rhetorical question. We want you to take a minute to identify your very first memory. After you have rummaged through your old-memories store, write down the specifics of the memory. What exactly happened? When? Who was—and was not—there? What about your memory is crystal-clear, and what is missing or foggy? After you've settled upon a version of the experience, shift your focus to the thoughts, especially the feelings surrounding them. Be patient. It's likely that details will surface at their own pace. Once you're comfortable that you've recaptured your first memory, continue on with your reading and rejoin us.

Austrian psychologist Alfred Adler felt that a person's first memory was a window into the rest of his or her life.[3] During his initial session, Adler often asked his therapeutic clients about their first memories and then used the memories as a way to understand their present. For example, if an anxious client's first memory was of being abandoned by his mother at an orphanage, Adler would interpret his current anxiety differently than if the person's first memory was of the day when a baby sibling arrived home from the hospital. Adler was only mildly concerned with the veracity of those memories, as he typically could not confirm or negate them without independent evidence. He understood that what the person believed to be true was actually more important than the objective, factual truth, if such a thing actually exists. After all, people live their lives based upon their personal memories—based upon what they believe to be true—not upon an officially sanctioned version of events recorded in an objective history. For Adler, the past was important, but it was a reinterpretation of events—a reconstruction—based on present thoughts and feelings. In other words, your past can shape your current thoughts, feelings, and actions, and those current thoughts, feelings, and actions, in turn, can shape memories of the past.

A MEMORY OF JOHN BOYD'S

My first memory is of sitting on a worn sofa with my dad when I was about three years old, watching a cops-and-robbers show on TV. During a chase scene, a bad guy is cornered on the roof of a metal warehouse. Instead of giving up, he leaps onto a pile of cardboard boxes and garbage in the alleyway below. After a graceful fall, he rolls off the boxes and eludes the cops.

On seeing the bad guy's stunt, I stood up on the sofa cushion, dived into the air, and did a perfect belly flop onto the hard floor below. The sudden jolt at the end of the jump was much less fun than it had looked on TV, and I remember thinking, That didn't work out like I thought it would. The memory was confirmed by my father, who also remembers waiting for me to begin crying after the jump. Instead, I rose from the floor with a look of puzzlement and surprise, quietly climbed back onto the sofa, and returned to watching TV. I have been testing reality in my personal and professional lives ever since.

What does your first memory reveal about you? In what ways are you still like the younger self in your memory? How are you different? You might ask guests at a dinner party to relate their first memories to the group. After going around the table or room, share Adler's theory with the other guests, then go back around the room and explore how each person's first memory relates to the person he or she is today. When we authors have done this, our friends often identify connections and unearth interesting meanings that the narrator never considered. Of course, there are no right or wrong answers to this game, and it is even possible that the event in your memory did not happen as you recall it, as we will soon see.

PSYCHOLOGY'S PAST: DETERMINISM, ANALYSIS, AND BEHAVIORISM

With Earth's first Clay They did the Last Man knead,
And there of the Last Harvest sow'd the Seed:
And the first Morning of Creation wrote
What the Last Dawn of Reckoning shall read.

Yesterday This Day's Madness did prepare;
To-morrow's Silence, Triumph, or Despair:
Drink! for you know not whence you came, nor why:
Drink! for you know not why you go, nor where.
—Omar Khayyám[4]

Psychological determinism asserts that every thought and feeling we have and every action we perform is caused by events in the past. Although determinism may seem incompatible with the feeling that you exercised free will in choosing what you ate for breakfast this morning, science is based upon it. The goals of science are to describe, understand, *predict*, and, when prudent, control ourselves and our world—ideally, for the better. Accurate prediction requires that relationships identified in the past and the present will also be valid in the future. Imagine trying to predict the path of a billiard ball if the laws of physics changed every time you struck one. Or if traffic flowed randomly without regard for lights or signs when you tried to cross the street. Fortunately, the laws of nature are relatively constant and we are able to use the scientific method to reveal stable physical and psychological relationships, even to identify the causes of instability. In particular, two psychological schools of thought— psychoanalysis and behaviorism—stress the importance of the past in determining the course of our lives, just as the laws of physics determine the trajectory of billiard balls.

Early in his career, Sigmund Freud was an ambitious Viennese neurologist who sought to treat people whom no other medical professionals could—or would—help. These people suffered from serious conditions such as paralysis, blindness, fainting spells, and despondency, and they had exhausted all other treatment options available at the time. Before Freud came along, these people were left to fight their illnesses on their own, much as Phil was when he suffered from whooping cough. Freud sought to help these nineteenth-century middle-class "untouchables" and, in so doing, made a unique name for himself.[5]

Initially, Freud was unsure how to treat these intractable cases. With little precedent to guide him, he began by listening to his clients. He let them take the lead in their own treatment by telling him their personal stories, which invariably took him into the chambers of their pasts. During a typical session, Freud spoke very little himself but listened attentively and nonjudgmentally as his clients talked about their pasts or whatever they wanted. This treatment was so successful that one of Freud's early clients called it "the talking cure," likening it to the effect of a chimney sweep removing the psychological soot that had accumulated from heated moments long ago. Although modern psychology and psychiatry have abandoned many of Freud's theories, his sensitive, nonjudgmental listening approach remains the core of most modern therapeutic strategies.

Personal experiences are not the only contribution of the past to one's psychological life, however. Freud felt that the past also expressed itself through the *Id*. In Freud's original German, the *Id* is actually the *Es*, which is the German pronoun for "It." English translators unfortunately emphasized the medical aspect of Freud's work and, as a result, translated "Es" not into the English "It" but into the Latin "Id," which has contributed to the common misconception of Freud as an intellectual out of touch with the suffering of real people. For Freud, however, the It described the deep, dark, ancestral, immature, and instinctual part of each of us. The It is timeless.[6]

The interaction of the It with two other aspects of personality—the "I" (or *Ego*) and the "above-I" (or *Superego*)—determines what we think, feel, and do.[7] While the It is governed by our ancestral instinctual past, and also by the "pleasure principle," the I is pragmatically governed by the social constraints of the present. As you can imagine, the competing goals of the It and the I often put them in conflict. The It wants to get its way now—like a spoiled child—while the I recognizes that we often have desires, wants, and needs that are not in our best interest to pursue. Translated into Stephen Stills lyrics, the It would be satisfied only by loving the one it wants, while the I would be content to love the one it's with.

Looming over both the It and the I is the above-I, which contains moral principles instilled by parents, religion, and culture. The above-I is formed in childhood and driven by shoulds, oughts, and musts that contain implicit if-then relationships. If you find a wallet on the street, your above-I may tell you that you must return it. You learned these if-then relationships in the past, but they govern how you must behave now and in the future.

In addition to his medical training, Freud was a sagacious social critic, and he quickly realized that the content of his clients' narratives were associated with areas of life that were not openly discussed in Viennese society—sex foremost among them. Often his clients would express thoughts and feelings that were socially inappropriate, but the benefit they felt from discussing "taboo" topics led Freud to formulate the "fundamental rule" of psychoanalysis: that a client be completely honest and candid when sharing thoughts, feelings, and behavior without censoring them.

Freud felt that disagreeable, even insignificant, and nonsensical thoughts were important in the therapeutic process. As he saw it, his role as a therapist was to lead his clients on an archaeological expedition of their past, and—just as a real archaeologist at a dig would—act as an interpreter and guide for the client. Thus, Freud is often described as an "archaeologist of the soul." Much of what Freud and his clients found was not pretty—in fact, much of it was ugly—but in Freud's view, however ugly, those conceptions of past events determined the present. Although he sought to understand the future, Freud devoted most of his life to excavating repressed past experiences and reinterpreting them in the light of the present.[8] Through a client's reliving and reinterpreting the past under his guidance, Freud strove to relieve emotional disorders and mental illness, thus transforming misery into common unhappiness and healthier functioning.[9,10]

The behaviorist school of psychology believed that their principles could lead to utopian developments.[11] The behaviorists—led by John Watson and B. F. Skinner[12]—took psychological determinism to an extreme. They confidently declared that human behavior is completely determined by the rewards and punishments experienced in the past. People spend their lives developing thoughts and feelings, and performing behaviors that they expect will lead to rewards and lead away from punishment. Behaviorists also insisted that thought and interpretation play little role in determining behavior. For behaviorists, prior actual *experiences* cause thoughts, feelings, and behavior; thoughts and feelings do not cause behavior.[13] In a later version of behaviorist thought, B. F. Skinner maintained the primacy of the past and went on to assert that the future is irrelevant in the determination of behavior. He wrote:

> Most thoughtful people agree that the world is in serious trouble . . . the earth grows steadily less habitable; and all this is exacerbated by a burgeoning population that resists control. . . . Why is more not being done? . . . We are being asked to do something about the future. But the future does not exist. It cannot act upon us; we cannot act upon it.[14]

Freud's and the behaviorists' views of the past led them to develop different forms of psychotherapy. For Freud, therapy consisted of an honest exploration and reinterpretation of the past. This process would not change what happened in the past but would change a client's attitudes toward past experiences.

The behaviorists, in contrast, felt that mental health could be controlled by a system of reward and punishment. For example, if you reported to a behavioral therapist that you had a history of turbulent romantic relationships, the therapist would explore what rewards you receive from maintaining such relationships. Although the rewards may not be obvious or even rational, behaviorists insist that they are there or were there in the past. For instance, some parents will hold their own real or imagined illnesses over their children's heads to get them to behave as they want ("Don't marry/move away/go to that school, or it will give your mother/father a heart attack"). The parents are invested in being ill to get their way. Behavioral therapy involves extinguishing maladaptive thoughts and behaviors and replacing them with healthier ones by adjusting the rewards and punishments.

RECONSTRUCTING THE PAST

Most people assume that their memories accurately capture what happened in the past and that these memories are permanent. Unfortunately, memories do change over time. They are not an objective record of the past, as though a video of an event had been saved on a mental hard disk. Rather, memories are reconstructed, and their reconstruction is influenced by current attitudes, beliefs, and available information. This reconstructive nature of the past means that how we think and feel today influences how we remember yesterday. Even such subtle influences as the way in which we are asked about the past can dramatically influence our memory of "what really happened."

In a famous study that showed the reconstructive nature of memory by Elizabeth Loftus, two groups of participants were shown a videotape of an accident involving two cars. The researchers then changed one thing—the wording that was used to ask each group how fast the cars were traveling when they collided. One group was asked "How fast were the cars going when they *smashed into* each other?" This group reported that the cars were going about forty-one miles per hour, on average. Those in the second group were asked "How fast were the cars going when they *contacted* each other?" The people in this group, who had seen the same scene as those in group one, reported that the cars were going only about thirty-two miles per hour, on average. Participants were then asked whether they remembered seeing broken glass after the collision. Despite the fact that there was no broken glass, three times as many participants in the "smashed" group than in the "contacted" group reported seeing the nonexistent broken glass.[15]

Clearly, the participants in this study had not stored a videolike memory of the accident that they could play back at will. They had stored a rough impression of the accident and, when asked to recall specifics, filled in details based on information available to them in the present. For example, participants in the "smashed" group reconstructed their memory so that it was consistent with a more violent collision, with the cars going faster and the broken glass that often results from such a collision. In contrast, participants in the "contacted" group remembered the cars going more slowly and, consistent with the slower speed, no broken glass that would accompany a more violent crash. Such leading questions are used every day by skillful trial attorneys.

Remembering Things That Did Not Occur

In the study described above, some participants in both the "smashed" and the "contacted" groups remembered seeing broken glass after the collision, even though there was no broken glass in the videotape. In subsequent research, Loftus and her colleagues repeatedly demonstrated that creating such "false memories" is surprisingly easy to do. In one study, participants were shown a print advertisement for Disneyland that asked the reader to recall wonderful earlier experiences at Disneyland, such as singing "It's a Small World After All," running from ride to ride, and shaking hands with Bugs Bunny. The description was so warm, glowing, and fuzzy that many participants undoubtedly paid a visit to Disneyland after the study.

But there was a mistake in the ad that had been inserted intentionally by researchers interested in its effect on readers: Bugs Bunny is a Warner Bros. character, not a Disney character. Bugs Bunny has thus never visited Disneyland. When participants were later asked about their own memories of visiting Disneyland, however, 16 percent remembered shaking hands with Bugs Bunny, despite the fact that this action could not have possibly occurred.[16]

What's the harm in remembering something positively that did not occur? There probably isn't any, unless you plan to return to Disneyland so that you can introduce your kids to Bugs Bunny. But what about negative events? Can people remember negative events that did not occur? Based upon additional research by Loftus and other psychologists, the answer is clearly yes.[17] In one study, people were asked to describe four separate memories that had been previously related to researchers by a relative of the participant. Three of the four memories were true and had been shared by the relative. The fourth memory—of the participant being lost in a mall at about the age of five, which the relatives confirmed had not happened—had *not* ever happened. In follow-up interviews, participants remembered most of the events that had taken place, but fully 25 percent of them also vividly remembered being lost in the mall, crying, and being found by an elderly woman. One fourth of the participants remembered a false traumatic event that had not oc-curred! To be fair, participants remembered more details about the true memories, and they reported that the true memories were clearer. Nonetheless, many people remembered false events as though they had personally experienced them.[18]

Remembering Things Forgotten

At the time of Loftus's work, most therapists assumed that memo-ries could be repressed for years and then recovered. Belief in re-pressed memories had been around for so long that everyone assumed it to be true. Repressed memories were central to Freud's theory about the nature of unconscious processes, and since his time, no one had felt it necessary to prove their existence. As the possibility of implanting false memories became evident, believers in repressed memories, such as those in the Recovered Memories Project,[19] began to collect evidence demonstrating that repressed memories can, in fact, be recovered. Researchers even made progress in identifying the brain systems involved in repression.[20] In retro-spect, the data had always been there. For example, the fact that war veterans often forget traumatic battles had been known for cen-turies. The syndrome that is now called post-traumatic stress disor-der (PTSD)—a condition that many veterans of the Iraq war now suffer—was called traumatic war neurosis during World War II, shell shock in World War I, and nostalgia during the American Civil War.[21]

In one of the best studies on recovered memory, 129 adult women who had suffered childhood sexual abuse were identified through medical and social service records. When interviewed an average of seventeen years after the abuse, 38 percent of the women failed to recall the abuse.[22] Other researchers have taken the opposite ap-proach. Instead of identifying women who are known to have suf-fered sexual abuse based upon records and then asking them if they remember the abuse, psychologist Jonathan Schooler and others have identified women who have uncovered memories of childhood sexual abuse and then found corroborating evidence for the abuse.

To date, the Recovered Memory Project has documented more than one hundred cases of memories recovered many years after they were initially experienced and repressed from conscious awareness.

Recovering Valid Memories Versus Implanting False Memories

During the 1990s, discussion of the veracity of memories moved from psychology departments to the media. At the same time Loftus and others were demonstrating that false memories can be implanted, other psychologists and therapists were recovering memories of childhood abuse and trauma. The clients and therapists who recovered the memories believed those memories to be true. Others believed that the recovered memories had been planted by unwitting therapists, counselors, and social workers. Soon the "discussion" escalated into a vitriolic war. Therapists and psychologists accused one another of callousness and ignoring the data. Popular books such as *The Courage to Heal* encouraged readers to recover lost memories of childhood sexual abuse.[23] Such books advised (falsely) that such memories were more likely to be true, the stronger the emotions associated with them. Those relatives accused of perpetrating these abuses were typically shocked, and when put in the media and legal spotlight, their lives were devastated.

Battle lines were drawn. On one side, advocates of recovered memory therapy believed that the memories their clients uncovered were true and the memories should be admitted as legal evidence. In one memorable case, a prominent businessman, George Franklin, was convicted for the murder of his daughter's friend that had occurred over twenty years earlier; the conviction was based largely upon his daughter's recovered memories of homicide and incest. The daughter, Eileen, had been eight at the time of the murder and claimed to have repressed memories of the murder and abuse for over twenty years. She maintained that she recovered the traumatic memories suddenly, when her own daughter neared the age at which her friend had been killed, and she was reminded of her childhood friend. Mr. Franklin spent six years in jail before his conviction was overturned. He was declared innocent, but his career was ruined.

On the other side of the battle was the False Memory Syndrome Foundation,[24] founded by family members accused of childhood sexual abuse by their adult children. The foundation argued forcefully that recovered memories were not true and were often planted. Like the individuals who recovered false memories, families accused of abuse felt pain and humiliation. Imagine receiving the letter below from one of your children:

> *Mom and Dad,*
>
> *Hi! Just thought I would drop you a line to say hi! I have been so busy lately I have forgotten to tell you guys how much I love you. You two have done so much for me. . . . You have continually supported me, loved me, and helped me work through my various problems and adventures. . . . I just wanted you guys to know that you are appreciated. I seldom tell you how much you guys mean to me. . . . I love you more than words can say.*
>
> Love "C"

Imagine later receiving this letter from the same child:

> *Dear First Name and Last Name,*
>
> *Why am I writing this letter: To state the truth—Dad I remember just about everything you did to me. Whether you remember it or not is immaterial—what's important is I remember. I had this experience the other day of regressing until I was a child just barely verbal. I was screaming and crying and absolutely hysterical. I was afraid that you were going to come and get me and torture me. That is what sexual abuse is to a child—the worst torture. . . . I needed your protection, guidance and understanding. Instead I got hatred, violation, humiliation and abuse. I don't have to forgive you. . . . I no longer give you the honor of being my father.*
>
> "C"[25]

The woman who wrote the letter above is obviously suffering tremendous pain—whether or not her memories are true. An innocent mother and father would be equally devastated. The reader cannot help but feel sympathy for those involved, but for whom? A woman who was abused by her father or a wrongly accused father? Research has demonstrated that it is possible to implant false memories simply by asking leading questions about the past. Therefore, it is likely that some events recalled in "recovered memories" never happened. Other research, however, clearly shows that memories can be repressed and later recovered. What percent of recovered memories are false? you ask. No one will ever know. No matter which side was "right," the clear losers in this war of memories were the many people who were thrown into the fray by overly eager therapists, social workers, pop psych authors, and lawyers. Negative memories hurt, whether or not they are real.

DOES THE OBJECTIVE PAST MATTER?

Our memories are fallible. We can forget things that actually happened, and we can remember things that did not. Despite the failings of memory, past events that objectively occurred may still play a substantial role in determining who we are. It is possible that, although we can't remember the past, our lives are fundamentally determined by it.[26] Yet psychologists have increasingly begun to question this assumption, pointing to the difficulty of establishing a clear relationship between negative past events and negative outcomes as well as positive past events—such as interventions—and positive outcomes.[27] Martin Seligman, past president of the American Psychological Association, writes:

> I think that the events of childhood are overrated; in fact, I think past history in general is overrated. It has turned out to be difficult to find even small effects of childhood events on adult personality, and there is no evidence at all of large—to say nothing of determining—effects.
>
> The major traumas of childhood may have some influence on adult personality, but only a barely detectable one. Bad childhood events, in short, do not mandate adult troubles.

There is no justification in these studies for blaming your adult depression, anxiety, bad marriage, drug use, sexual problems, unemployment, aggression against your children, alcoholism, or anger on what happened to you as a child.[28]

So, which is it? Does the past determine our lives or is the past overrated?

We authors believe that the past matters, but it matters less than Freud and the behaviorists claimed. Everyone is affected by the factual past but not completely determined by it. And it is not the events of the past that most strongly influence our lives. *Your attitudes toward events in the past matter more than the events themselves.* This distinction between the past and your current interpretation of it is critical, because it offers hope for change. *You cannot change what happened in the past, but you can change your attitudes toward what happened.* Sometimes changing the frame can alter the way you see the picture.

Your Attitudes Toward the Past Matter

Time-out One: Relationships between Attitudes toward the Past and Psychological and Behavioral Characteristics

Behavioral Characteristics	People High in Past-negative Are	People High in Past-positive Are
Aggression	More aggressive	Less aggressive
Anxiety	More anxious	Less anxious
Conscientiousness	Less conscientious	More conscientious
Consideration of future consequences	Less consideration	Not different
Creativity	Not different	More creative
Depression	More depressed	Less depressed
Emotional stability	Less stable	More stable
Energy	Less energy	More energy
Exercise	Less often	Not different
Friendliness	Less friendly	More friendly

Behavioral Characteristic	People High in Past-negative Are	People High in Past-positive Are
Gambling	More positive toward gambling	Not different
Happiness	Less happy	More happy
Impulse control	Less control	Not different
Ego control	Less control	Not different
Frequency of lying	More lying	Not different
Novelty seeking	More novelty-seeking	Not different
Reward dependence	Not different	More reward dependence
Self-esteem	Less self-esteem	More self-esteem
Shyness	More shy	Less shy
Frequency of stealing	More stealing	Not different
Temper	More temper	Not different

Psychologists have demonstrated that no one can be certain about what happened in the past, but our research has shown that what people believe about the past influences how they think, feel, and behave in the present. People who have positive attitudes about the past—whether or not these attitudes are based upon accurate memories—tend to be happier, healthier, and more successful than people who have negative attitudes toward the past. Of course, everyone experiences both positive and negative events during life. As a result, most of us carry both positive and negative attitudes toward the past.

Time-out One illustrates the ways in which beliefs about the past affect people's lives in the present. The column labeled "Past-negative" compares people who score high on the past-negative scale of the ZTPI with people who score low. For example, people with high past-negative scores tend to be more aggressive than people who score low. For certain characteristics, there are no differences between high and low scores, but for others, there are some critical differences that put past-negative people at psychological risk. Both of your authors' scores on the past-negative time perspective are 1.9 on the 1–5 point scale. We therefore do not have strong negative attitudes toward the past.

The column labeled "Past-positive" compares people who score high on the past-positive with people who score low on this time perspective. For example, people who score high on the past-positive tend to be less anxious than people who score low. Phil's score on the past-positive time perspective is a perfect 5.0. John's score is a near-perfect 4.8. We both thus have relatively strong positive attitudes toward the past.

Psychologists Bob Emmons and Mike McCullough discovered that attitudes toward the past are key to the development of gratitude, which allows you to appreciate your life in the present. Their work and our work on the past-positive time perspective suggests that positive attitudes toward the past are associated with greater happiness and health. In one study, McCullough and Emmons assigned a class of two hundred students to one of three groups. One group—the "grateful" group—was asked to think back over the past week and write down five things in their lives for which they were thankful. A second group—the "hassles" group—was asked to list up to five hassles that occurred in the past week. The third group—the "objective events" group—was asked to write down five events that had an impact on them over the past week. All groups completed the their lists weekly for nine weeks. Students also made similar tallies of mood, physical symptoms (such as minor illnesses), reaction to social support, amount of time spent exercising, and overall mental health. At the end of the nine weeks, students in the gratitude group rated their lives more favorably and reported fewer physical illnesses than students in the hassles or objective events group, and they reported spending more time exercising than the students in the hassles group. They also had more positive emotion overall. McCullough and Emmons replicated their work using people suffering from neuromuscular disease. Again, participants in the gratitude group reported greater satisfaction with their lives, more optimism regarding the upcoming week, and greater connection with others. They also reported getting more hours of sleep and being more refreshed upon waking.

Time-out Two: Measuring Attitudes Toward the Past

The Past-positive Time Perspective	The Gratitude Survey	The Past-negative Time Perspective
It gives me pleasure to think about my past.	I have so much in life to be thankful for.	I think about the bad things that have happened to me in the past.
I get nostalgic about my childhood.	If I had to list everything that I felt grateful for, it would be a very long list.	Painful past experiences keep being replayed in my mind.
Happy memories of good times spring readily to mind.	When I look at the world, I don't see much to be grateful for.*	It's hard for me to forget unpleasant images of my youth.
On balance, there is much more good to recall than bad in my past.	I am grateful to a wide variety of people.	I often think of what I should have done differently in my life.
I enjoy stories about how things used to be in the "good old times."	As I get older, I find myself more able to appreciate the people, events, and situations that have been part of my life history.	I think about the good things that I have missed out on in my life.
Familiar childhood sights, sounds, and smells often bring back a flood of wonderful memories.	Long amounts of time can go by before I feel grateful to something or someone.*	I've made mistakes in the past that I wish that I could undo.
I like family rituals and traditions that are regularly repeated.		I've taken my share of abuse and rejection in the past.
I find myself tuning out when family members talk about the way things used to be.*		Even when I am enjoying the present, I am drawn back to comparisons with similar past experiences.
The past has too many unpleasant memories that I prefer not to think about.*		Things rarely work out as I expected.
		My decisions are mostly influenced by people and things around me.

*These statements come from the ZPTI; the starred statements are reversed.

A POSITIVE RECONSTRUCTION OF THE PAST

When we met Edie Eger, she was a glowing sixty-eight-year-old who exuded a joy for life. To the Stanford psychology class to which she spoke, she made aging seem fun. Her voice grew dark, however, as she recounted her arrival at the Auschwitz concentration camp in 1944 at the age of sixteen. After stepping from the cattle car in which she and her family had traveled from Hungary, prisoners were split into two lines. The infamous Dr. Mengele, "the angel of death," pointed to the line on the left, and Edie began to follow her mother toward the line. Mengele then yelled and directed Edie and her sister to the other line, on the right. The line on the left was for the "expendables," the elderly and sickly. The line on the right led to slave labor and the chance to live one more day. Later—while still standing in line—Edie asked a woman next to her when she would see her mother again. The woman pointed to a plume of smoke rising from the ovens and said, "You can see her there. She is burning. You better speak of her in the past tense." Edie clung to her younger sister, who said, "The soul never dies." They never saw their mother again.

Many people would have been overwhelmed by this and other horrifying experiences, and no one would blame them for it—but not Edie. She also told the story of a time when her sister was starving. Edie climbed over a wall and sneaked into the guards' garden to search for food. Before finding any, Edie was spotted by a guard. The guards had strict orders to shoot on sight any prisoner who left the yard, but Edie made it safely back over the wall unscathed. The next day, during a lineup, the guard who had seen but not recognized her asked the person who had attempted to steal the guards' food to step forward. Edie knew that stepping forward could cost her life, but she also knew that if she didn't step forward, someone else might be blamed for her act. So Edie bravely stepped forward and identified herself. The guard approached her slowly and said, "You must have been very hungry to try something like that. Here, take this." He handed her a loaf of bread and sent her back to her place in line. There would be no negative repercussions. At the end of the story, Edie faced the class and asked, "How do you explain that?"

Edie also recounted the important role that humor played in the camps. On one occasion, the women prisoners held an impromptu "best boobs" contest. At first, the story appeared an odd digression, but Edie made sense of this event, too. Even at her age, Edie was proud to have won the competition.

We authors have visited some of the concentration camps. We have seen the barracks and the gas chambers. And we have been fortunate to meet people who lived through their experiences in them. To some small extent, we understand the terrible suffering that this woman—then only a girl—endured. The events were so painful that Edie did not share them with others for thirty years. Her past was horrific, yet she took the best from it and encouraged others to do the same, a testament to the power that each of us has to reconstruct and reinterpret the past. As a psychotherapist, she now empowers others whose lives have been filled with various forms of suffering to go beyond surviving to thriving. Edie's final words to our psychology class were these: "I am all about life and living, not death and dying, although death is part of life."

CHANGING YOUR ATTITUDES TOWARD THE PAST

You cannot change the past, but you can change your attitudes toward it. To begin the process of proactively reconstructing your past, please complete the Who Was I? test. This test consists of the same question—who was I?—asked twenty times in succession. Don't worry if you can't answer all twenty questions, but do take your time trying. List the twenty most important ways that you would describe yourself as you were in the past. No one but you ever has to see this list, so there is no need to make yourself look better or worse than you really were. Be sure to hold on to this test, because you will return to it in a few weeks.

Time-out Three: The Who Was I? Test

1. I was: _____

2. I was: _____

3. I was: _____

4. I was: _____

5. I was: _____

6. I was: _____

7. I was: _____

8. I was: _____

9. I was: _____

10. I was: _____

11. I was: _____

12. I was: _____

13. I was: _____

14. I was: _____

15. I was: _____

16. I was: _____

17. I was: _____

18. I was: _____

19. I was: _____

20. I was: _____

Once you have completed the Who Was I? test, please complete the Reconstructing a Positive Past worksheet on the next page. The three events that you choose to list can be any you like, but you should choose events that you continue to associate with negative emotions, such as guilt, shame, humiliation, sadness, and fear. Remember that the events are past; they do not determine who you are today, and *you can* change your attitudes toward them. Also be assured that reinterpreting the past is not disrespectful to others who may be present in your memories. Rather, it is respectful. Reinterpreting the past simply gives you control over your past, rather than allowing your past to control you. Letting go and moving forward does not mean that the past is forgotten—it is just made more agreeable.

Time-out Four: Reconstructing a Positive Past Worksheet

List three significant negative events that have occurred in your life:

Event 1. _____

Event 2. _____

Event 3. _____

What positive messages can be taken from these events?
(e.g.: Because you made it through challenging events in the past, you know you will make it through challenging events in the future.)

Event 1. _____

Event 2. _____

Event 3. _____

How can these lessons improve your future?
(e.g.: You may have learned to avoid similar situations in the future, or you may have learned how to cope with similar situations more effectively.)

Event 1. _____

Event 2. _____

Event 3. _____

Once you've completed the Reconstructing a Positive Past work-sheet, complete a Gratitude List each day for two weeks. At the end of each day, simply write a list of the things for which you were grateful that day. The list can be as long or as short as you like. You may want to keep a pen and pad on your nightstand to remind you to complete the task.

After completing a Gratitude List each day for two weeks, complete the Who Was I? test again. Once you've completed it, take out the last Who Was I? test that you completed. For each of the twenty questions on both tests, give yourself a "+" if your answer reflected a positive attitude toward the past, a "0" if your answer reflected a neutral attitude toward the past, and a "-" if your answer reflected a negative attitude toward the past. Count up the number of "+" and "-" signs that you received on each test. For each time you took the test, subtract the number of "-" that you received from the number of "+" that you received. Over the course of two weeks, your score should have increased to become more positive. If it has not, don't despair. Your past did not happen overnight, and it is likely that change will take time as well. Rest assured that you will change, and when you do, you will be better prepared to nudge yourself into a more positive direction, into a happier time zone. Remember that we are working to change the course of the great river of your life, and that small efforts—given time—can lead to substantial change. And no matter how you scored, completing a Gratitude List daily may lighten your mood and improve your health.

THE GOOD IN THE PAST

At this point in our journey through time, it may seem as though the past is more trouble than it is worth: You can seldom be certain that your memories of it are accurate, and it can cause pain to your-self and others. So what good is the past? First of all, our pasts pro-vide us with continuity and a sense of self. Without the past, our lives would be as unpredictable as the course of a billiard ball for which the laws of physics constantly changed. For those of us who have positive attitudes toward the past, it can be a source of happiness. Just as remembering negative events can elicit negative emotions, remembering positive events can elicit positive emotions. As Martial, a first-century Roman poet, wrote, "To be able to enjoy one's past life is to live twice."[29] Therefore, fostering positive attitudes may be as important as eliminating negative ones.

The past is also our best predictor of the future. It's notoriously imperfect, but it is all that we have. We can be certain that some relationships uncovered from the past will hold true in the future. The challenge is to figure out which relationships they are. As Freud wrote, "The less a man knows about the past and the present the more insecure must prove to be his judgment of the future."[30] Freud is not the only one to make this observation. The American patriot Patrick Henry remarked, "I have but one lamp by which my feet are guided, and that is the lamp of experience. I know no way of judging of the future but by the past."[31]

What's Bad About Living in the Past?

Whether you are biased toward a positive or negative remembrance of the past, your perspective provides backward-looking orientation, not a forward focus. The past may give you a sense of security, especially if your recollections are good ones. However, new adventures lie ahead. If you are stuck in the past, you are less likely to take chances, to make new friends, to try new foods, or to expose yourself to new music and art. You want the status quo and abhor change.

If the people in a culture that uses the past to evaluate current situations share a past trauma, they are likely to want revenge—even if the crimes against them were committed many decades ago. The perceived perpetrators are not forgiven; they must be punished. This vendetta mentality undercuts attempts at peaceful reconciliation and promotes violence and warfare as new generations are obligated to avenge or pay for crimes against their parents or grandparents.

To the extent that people share positive views of the past, they seek to maintain the status quo culturally and politically. They do not want change; rather, they seek to conserve and re-create in the present what was good in the past. This view may blind them to newer, better ways of doing things. In a global economy, nations that live in the past will be left behind.

MAINTAINING A POSITIVE PAST

Phil was stuck in a traffic jam on the outskirts of Naples, Italy, one Sunday. While he was surprised at the Sunday traffic, his driver was not. In that city, as in many European countries, people often double-park while buying flowers to take to the graves of their loved ones. Most families have a member who regularly pays respect to their dead, who are never forgotten. On any given day, most grave sites are adorned with freshly cut flowers. By contrast, it takes a national holiday for floral abundance to grace cemeteries in the United States. Over time, acts like these become cultural traditions, like big Sunday family dinners.

Israeli time researcher Rachel Karniol believes that although the past can be a foe to humankind, there is also substantial evidence that the past is in many ways a friend. She notes that:

> The relation of the past to the present and imagined future is a two-way street, with reciprocal connections between people's goals and recollections. The past can come to mind uninvited, color the present, and push individuals into action: people can use their memories to guide their selection of goals and plans; and people can use their memories to help them achieve their chosen goals. Finally, goals can affect how people retrieve, construct, and interpret their memories.[32]

You can use the power of the past to create a secure base from which to envision a future where you can make healthier, safer, more meaningful decisions. Two researchers at the University of California, Berkeley, were surprised to discover that many actively injecting drug users reported "doing nothing" all day. This meant "nothing new," "nothing different," "nothing important." Those who held this view of their past were also at higher risk than those drug users whose day included doing "something"; the first group reported more needle sharing and less condom use. Essential to recovery from drug abuse is a fixed daily schedule in which one's time is highly structured.

The researchers Julie Goldberg and Christina Maslach[33] also found that the ways in which people think about their past is related to their ability to imagine their future. To test this view, they surveyed nearly three hundred undergraduate students who completed our ZTPI as well as a basic scale measuring the five major dimensions of personality, the Big Five Questionnaire (BFQ). Before outlining a sample of their provocative results, it is important to note that our time perspective measure explained behavioral differences, regardless of personality, sex, or ethnicity.

- Those who reported most involvement with their families were most likely to be highly past-positive. They saw their families regularly for no special reason. They were also more involved in family traditions and planned to continue practicing them in the future. They entertained a broader sense of extended family going back over more generations than did those with different time perspectives.

- Those who are engaged in family traditions from the past have both a higher past-positive and a higher future orientation than those who do not continue to honor those traditions.

- Past familial experiences influence future goal-setting. The students who had described specific goals one or five years ahead wrote that family traditions had directed them to make meaningful decisions in their lives.

- Finally, this research found that higher scores on the past-positive time perspective were related to setting specific one-year goals, to setting five-year goals, and even to writing about more specific plans for next week.

  Involvement with family traditions and regular family contact contribute both to developing a positive-past time frame and to shaping a more viable vision of the future.

If holocaust survivors are able to retain a positive outlook on life and to see the good in the past, so can you. If people who suffer from neuromuscular diseases are able to find things for which they are grateful—and by so doing increase their happiness—so can you. By changing the way you think about your past, you can change your future. You don't need to repress memories or to avoid the negative things that you have experienced in your life. In fact, you should remember the negative things that have happened so you can avoid repeating them. But you can also work to change your attitudes toward negative past experiences and to emphasize the positive memories and attitudes that you already have. You can free yourself from your past and embrace the future by letting go of negative attitudes and nurturing positive attitudes toward the past. According to the Dalai Lama, happiness is not a static state that we attain. It is an elusive goal that we must constantly pursue.[34] So it is with the past. Even a happy past is under constant reconstruction. By rebuilding your past upon a foundation of positive attitudes, you can reclaim it for yourself, and in so doing, free yourself for the pursuit of happiness in the present and the future.

four

THE PRESENT

An Instant for All That Is Real

Remember that man's life lies all within this present,
as 'fwere but a hair's-breadth of time;
as for the rest, the past is gone, the future yet unseen.
Short, therefore, is man's life,
and narrow is the corner of the earth wherein he dwells.
                    —*Marcus Aurelius* (Meditations, *III, 10*)

One life—a little gleam of time between two Eternities.
                    —*Thomas Carlyle*

When we are infants, biological urges dominate our lives. All that exists is the here and now. Our brains have not yet developed their capacity for storing and recalling memories, so we have little sense of past. Nor has the brain's frontal cortex developed sufficiently to enable us to plan for future events or to imagine alternative scenarios. A baby is a little present-oriented hedonist who wants nothing more than to get pleasure and avoid pain.

Our lives start with a natural focus on the present, but some people continue to focus on present biological stimulation into adulthood, responding only to events happening in their immediate physical and social environment. Others, as we saw in the last chapter, base their decisions and actions on memories rather than on current experience. Still others, as we shall see in the following chapter, base decisions on their expectations of future scenarios, suppressing present reality in favor of anticipated contingencies. For them, two birds in the bush are worth one in hand. As with other time perspectives, an excessive present orientation has a number of positive elements associated with it. However, living in accordance with extreme bias exacts a toll on the quality of life that often outweighs whatever benefits it may offer. This is a paradox of time: Some present orientation is needed to enjoy life. Too much present orientation can rob life of happiness.

WHAT MAKES SOMEONE PRESENT-ORIENTED?

In a society that is politically and economically unstable, you cannot predict the future from the vantage of the present. You work hard and put money in the bank to save for a rainy day, but inflation suddenly soars and makes your money worthless. The rules of the game of life seem to change randomly, so why would you invest in the future? You probably would not. You would focus on the present. People in volatile economies do not invest, because it is better to spend now than have their earnings lose value tomorrow. When people do not invest in savings or put their money into insurance policies, those institutions do not have sufficient funds to provide mortgage and business loans. This, in turn, means there is less cash for construction or new business ventures and less overall opportunity.

Political and economic instability also causes instability within families and causes people to trust only what they can hold in their hands. The development of a future orientation requires stability and consistency in the present, or people cannot make reasonable estimates of the future consequences of their actions. Promises of what is inconceivable and out of sight mean little. The less people can rely on the promises of government, institutions, and families, the more they eschew the future and focus on the present, creating a world of yes and no, black and white, is and is not, rather than one filled with maybes, contingencies, and probabilities. Present-oriented people do not use basic if-then reasoning—i.e., what causes or leads to what—and therefore can be at a disadvantage in bargaining and negotiating, in conflict resolution, and in academic and professional settings. In short, they may be at a disadvantage in the complex postmodern world.

Less educated people are more likely to live in the present. Education helps to develop a sense of the past through the study of history, through studying for tests and grades that determine success or failure, and through the need to delay gratification. Societies that offer less opportunity for education are likely to have more citizens whose focus is limited to the present. This is especially the case where even minimal educational resources are unavailable for women; when women's educational level advances, their children and social class also advance.

Social class is both a contributor to and a consequence of time perspective. Future orientation is a prerequisite for membership in the middle class.[1] Ambition and need for achievement drive a future orientation that focuses on work, savings, and planning for a continually better life through one's efforts. A broad-based middle class stabilizes a nation and enhances the gross national product through its work ethic and its investment in the future of its children. Present-oriented people are likely to be less concerned with work and more cynical about current efforts paying off in the future. They are also more distrustful of society, institutions, and families, all of which prevent movement up the social-class ladder. Living in the present time zone means a greater likelihood of being in the lower class in any society.

In contrast to the lower and middle classes, the rich or upper class can afford to take any time perspective they want. Some are the recipients of old money inherited from a family legacy that stressed adherence to past tradition and future planning. The nouveau riche worked hard for their social gains; they came up with new technology or inventions, or they earned stock options from Yahoo!, Apple, or Microsoft early on. Present-oriented top athletes or rock stars also worked hard for their money, but many also retained a present perspective that biases them toward addictive behaviors.

Lifestyle differences and social aspirations are *learned* methods of dealing with the options available, not inherent differences based on genetic or brain-based inequality. You can modify your time perspective to become more balanced and free yourself from learned biases that prevent you from realizing your fullest potential. Yet many future-oriented people—lay, public, and professionals alike—hold prejudices about the innate origins of present orientation among the lower class. In his book *The Unheavenly City*, the economist Edward Banfield argued that the lower class is present-oriented to a pathological extent:

> The term normal . . . refer[s] to class culture that is not lower class. The implication that lower class culture is pathological seems fully warranted both because of the relatively high incidence of mental illness in the lower class, and also because human nature seems loath to accept a style of life that is so radically present-oriented. Some word is needed to designate the sector of the class cultural continuum that is not lower class, and no other word seems preferable on the whole.[2]

Banfield is future-oriented, and he obviously believes that everyone else should be, too. To him, present orientation is the cancer of the poor for which there is no cure, and those who are not future-oriented are abnormal. Attributing pathology to Presents, however, denies the value of remedial programs that might raise their educational and skill levels.

Acceptance of future orientation as the "normal" time perspective is not limited to Banfield. Our colleague Robert Levine, in his fascinating exploration *A Geography of Time*,[3] offers many vivid examples of how place influences purpose in life. In northern Italy, a movement (*La Lega*, headed by Umberto Bossi) has started in recent years to divide the country into separate states of north and south. The dividing line would include the prosperous cities of Milan, Turin, and Genoa and extend to just below Bologna and Florence. All the rest—Rome, Naples, and Sicily—would be designated the "other" Italy. The reason for this extreme circumcision is that hard-working northern Italians resent having to pay taxes that take care of their "lazy," "self-indulgent" southern neighbors. "We work, they play, and we pay for their fun" is the chant that political organizers might use to arouse their constituents to vote for division. The conflict between north and south is clearly rooted in time. The north produces most of Italy's wealth: big business, job opportunities, and a workforce whose future focus is shared by their German and Austrian neighbors.

Big business is not as willing to establish itself in the southernmost regions, where the Mafia still exacts payment from business large and small and can control unions. The absence of industry causes high unemployment, and valuing work becomes a lost virtue. Consider what it means to be unemployed in a small Sicilian town, where unemployment can run as high as 50 percent:

> As of now they're [young people] just left on their own, without training or the hope of a job, so they just give up and stand around in the squares or play cards in the bars. Early in the morning, if you take the bus for work, you see them hanging around, gambling for a cup of coffee. When the harvest's over you're usually jobless. So you wander all around town. . . . You joke around to pass the time. . . . Then you go back home and the wife is grumbling, there's nothing to eat, words fly. . . . So what do you do? Nothing. You go back to the bar. If you have some change, you gamble. If not, you watch. . . . We all want to change this way of life. But where do we start?[4]

This commentary of the Sicilian author Danilo Dolci, in *Sicilian Lives,* applies today to many pockets of poverty around the world.[5] Work structures daily life into orderly, predictable units, as do school and college. Being out of work or out of school wipes away that external structure and therefore demands an internally imposed sense of self-efficacy to navigate through each day. But that can-do sense does not develop fully if one is present-oriented. Without it, people doubt that they can change anything for the better. They become resigned to what is and do not strive to create a better what could be.

THE ECONOMICS OF DISCOUNTING THE FUTURE

Focusing on the present and discounting the future sometimes makes sense—for instance, when a present circumstance is a sure thing and the future is uncertain.[6] Imagine that you are given the choice between receiving a hundred dollars today or a hundred dollars a week from today. Which would you choose? Most people choose the hundred dollars today, because they can use the money now and they are not fully certain they will actually receive the money promised next week. Many things could happen between now and next week that could prevent the payment: The man who promised you the money could lose his job; he could be robbed, get sick, forget his promise, or decide to give it to someone else. Because of these uncertainties, you don't really value the money that you could receive next week as much as you value the money today. You *discount* the hundred dollars next week, so it is worth less.[7] If you are 80 percent certain that you'll receive the money next week, then in today's dollars, it would be worth about eighty dollars. But how can you really have any degree of certainty about your future chances?

Let's change the scenario: You are offered a hundred dollars today or a hundred and fifty dollars a week from today. Now the decision becomes interesting. Take the sure money and run, or wait and increase your gain. Some people still choose the money today. They discount the money next week so much that in their mind it is worth less. Others choose the money next week. They, too, discount the hundred and fifty, but they don't discount it as much. In their minds, the hundred and fifty may be worth only a hundred and twenty-five or a hundred and ten today, but it is still worth more than a hundred.

A solely present-oriented person would discount the future completely. He or she would choose the money today even if promised a thousand dollars next week. In his mind, the thousand dollars would be worth zero or much less than the sure hundred bucks. A future-oriented person, in contrast, would discount the future very little and probably choose even a small possible gain in the future over less sure money now. Of course, most people lie somewhere between these two extremes. Where do you fit? How much bigger would the future amount have to be than the current amount for you to wait? What would make you prize a bigger future despite its uncertainty over a smaller present certainty?

THREE WAYS OF BEING PRESENT-ORIENTED

People can be oriented toward the present in three ways: as present hedonists, present fatalists, and present holists. When we refer to people as Hedonists, Fatalists, or Holists, we are using shorthand to refer to people who are high on these three dimensions.

Time-out One: Relationships between Attitudes Toward the Present and Psychological and Behavioral Characteristics

Behavioral Characteristic	People High in Present Hedonism Are	People High in Present Fatalism Are
Aggression	More aggressive	More aggressive
Depression	More depressed	More depressed
Energy	More energy	Less energy
Wear a watch	Less likely	Not different
Exercise	More exercise	Not different
Gambling	More gambling	Not different
Friendliness	Not different	Not different
Conscientiousness	Less conscientious	Less conscientious
Emotional stability	Less emotionally stable	Less emotionally stable
Openness	Not different	Less open
Consideration of future consequences	Less concern for future consequences	Less concern for future consequences
Ego control	Less ego control	Less ego control
Impulse control	Less impulse control	Less impulse control
Novelty-seeking	More novelty-seeking	More novelty-seeking
Preference for consistency	Less preference for consistency	Less preference for consistency
Reward dependence	Not different	Not different

(continued)

Behavioral Characteristics	People High in Present Hedonism Are	People High in Present Fatalism Are
Self-esteem	Not different	Less self-esteem
Sensation-seeking	More sensation-seeking	More sensation-seeking
Anxiety	Not different	More anxious
Grade point average	Not different	Lower grade point average
Hours studied per week	Study less	Not different
Creativity	More creative	Less creative
Happiness	More happy	Less happy
Frequency of lying	Lie more	Lie more
Frequency of stealing	Steal more	Steal more
Shyness	Less shy	More shy
Temper	Not different	More temper

Present Hedonism

When we talk about living in the present, we usually mean being present-hedonistic. Hedonistic people enjoy all things that yield pleasure and avoid all things that cause pain. Beyond passive enjoyment, Hedonists actively seek pleasure. They arrange their choices in life around activities and relationships that are pleasurable, arousing, stimulating, exciting, and novel. They focus on immediate gratification, self-stimulation, and short-term payoffs. Such people avoid people and situations that are tedious, that require high effort and maintenance, or that are regularized or boring. They are playful and impulsive at all ages, undertaking play and pleasant leisure activities for their intrinsic worth and continuing them as long as they do not become boring.

Our research[8] found that hedonistic college-age students also seek novelty, sensations, and have a high level of energy. They are often engaged in many different sports and physical activities for as long as they stay healthy. On the negative side, they are likely to have undercontrolled egos, to prefer inconsistency in their lives, to have weak impulse control, and to be less conscientiousness and emotionally stable than others. On the positive side, they make good friends, lovers, and party guests. They enjoy other people as a source of stimulation, as long as the others are not boring, which they generally consider teachers and bosses to be.

Phil's score on the present-hedonistic factor is 3.5, which is much higher than it was before he retired. John's score is 2.9. (Both John and Phil would like to indulge their hedonistic impulses more fully in the future.)

Present Fatalism

Imagine that you are an uneducated mother or father trying to survive below the poverty level. You have lost your job. Your children are doing poorly in school. Your son is using drugs and is in a gang. Your teenage daughter is pregnant. Rent is past due. You are likely to be the last hired and the first fired when there are layoffs. What chances do you have of changing and improving your life? The realistic answer is little or none. Suppose further that you are an immigrant who could not find work in your home country. You are likely to be forced into a low-skilled job in which your self-esteem will be eroded as people treat you with the disdain or indifference that is commonly meted out to service workers. Over time, you are likely to begin to believe that nothing you do makes a difference to the future. While others are rewarded because of their privilege, entitlement, and connections, you can barely get by.

"My life path is controlled by forces I cannot influence." That inner voice rings loud and clear for people with a fatalist view of life, a kind of learned helplessness. Their behavior does not produce or even influence the outcomes they desire. Resignation and cynicism overwhelm hopefulness and optimism. They wait for their ship to come in, their luck to change, their number to pay off, but have nothing to bank their future on. In the end, the house always wins. Phil's score on the present-fatalistic time perspective is 1.1; John's is 1.7.

Many people adopt a Fatalist time perspective from religious beliefs that center on predestination. They believe that if our lives are all laid out in advance by a god's master plan, whatever happens is meant to be and is predetermined independent of individual actions. Some factions of the Islamic religion hold the belief that Allah is the master planner who has arranged for them and their family to be at His side in the next life—or not to be. This belief has specific repercussions on a daily basis. For instance, recently, during the holy pilgrimage to Mecca, hundreds died in a stampede. This had also happened in previous years, but most on the pilgrimage thought that these people were meant to die that day, either there or somewhere else. They did not assume that the authorities were at fault and should have planned ahead after the last stampede to take precautions. Nor did they think that security guards guiding the masses through the narrowed space could have averted the disaster. This fatalistic sentiment, tinged with a hint of pragmatism, is revealed in a famous Muslim proverb: "Trust in Allah, but tie your camel."

Even functioning college students attending classes at a good California college can become Fatalists. It is unclear why young people embrace such attitudes toward time so early in their lives, but it is abundantly clear that doing so negatively affects their health and their future. For such students, the more extreme their fatalistic orientation, the more aggressive, anxious, and depressed they are. Fatalistic students are also less concerned about future consequences, have less ego control, less energy, and lower self-esteem. They are also less conscientious, less emotionally stable, and less happy. Surprisingly, these young men and women are also high on novelty-seeking. Searching for something new may seem to them a means to offset the predictably negative course life has charted for them. It could also open them to trying new ways of getting revenge against society or its representatives for their unhappiness.

Such a present-fatalistic orientation may have figured in the massacre at Virginia Tech University's Blacksburg campus in April 2007. Seung-Hui Cho, the twenty-three-old student from South Korea who killed thirty-two other students and teachers and wounded another twenty-five before committing suicide, made a video before the massacre that was filled with anger about being rejected, ignored, humiliated, and isolated by his peers and faculty. A fatalistic manifesto of his rage against the indifference and humiliation he felt vividly describes his pain and also his inability to relate to others or feel compassion:

> Do you know what it feels like to be spit on your face and to have trash shoved down your throat? Do you know what it feels like to dig your own grave? . . . Do you know what it feels like to be humiliated and be impaled upon on a cross? And left to bleed to death for your amusement? . . . I didn't have to do this. . . . I could have fled. But no, I will no longer run. When the time came, I did it. I had to. . . . You had a hundred billion chances and ways to have avoided today, but you decided to spill my blood. You forced me into a corner and gave me only one option. The decision was yours. Now you have blood on your hands that will never wash off.[9]

For poor kids growing up in inner-city ghettos, a sense of fatalism pervades everything, and with good reason. The prevalence of drugs and weapons in their communities leads to high homicide levels. A recent report on the rise in youth killings in Oakland, California, found that fatalism was rampant: "Young people in some of the city's most crime-plagued neighborhoods said there is a sense of fatalism among those who turn to drug dealing and gangs." Having little education, no access to well-paying jobs, and criminal records that make them unemployable, they have no place to go but down. "They live like they're hopeless. Most of the dope guys don't think they're going to live past thirty-five," said a youngster who watches their dealings and watches them grow old fast.[10]

Holistic Present

This third attitude toward the present is very different from either present fatalism or present hedonism. Holism is the absolute present, a concept central to Buddhism and meditation, and is very different from the Western linear view of time. The absolute present contains both past and future. The present is neither a slave to the past nor a means to the future. Daily meditation gives the practitioner the experience of being in the present moment, unfiltered through the lenses of the past or future.

By opening your mind fully to the present moment, you give up longing and desire for future possibilities and surrender past regrets and obligations. This form of present attention or mindfulness can fill your entire being, replacing your sense of past and future with a sense of everything being one and the same. This is why we have called it the holistic present. With this perspective, the past, the present, the future, the physical, the mental, and the spiritual elements in life are not separate but closely interconnected within you. The holistic present reflects neither the pleasure-seeking of present hedonism nor the cynicism and resignation of present fatalism.

Sanskrit, India's classical language, captures that unique attitude toward time in this ancient saying:

> *Yesterday is already a dream*
> *And tomorrow but a vision*
> *But today well lived makes every yesterday a dream of*
> *happiness*
> *And every tomorrow a vision of hope.*

Although the holistic present is not common to Western thinking, many Western philosophers and theologians have written about it as something of an ideal. Certainly, the great poets Shakespeare, Donne, and Robert Herrick ("Gather ye rosebuds while ye may") wrote of the need for mindfulness of our mortality and duties and enjoyment of life in the present. The fourteenth-century Cawdor Castle in Scotland (Macbeth's territory) has engraved over its entrance: BE MINDFUL. All that is tangible and real in this world undeniably exists in the present. Among a long, distinguished list of psychologists and philosophers, William James, Kurt Lewin, and Karl Heidegger all stressed the role of the present and free will in human behavior. Free will, after all, is intentional action in the present that asserts a belief or thought. The present also contains the reconstruction of time that has passed and the construction of virtual time that will soon be present. The past and future are abstractions, mental constructions that are subject to distortion, wishful thinking, and the psychological disorders of depression, anxiety, and worry. The holistic present is a healthy perspective to have.

A FAST TRACK INTO THE PRESENT TIME ZONE

Religious beliefs and practices, socioeconomic limitations, geography, culture, and instability can motivate you to adopt any of the three forms of present orientation outlined here. But there is another quick and easy path to present orientation: drugs. Psychoactive drugs alter our consciousness in ways that drop the mental walls around full-bore present-tense experience. Past and future concerns and rational modes of thinking are suspended, while the mind's eye looks inward to a limitless present. Let us describe an unusual experience John had with drugs and time.

While preparing to teach an introductory psychology class at Stanford, Phil received a letter from the rector of the University of Peru, offering to give a lecture on his area of expertise—the psychology of shamanism—and also to perform a traditional Peruvian tea ceremony after the lecture. Phil accepted the offer, not knowing that the tea to be served was hallucinogetic. John, who was the head teaching assistant for the class, agreed to attend the tea ceremony and was put in charge of the event. Here is the rest of the story in John's words:

> The tea ceremony was held at nine P.M. in the psychology department lounge. I arranged to turn the lounge into an urban version of a Peruvian rain forest by removing furniture and concealing all sources of light. As the ceremony began, a single candle positioned in front of the rector illuminated the lounge, and about thirty students and their individually assigned personal attendants sat in a loose circle around the perimeter.

Earlier in the day, I had told friends that I did not plan to drink the tea. Like Phil, I had too much other work to do later that night. Nevertheless, as the tea was poured for each person individually, I decided that since I was stuck at the ceremony, I might as well try to enjoy it. In retrospect, it was one of the most present-oriented decisions that I have ever made.

As an attendant handed me a stone cup containing my portion of tea, he said, "The doctor says that this is for you and Professor Zimbardo." I'm still not completely clear about what this meant, but I suspect that I was given an extra-large portion of tea intended for both Phil and me. The drink tasted like a mixture of roots and dirt, seasoned with a hint of brown sugar. It didn't taste good, but it wasn't that bad, either.

The next thirty to forty-five minutes were filled with the sounds of people vomiting into bowls in front of them. No one went to the bathroom, no one got up, and no one seemed to be concerned with the vomiting. I did not get sick, but I did experience sudden anxiety regarding the potential future consequences of this unusual tea ceremony taking place on Stanford's campus. I thought that I would be expelled from school and given a short jail term, with substantial community service to amend for my giving in to the temptation to partake of the mysterious tea. My anxiety did not completely subside until I watched my left forearm dissolve into my left leg. Shortly thereafter, the white-clothed helpers of the rector/shaman began to dance, drum, and chant around the room. They were careful to attend to the members of the group who appeared to be reacting particularly strongly to the powerful hallucinogen.

Sightings of wild but not threatening jungle animals came into my vision. My body parts changed shape, stretching, contracting, and dissolving. A warm feeling of contentment flowed over and through me. I could feel my lips stretch into the biggest grin imaginable. Over six hours later, after what seemed at most like mere minutes, the shaman rose to his feet, and the chanting stopped. Suddenly, everyone in the audience sat up. No one had fallen asleep. The candle was extinguished and the lights turned back on. All but one of the students reported having gone on an extraordinarily beautiful trip. The exception was a student whose visions had been too real for comfort and who had gotten frightened.

John's sense of time had been totally altered from his usual to-do-list future focus into a magically expanded present. The Ayahuasca tea ceremony illustrates several important aspects of time perspective. First, it shows that a dominant future orientation can blind smart, well-intentioned people to near-term consequences. John and Phil were both looking beyond the little tea ceremony to the usual schoolwork that they needed to do, but they wanted to appease the guest speaker, be good hosts to their distinguished foreign guest, and provide a special event for their students. Their preoccupation with the future prevented them from making a full appraisal of what might happen in the present. In retrospect, it is unlikely that either of them would have allowed the ceremony to be held had they taken the time to inquire more fully about the kind of tea used; they had expected something more like a Japanese tea ceremony with music and dancing. Wrong!

Second, John's present-oriented decision to participate in the ceremony ran counter to his more typical future orientation, but it led to a night during which future focus melted into a totally present experience. Although Phil nearly got into trouble with the authorities because of the student who complained about being upset by what he had experienced, John could not wipe the toothy grin from his face for several days, evidence of the enduring power of the magic potion. Finally, it confirms, as have many other shamanic and drug experiences, that psychoactive substances can have a profound effect on our perception of time.

A Controlled Legal Trip into an Expanded Present

The problems associated with taking drugs such as LSD, marijuana, peyote, or DMT (the psychoactive ingredient in Ayahuasca tea) to alter your sense of time include the loss of volitional control, the

uncertain duration and jail time if you are caught by the authorities. A better alternative is using hypnosis to do the same thing,
cheaper, faster, and with controlled duration. And it's legal.

Hypnosis is a state of altered consciousness induced by verbal
suggestions that enhance concentration and minimize distracting
thoughts and feelings. Individuals vary in the degree to which they
are susceptible to hypnotic procedures. Low-hypnotizable people
cannot be hypnotized by the best stage hypnotists, while those who
are highly hypnotizable can readily go into a hypnotic state in response to suggestions from anyone they trust, including themselves.
The power of this tool for changing how the mind functions resides
entirely within the individual and not in the hypnotist.[11]

THE PRESENT IS EXPANDING:
PHIL'S PERSONAL TRIP BACK IN TIME

I escaped the hedonism and fatalism of my Sicilian family roots and
life in New York City's South Bronx ghetto, where I was born and
raised. Most of those around me lived for the moment, acting impulsively, sacrificing discipline and planned routines for the excitement
of immediate gratification and endless playtime. My father, when
employed, might blow most of his week's meager salary gambling on
prizefights, or buying rounds of drinks at the local bar that, unfortunately for my mother, happened to be located between the subway
station and home. My mother slipped into a fatalistic mode of thinking as a result. Life went on no matter what one did. As long as it
was somehow possible to put food on the table, she felt, you grinned
and bore it and didn't try to change human nature. Few from my
neighborhood went to college, and if they finished high school, they
went right into low-paying service jobs. Because those jobs were
boring, weekends were for partying, getting down and dirty, doing
daring deeds, and living as though Monday would never arrive.

Because school was clean, orderly, filled with predictable routines
and easily met challenges if you just paid attention and did the homework, I loved being a student. Dedicated teachers, who seem to me

now more like missionaries, encouraged my diligence and perseverance with gold stars and teacher's-pet status. Success bred ever more success, and that in turn allowed me to slip out of a present-time perspective and comfortably into a future one. Of course, that made me a homeboy anomaly: My father actually urged me to study less so I would not burn out my eyes. My friends only tolerated my work ethic because I was such a good athlete on the neighborhood teams.

Yet over the years, my life became all work, without any self-indulgent time-outs. Daily to-do lists grew ever longer, and each completed task gave rise to a new challenge, bred more tasks, more obligations. My mantra was "Yes, I can do that, too." The good thing about being so future-oriented was that I was a successful student and, later, an even more successful college professor. The hard work paid off when I was summoned to rise from the depths of an untenured assistant professorship at New York University to become a tenured full professor in Stanford's premier psychology department— all in one big cross-country leap. The bad thing about being a slave to the rigors of a future-time orientation was that work dominated everything else. There was little time left over for family, friends, listening to music that I loved, watching TV or movies, engaging in hobbies and sports, enjoying nature, or simply having fun. In essence, my future-time perspective turned the paradise that is Stanford University into a bleak Bronx basement laboratory where I was both Dr. Frankenstein and his time-bound monster.

After several years at Stanford, I needed to change. I was highly hypnotizable and had been certified as a practitioner of hypnosis in order to use it in research designed to vary emotional and cognitive states. I decided to become my own experimental subject in an attempt to loosen the grip that the future had on my life and try to introduce some of what I knew to be best in a present orientation. I felt that my extreme future orientation constrained my creativity and limited my imagination. So I encouraged a colleague to hypnotize me and, while I was deeply hypnotized, to suggest that:

The past and the future are becoming remote, dim, and insignificant in your mind.

The present is expanding.

The present is expanding to fill up your mind and body.

You will experience these changes until you hear me say "That's all for now." Then your usual sense of time will return.

I wondered briefly as I received this suggestion whether it could indeed penetrate my mind and transform my sturdy psychological clock, as it does in Salvador Dalí's paintings of time and memory distortion. As I waited patiently for something to happen, I first noticed a sudden lightness of being. My heavy body seemed to be lifting up off the chair, not held down by gravity. I looked at the painting on the wall, and its colors now shone brilliantly, with amazing vividness. My lips moistened, and visions of banana splits, malted milks, and pizza danced through my head. This struck me as funny, and I laughed loudly. This released laughter triggered the opposite emotion. I teared up over the loss of a friend. All those emotions went as quickly as they came, and soon I wanted to get up and run. I felt like doing something daring just for the fun of it. My heart was beating fast as I anticipated that something good was about to happen. Just then, as I took in a deep breath, the smell of flowers and freshly mowed grass filled my nostrils, and I relaxed really deeply.

At the signal, Phil returned to his former self and realized that he had not imagined the flowers and cut grass; the smell was coming through the open window from the garden. He had failed to notice the sweet scent when he had been in his usual future-oriented mind-set. Similarly, he had not noticed the picture's vivid colors before. The sensual sensations occurred only when his time sense was expanded. Phil further realized that the world of academia suppresses the public show of emotion in favor of cool rationality. It felt good to laugh and to cry! Overall, he felt like a sensual creature, his senses open to admit all stimuli, his muscles tuned to bodily processes. His desire to run, play, do daring deeds, and express strong emotions made him feel like a kid back in the Bronx when play dominated. However, Phil had not taken physical risks as a child or adult, so he was surprised by that urge.

It worked. The hypnotic induction enabled Phil to modify his excessive future orientation. During the session, Phil thought and felt differently. He redonned the familiar garment of present orientation and vowed to work at blending more of that good feeling into his too well-established future orientation. Phil wondered, however, as experimental researchers do, whether his transformation was idiosyncratic. Was what had happened limited to something weird or special about him? Could it be reproduced in others who were also hypnotizable? That thought initiated an experiment that we designed to determine whether such time perspective variations are reproducible and measurable with quantitative data.[12]

Liberating Behavior from Time-bound Control

A group of highly hypnotizable Stanford male and female students participated in the study. Each participant was given three tasks designed to measure changes in language use, thought, emotionality, and sensuous involvement. Initially, they all completed a story about their perception and interpretation of an ambiguous scene on a standard TAT card (the thematic apperception test [TAT] is a common psychological test). Then came one of four experimental manipulations. One group received training in rapid, deep hypnotic induction and the tape-recorded instruction: "Allow the present to expand and the past and future to become distant and insignificant." They were the primary focus during the experimental procedure. A control group received this instruction, but not while they were hypnotized, and were told only to imagine how hypnotized subjects would respond to it. A second control group got this instruction without any mention of hypnosis, while a third control group was merely told to think about their conception of time.

After the manipulation, participants completed another story about a different but comparable ambiguous scene. The stories were analyzed for verb use and references to past, present, or future events. Affective displays were recorded as smiling and laughing as they listened to the humorous but unexpectedly obscene tape-recorded promotion for a movie. Finally, participants were given a mound of clay and invited to make something out of it. At the end of a fixed time, when they had finished their product, participants returned to their cubicles.

Expanding their present orientation through hypnotism did indeed liberate their behavior from the usual time-bound constraints. They became expansively focused on the present. They changed their language—and therefore their thinking, since language reflects thought—using significantly more present-tense verbs, more references to present events, and fewer references to the past. They laughed significantly more than the other groups, who merely smiled when listening to the obscene comedy material. Further, because members of the other groups chose to make specific objects with their clay, they were ready and proud to show their objects to the experimenter when he told them to finish. However, those in the expanded present condition never finished because they were playing with the gooey clay and not making a *thing* out of it. When the experimenter left the room, his instruction to finish up and go back to the cubicles was immediately lost, as the pleasure of playing with the clay dominated the present moment.

In addition to specifically measuring these reactions, the experimenters observed that many participants in the expanded present condition changed their handwriting on their TAT stories to a more stretched-out, expansive style. Some even lost linear sequence, writing from left to right, placing words hit-or-miss down the page. Similarly, in writing their reactions to the obscene comedy tape, many of them reflected the obscene style in their language. For example, one participant in the expanded present condition wrote, "At first I was disgusted listening to those stupid f—kers, but when they started screwing up, it blew my nose." No one in the other conditions used obscenity in responses that would be seen by the experimenter, who was also their teacher. When they had finished with the clay assignment, all participants except those in the expanded present condition wiped the sticky clay from their hands with paper towels. None of the participants in the expanded present condition wiped his hands on the towels, but a few wiped their hands on their shirts and dresses. It was evident that the hypnotic induction had entranced the students in the *process* of playing with the clay and distracted them from any concern for the future-planned *product* that would come out of it. Said one, "The clay was very soft and moist. It felt nice to dig my fingers into it. When I was working with it, the shape just happened. There was very little effort involved. It just kind of worked itself out."

This research shows that our time perspectives are not determined by nature or by some cosmic clock setter, but are learned ways of relating to our physical, biological, social, and cultural environments. That view opens the way to modifying time perspective with various strategies. Hypnotically induced changes, as this study shows, may get people back to the present-orientation they had experienced as children. In Chapter Eleven, we shall explore other strategies and tactics enabling people to step outside a time zone that has become detrimental in order to develop an optimally balanced time perspective.

Time is the most indefinable yet paradoxical of things; the past is gone, the future has not yet come, and the present becomes the past even while we attempt to define it, and like a flash of lightning, at once exists and expires.
—Kugelmass, 1967[13]

WHAT IS GOOD AND WHAT IS BAD ABOUT LIFE IN THE PRESENT LANE?

As with the other time perspectives, the present perspective has both good and bad effects, though the good generally offset the bad. In general, Hedonists live active, high-intensity lives, filled with as much excitement, novelty, and spontaneity as possible. They engage in diverse activities, in many sports and hobbies. They learn early to make friends and lovers easily and frequently and are apt to fill their lives with people whom they find stimulating and with possessions they can show off. If they have enough money, they take great joy in living, appreciating the nature, animals, and people around them. People like to be with them because, like children, they have an open-eyed readiness to connect and an intensity that comes from being totally in the moment. The demands of the to-do list never dilute their here and now; in fact, they generally do not make lists, and when they do, they forget to check them.

A central core of their psychological makeup is sensuality. They are always open to sensory input, taking time to smell the proverbial roses and to touch. Sensuality merges with sexuality, and they enjoy sexual activities of all sorts. Present-oriented high school students reported enjoying R- and X-rated movies and pornography more than their future-oriented classmates did. They also described the most important characteristic of a potential mate as "exciting."

It is not surprising, then, that these Presents enjoy improvisation more than planned activities or replaying memories. Patricia Ryan Madson, a leading proponent of incorporating elements of improvisation into everyday life, writes:

> Long before there was planning, there was improvising. For millennia humans functioned naturally only by thinking on their feet, problem-solving in the here and how. . . . At some point, however, survival demanded planning: the cave folk who wolfed down just the berries at hand and trout only as it swam by didn't make it through long, freezing winters. To stay alive, early man needed to cultivate the capacity to think ahead and stow away food for the lean times. This development in human history marked the end of improvising as our primary modus vivendi. Enter the appointment calendar. We learned to worry about the future. . . . Leapfrogging thousands of years into the present, we find ourselves nearly strangled by this planning instinct.[14]

Improvisers require a fine sense of timing and the ability to make something new happen on the spot. Naturally, these performers bring to each session the knowledge of what others have done in the past in order to know what not to repeat as well as what to build upon, extend, and enhance. But being able to use the past as a scaffold and not a blueprint marks the creative performer as one who can improvise in ways that go beyond the past into new realms. For comedians, it means allowing themselves to be totally open to the mood and reactions of the audience, and for jazz musicians, to be totally open to their feelings and "online" mental processes.

Go for the Flow

A present orientation can help you become fully immersed in inner and outer experiences as you work or perform activities, but it is not essential. We know that future-oriented folks can also become totally absorbed in their work. For example, futures can get into a "flow" experience in the middle of giving a particularly enjoyable lecture. Psychologist Mihaly Csikszentmihályi identifies flow as a special state of mind in which there is total absorption for a period of time in a given activity. The main characteristics of flow are:

- *Clear goals* (expectations and rules are discernible, and goals are attainable and align appropriately with one's abilities).

- *Focusing,* a high degree of concentration on a limited field of attention (a person engaged in the activity will have the opportunity to focus and to delve deeply into it).

- A loss of the feeling of self-consciousness, the merging of action and awareness.

- *Distorted sense of time*—one's subjective experience of time is altered. Direct and immediate *feedback* (successes and failures in the course of the activity are apparent so that behavior can be adjusted as needed).

- *Balance between ability level and challenge* (the activity is neither too easy nor too difficult).

- A sense of personal *control* over the situation or activity.

- The activity is *intrinsically rewarding,* so there is an effortlessness of action.[15]

Flow is involvement in the *process* of whatever you are doing. When in flow, you are not focused on the *product* of the process in which you are engaged. When we are concerned about the product, we worry about how it will be judged, evaluated, accepted, or rejected. Our ego is put on the line. Worries can then feed back and disturb the process of creating new ideas, new visions, and new products. We demonstrated in a laboratory that present hedonists, who more often than not readily slip into flow states, are most creative when they are encouraged to perform within a process orientation, and least when given a product orientation.[16] Do you think that future-oriented individuals perform best when given a process or a product focus?

In a study in our laboratory, male and female college students were selected because they were either high on hedonism or high on future orientation. They were asked to paint a color picture of a basket of flowers. Half of each group was told that judges in the art department would evaluate their efforts. The other half was told to focus on the artistic process itself. After participants finished, several graduate art students judged all the paintings on two dimensions: technical merit (best uses of color, space, layout, etc.), and creativity (originality, novel use of color and design, etc.). They did so unaware of the differences in task focus or time perspective.

Sure enough, present hedonists painting in the process condition were most creative. Futures painting in the product condition produced paintings with the most technical merit. When present-oriented participants focused on their product, they performed most poorly on measures of creativity and technical merit. These findings suggest that creativity is fostered when people are encouraged to tune in to the creative process, especially when they are disposed toward the present, while the technically best outcomes are encouraged in those who are already future-oriented when they are aware that the products they produce will be evaluated. Here are some examples of the differences in these artistic productions, so you can judge for yourself.

A future-product painting.

Two examples of present-process art paintings.

A present-product painting by a present-oriented artist who did not like being forced to paint under the constraints of the product focus.

WHAT IS BAD ABOUT THE PRESENT?

"Live fast, die young, and leave a good-looking corpse" was the tough-guy epitaph of the hero in the novel *Knock on Any Door*. It could just as easily be the motto of young Hedonists. What could go wrong with someone who is impulsive, spontaneous, and aggressive; who is willing to take risks; who acts without fully anticipating consequences; who does not learn from past failures; who rarely does a cost-benefit analysis of his decisions before acting; and who is unable to delay gratification? A great deal can go wrong.

Hedonists compromise their health by not getting regular medical and dental checkups, not getting breast cancer testing, and not flossing their teeth regularly. They are less likely than others to eat healthy foods if they don't like the taste. Their high energy keeps them going longer, like the Energizer Bunny, but they are often sleep-deprived. Presents are more likely than those with the other time perspectives to smoke, drink alcohol, get drunk, and take risks driving cars, bikes, and skateboards. To make matters worse, there is a highly significant correlation between being present-oriented and car racing, driving while drunk, and not wearing seat belts while driving. Research with high school students was repeated with a large sample of more than twelve hundred college students from Stanford and Cornell universities and yielded the same pattern of results: Present orientation is significantly associated with risky driving and alcohol use. This was found to be the case in both of these East and West Coast prestigious schools. Moreover, hedonistic female students at both colleges were no different from their male counterparts in their high use of alcohol and risky driving habits. Correlation between these behaviors and future orientation was negative or nil.[17]

At Risk for Every Addiction

Common to all addictions—drugs, alcohol, gambling, sex, and food—is the immediate high they offer. They also often combine biological and social arousal. Because the aversive consequences of addictions are delayed, usually over long periods, and most people who become addicted know *intellectually* that there are costs and pains to weigh against the momentary gains, you might expect that their behavior would be influenced by their knowledge. But that abstract knowledge about future consequences never feeds back to influence current decisions and concrete actions; discount it, relegate it to a vague probability, and deny it as personally irrelevant. Those with present biases don't use contingency or probabilistic thinking, don't engage in long-term cost-benefit analyses, and are likely to affiliate with others who deal with decisions in the same way—"Just do it!"

A recent study comparing thirty-four heroin addicts in a treatment program with fifty-nine non-drug-using controls found that addicts were significantly higher on our scales of present hedonism and fatalism, and significantly lower in future orientation.[18] But how can time perspective end up oiling the slippery slope to drug addiction? Don't they know the long-term negative consequences associated with continued drug use? Sure they do, but that is a way-out then, and the high from drugs is a nearby now. This research went further in demonstrating that, compared to controls, heroin addicts were insensitive to the future consequences of many of their actions. They were less likely to predict far into the future or to organize events systematically. For example, in a card game, the addicts played from a deck that gave them immediate large rewards but resulted in large delayed punishments and overall net loss. It is as though they were using binoculars backward, making the visual field of the future small and remote, and not allowing it to affect current decisions and actions.

Another study with more than four hundred elementary school students, average age twelve, compared their early substance use with their time perspective and other measures of coping. Sure enough, present orientation was significantly associated with substance abuse, and future orientation inversely associated to substance abuse. These relationships held regardless of the sex or ethnicity of the students. The researchers conclude: "Future orientation was generally related to higher levels of adaptive outcomes, such as perceived control, positive well-being, and adaptive coping dimensions, particularly behavioral coping. In contrast, present orientation was related to recent negative events, lack of perceived control, and maladaptive coping dimensions, including anger, withdrawal, and helplessness." [19]

The enormous costs to the addicted, their families, and nations around the world have prompted extensive anti-addiction advertising campaigns and various school programs against smoking, taking drugs, and premarital sex. Two of the most well-known federally funded programs (to the tune of hundreds of millions annually) were found recently to be resoundingly unsuccessful. The DARE program, "Just Say No to Drugs," was applauded by parents, principals, teachers, students, and the police who brought these role-playing exercises into classrooms in many states. The most heavily funded national program in the United States, it reaches twenty-six million children across fifty-four different countries. When the question of "Does the program work?" is framed in terms of measurable reductions in smoking and drug use by kids who took part in the program, rather than in feel-good terms, no differences have been found. Seven studies and a meta-analysis of them all revealed that the DARE program had absolutely no effect on these behaviors.[20] Similar results are being reported with the much touted sexual abstinence school programs, which promote virginity promises. A comprehensive study of many of these programs found no sign that they delay sexual activity.[21] A major conclusion was that "No program was able to demonstrate a positive impact on sexual behavior over time." In addition, the lack of information about contraception use in the abstinence programs made it more likely for those girls to have unplanned pregnancies than those in other sex education programs. "Abstinence" youth also tried oral and anal activities more frequently because, in some of these programs, sex was defined primarily as vaginal intercourse.

What is wrong with all such programs and their related advertising campaigns? They focus on aversive future consequences that work for future-oriented people but *not* for present-oriented—the target audience. They also focus on personal willpower, resolve, and character, which fails to recognize powerful situational and social forces in the present behavioral context that influence Hedonists and Fatalists more than they do others. Role-playing and promises in a schoolroom become pale reminders of shoulds and oughts when kids are at a party or rock concert, in the backseat of a car, or just hanging out. We bet that a reanalysis of the data in these evaluation studies would show they work only for those students identified as future- or past-oriented, with little or no effect on the presents. It is time for time perspective to be recognized as a key ingredient for "leading us not into temptation."

"180 Trillion Leisure Hours Lost to Work Last Year"

"The majority of American adults find work cutting into the middle of their days—exactly when leisure is most effective." This spoof in the satirical weekly *The Onion* (July 12, 2007) captures how many Presents really feel. Work is the antithesis of play, and most work requires discipline, perseverance, long hours, and delayed gratification, not typical present attributes. Tomorrow is soon enough for them. Procrastination is the name of the game.

Among students, those biased toward the present are most likely to be late signing up for required assignments, late starting and completing assignments, and no-shows for appointments.[22] This carries over into requiring more extensions for assignments and receiving more course incompletes, which adversely affects academic performance. In our large introductory psychology course at Stanford, where grades are based entirely on objective multiple-choice tests, time perspective figured in to how well students did. The lowest grades were found among the Fatalists, and the next lowest were among the Hedonists. The futures sat high atop the distribution. In general, presents score better in courses they like than ones they don't. For futures, liking is irrelevant, because they realize their GPA combines both.

If this is true among students smart enough to get into selective universities such as Stanford, it is probably even more so in high schools and middle schools. Students who are highly present-oriented have more failures, remedial class assignments, truancy, and dropouts. Given that socioeconomic class is related to time perspective, with lower-class people more present- than future-oriented, the high dropout rates of minority students may be attributable more to unfavorable time perspectives than to lack of ability.

SEX, DRUGS, ROCK AND ROLL: THE SIXTIES TIME REVOLUTION

We were struck by a headline in our local paper that proclaimed, "Japanese teens pick night life over class." The subhead continued, "New generation shuns future in favor of nonstop fun."[23] The news report continued to describe a new trend in a country noted for its intense future-oriented work ethic and its deep respect for the past. Before now, present hedonism was a rarity in Japan, where people took fewer days off for vacation than any other industrialized nation, and parents were traditionally obsessed with getting their children admitted to the best schools and paid handsomely for after-school and weekend tutoring in "Juku" or "cram" schools. In this remarkable new trend, students drop out of high school or do not go to college at all, preferring instead to shop, hang out with friends, sleep late, and go nightclubbing.

Around the world, youths are rebelling against conventional attitudes toward time imposed by earlier generations. It is not a new phenomenon and follows on an earlier version in the sixties—the sex, drugs, rock-and-roll hippie generation's social-time revolution. Timothy Leary, Harvard psychology professor turned LSD guru, advocated three paths for young people to follow: "Turn on, tune in, and drop out." Turn on to mind-altering drugs that would change their perceptions and consciousness; tune in to the playful child within them, to the inner self that rejects meaningless, boring work regimens as the way of the world; and drop out of the conforming, middle-class, future-oriented consumer society controlled by the military-industrial establishment. This manifesto intended to transform society into both a present-hedonistic state and an expansive holistic-present state.

Sexually transmitted diseases killed the free-sex era, however. Laws killed drug experimentation. Hunger killed play that did not pay the food bill or rent. Nonetheless, the ideals of putting more pleasure in one's life and taking time out of the press of daily existence to enjoy friends, nature, and one's self are still worthy.

Tuning in to the Present

Time-out Two: The Who Am I? Test

Please answer each of the following questions. Be sure to give a new answer to each question.

1. I am: _____

2. I am: _____

3. I am: _____

4. I am: _____

5. I am: _____

6. When am I: _____

7. When am I: _____

8. When am I: _____

9. When am I: _____

10. When am I: _____

11. Where am I: _____

12. Where am I: _____

13. Where am I: _____

14. Where am I: _____

15. Where am I: _____

16. How do I feel: _____

17. How do I feel: _____

18. How do I feel: _____

19. How do I feel: _____

20. How do I feel: _____

There are countless techniques for promoting present orientation. Some of them, such as meditation, yoga, and self-hypnosis, have been used for hundreds, if not thousands, of years. If you currently practice one of these techniques, terrific! If you do not, we encourage you to learn one. While your authors defer to experts who teach these techniques, we do want to offer one simple way of becoming engrossed in the present. It is slightly modified version of the Who Was I? test found in the preceding chapter.

In its original form, the Who Am I? test asked respondents to answer the same question—Who Am I?—twenty times in a row. The developers of the test claimed that each successive response to the question revealed deeper layers of psychological meaning. For our current purposes, we will not insist that you answer all twenty iterations of the questions, but we will ask that you answer multiple variations.

Start by asking the original question, Who Am I?, in as many ways as you can. List the ways on the exercise box provided. Be sure to focus on who you are today, not who you were yesterday or who you will be tomorrow. Also remember that this is not a speed test. Take your time and let thoughts and feelings surface at their own rate.

When you have exhausted your reservoir of answers, move on to the question of When Are You? Obvious answers include the date, the time, and the day of the week, but be inventive. When are you in the course of your career, your relationship, and your life? When you've exhausted your reservoir of answers, move on to the question of Where Are You? Again, there are obvious answers, but force yourself to stretch beyond them. Notice the new and the old around you. Notice the sights, the sounds, and the smells. What surprises you? What is familiar? What do you like and what do you dislike about your surroundings?

Once you've run out of answers or gotten bored with the question of Where Are You?, move on to the final and most challenging question: How Do You Feel? Push through the hackneyed answers that surely spring to mind and open yourself to the possibility that you really do feel. If you do, what is it that you feel? Are you stressed, sad, happy, horny, hungry, confident, insecure, full, proud, or all of the above? Give yourself time for your answers to reveal themselves. Often people have difficulty feeling anything at all, and when they do feel something, they often can't immediately label what they are feeling. As with everything else, it takes time to feel.

This simple exercise obviously cannot replace the regular practice of meditation, yoga, or self-hypnosis, but you can repeat it anywhere and anytime that you like. You don't even need a piece of paper. Simply asking yourself Who Am I?, When Am I?, Where Am I?, and How Do I Feel? is enough.

PUNCTUALITY: YOU HAD BETTER BE ON TIME OR ELSE

What happens when many people in any society live in the present?
They are all late! They are never on time! They forget the appointment or underestimate the transit time. They do things that are
more interesting and do not consider punctuality a virtue but a
limitation. This phenomenon of punctuality practiced by uptight
urbanites is common in many countries and cultures. In Phil's
words:

> I was about to give a workshop to psychiatrists and clinical psycholo-
> gists at a convention in Ixtapa, Mexico. Only two were there at the
> appointed time. Both were Americans. The talk was delayed half an
> hour until enough participants drifted in after their late lunch. Others
> continued to amble in even an hour later, and some did so right up to
> the designated termination time at four P.M. Mind you, they did not
> slink in, embarrassed that they were late for this special event, but
> usually interrupted with an open greeting: "Hola, Zimbardo!" They
> were operating on Mexican time. I was following Gringo time.

In Peru, this cultural habit of ignoring clocks is called *La hora Pe-
ruana,* or "Peruvian time." Our colleague Robert Levine, author of
A Geography of Time, says that most of Latin America is dominated
by a different way of timekeeping. People tend to live life on event
time, not on clock time. Social and personal events always take priority over clock-timed events. Parties do not begin at the invitation
time; rather, they begin at whatever time most people decide to
attend.

This lack of punctuality is more than an inconvenience for those
who are on time and forced to wait for the latecomers to arrive.
It is costly to a nation's economy. A recent survey in Peru estimated
the cost of chronic tardiness at five billion dollars annually. On
average, each Peruvian is 107 hours late for jobs, schools, and other
appointments every year. Over 80 percent of Peruvians surveyed
thought that their compatriots were never punctual, or only sometimes.[24]

In 2007 Peruvian president Alan Garcia started a national campaign to counteract this human temporal drain on the economy. *La Hora sin Demora,* or "Time Without Delay," was its theme. On national television, he invited his countrymen to synchronize their watches. Psychologist Max Hernandez was asked to coordinate this massive behavior-change campaign. Despite a lot of media hoopla and promotions to make punctuality a virtue, Peruvians are still running late. Sometimes it is only *un minutito,* or one teensy minute, but that can actually mean an hour. A professor at Lima's Catholic University doubts this local custom can be changed because it is so widely practiced across all social classes. The elite show their disdain for following social mores, and this upper-class arrogance has spread to the masses. Even university professors routinely show up an hour after class is scheduled to begin.

In the U.S., a similar pattern of disregarding clock time, "the man's time," in favor of "people's time" used to be termed CPT, or "colored people's time." Clocks are stretched to fit human needs rather than the other way around, but that stretching can eventually snap when confronted with a future-oriented teacher, boss, job interviewer, or parent for whom being only a few minutes late is *late* and perceived as irresponsible, immature, inconsiderate, and unacceptable. Here is where clashes between time zones are misperceived as innate deficiencies in personal temperaments and traits.

In our next chapter, we will view the world from the perspective of those who have come to embrace a future orientation. As we saw earlier in the case of northern, future-oriented Italians wanting to rid their country of those less productive, present-oriented southerners, time perspective influences both individual modes of being and national destinies.

five

THE FUTURE

*Tomorrow Through
the Lens of Today*

I never think of the future. It comes soon enough.
—*Albert Einstein*

The future ain't what it used to be.
—*Yogi Berra*

Change is the law of life.
*And those who look only to the past or present are certain to miss
the future.*
—*John F. Kennedy*

Situated along the western coast of Africa near the equator, the Republic of Ghana enjoys a warm tropical climate. Yet one in three Ghanaians lives at or below the poverty level. A farmer who harvests cocoa, the main crop, earns about three hundred dollars a year. Soccer—or football, as most of the world calls it—is their passion. Football fever runs so hot in the Oregon-size country that national industries are required to shut down during important football matches so there will be enough energy to power the country's televisions. In Ghana, whenever the national team plays, the event is cause for a nationwide party. On the field, the men play fiercely and gracefully, demonstrating athletic creativity as well as an open disdain for regimentation, order, and timing. In a sense, they embody the joys of living a laid-back present-hedonistic lifestyle. As discussed in the previous chapter, geography is often associated with this temporal perspective. Indeed, one journalist covering the 2006 World Cup wrote, "The stereotype in soccer is that, the closer your country is to the equator, the more it plays a wild, loose, fast, creative, and undisciplined style of ball." That was indeed the Ghanaian style— until the team got a future-oriented coach.

In 2004 Ghana hired Ratomir Dujković, a Serb, as its fifth coach in two years. In addition to an impressive international football record, Dujković brought to the present-oriented Ghana team a European discipline that featured a highly focused future time perspective and insistence on hard work and punctuality. He quickly let the players know that he meant business by firing one of the best players for missing a training camp. Under his direction, for the first time in its history, Ghana qualified for the World Cup tournament, a massive achievement in itself. Of his players, Dujković said, "At first they resisted and came late to training, lunch, meetings—even games. But I persisted, habits changed, and now we are enjoying success."

Of the traits that Dujković instilled in his refashioned Ghanaian team—discipline, toughness, goal-scoring, and punctuality—perhaps the most important were high expectations of future success. Dujković's regimen inspired the team to believe that they could beat the best teams in the world. And they did! When they combined their present-oriented creativity with their newfound future desire to win, this underdog landed a stunning 2–0 victory over the powerful Czech Republic team. Next up—and down—was the USA National Team, in a 2–1 upset. Ghana was the only African team to reach round sixteen, where the world-class Brazilian team finally eliminated them, although some contend that they might have won if the match had not been so poorly officiated. Of their success, Dujković said, "For me, it's not a surprise. You should remember, I said before [the 2006 World Cup Tournament] that we're going to reach the semifinals." In retrospect, Dujković may wish that he had said they were going to reach the finals. As long as he was implanting future aspirations into the mental set of his players, he might have moved them all the way to the top.

The future, like the past, is never experienced directly. It is a psychologically constructed mental state. Fashioned out of our hopes, our fears, our expectations, and our aspirations, the future is essential scaffolding for success in school, business, the arts, and athletics. Talent, intelligence, and ability are necessary for success, but they are not sufficient. Discipline, perseverance, and a sense of personal efficacy are also required. Childhood prodigies of any kind, for instance, rarely become successes in adulthood unless they have the discipline to spend endless hours at their craft. Becoming future-oriented involves turning away from the comforts of present existence and instant pleasure, the youthful temptation to play all day. It directs us away from the certainties of the here and now, black and white, is or is not, to a world of imagined options, of probabilities, of if-thens. Futures view the past as a reservoir of mistakes to be rectified and successes to be repeated and expanded and have little use for an impulse-driven present.

The mantra of a future is "Meet tomorrow's deadline, complete all the necessary work before tonight's play." While presents avoid work and are vulnerable to sex, drugs, rock and roll, futures consider work a source of special pleasure. For them, tomorrow's anticipated gains and losses fuel today's decisions and actions. Gratification delayed for greater reward is always a better bet for futures, who will trade a bird in the hand for a flock in the future. Unlike their present-hedonistic peers who live in their bodies, the futures live in their minds, envisioning other selves, scenarios, rewards, and successes. The success of Western civilization in the past centuries can be traced to the prevalence of the future orientation of many populations.

Beliefs and expectations of the future in part determine what happens in the present by contributing to how people think, feel, and behave. Once the Ghanaian soccer team believed that it could defeat its more highly ranked competitors, it began to beat them. The soccer team's belief in its own strength and high level of performance may have made the members all work harder and longer in anticipation of success. In short, the team believed that it could influence the future by working hard in the present. When you want to achieve something and you believe that you can, you work harder.

It makes sense that belief in yourself would influence your behavior, but it turns out your conceptions of other people influence their behavior as well. In one study devoted to what has become known as the Pygmalion effect, the psychologist Robert Rosenthal told a group of teachers that he had identified a small number of children who were poised for a great intellectual growth spurt during the coming school year. In fact, Rosenthal had randomly selected those particular children, who were no more likely to experience an intellectual growth spurt than other children in the classes. Rosenthal and his team observed both the children and the teachers during the course of the school year, at the end of which all the children took standardized tests. On average, the children who had been identified as likely to experience a growth spurt scored higher than other students because the teachers' expectation of the children's performance influenced the way they interacted with those students and, ultimately, the way the students themselves behaved.

In another study on the effects of expectation, male and female college students were told that they were participating in a study of verbal communication. To minimize the effects of their sharing nonverbal cues, the boys and girls never met; communication took place over the phone. Each boy was given an identical packet of information that was supposed to help familiarize him with the girl with whom he was to speak. The packet contained a description of the girl's personality, what she liked and disliked, and what school she attended. Half of the boys received an "attractive" picture of their communication partner, while the other boys received an "unattractive" picture of her. In reality, the picture that they received had no relationship to the girl with whom they would speak but had been prescreened in an earlier experiment to distinguish between attractive and unattractive girls. Because of the manipulation, half the boys thought they were going to speak with an attractive girl, and half thought they were going to speak with an unattractive girl. The girls were given no information about the boys, including whether they believed the girls to be attractive or unattractive.

Mark Snyder and his research team who conducted this study

were interested in two variables. First, they wanted to see whether the boys with the supposedly attractive phone partners would behave differently from those with the supposedly unattractive partners; second, they wanted to see whether, if the boys did behave differently, their behavior affected the girls.

The phone communication between the boys and the girls was taped and then scored by blind raters. Within about thirty seconds, the raters could tell whether the couple was in the attractive or the unattractive category. With the attractive girls, the boys were more friendly, outgoing, funny, and energetic. The boys' expectation of what their communication partner looked like indeed influenced their behavior. Surprisingly, the boys' expectations also influenced the girls' behavior. Girls who were supposedly attractive were more friendly, outgoing, and funny than girls expected to be unattractive.

Our own expectations influence our behavior, and other people's expectations of us can influence our behavior as well. Expectations, of course, reside in the future, and in order for them to influence our behavior, they must be made present. If you scored lower than you would have liked on the future time perspective, don't worry. We will help you to become more future-oriented. If you are excessively or obsessively future-oriented, you need not worry. We will help you create better balance in your life. The poet Milton reminds us of the human mind's capacity to transform existence when he has the character Satan say in *Paradise Lost,* "The mind is its own place, and in itself can make a heaven of hell, a hell of heaven." And the visionary artist and sculptor Anselm Kiefer has said, "We cannot stand not to have a heaven in our minds." Instead of urging "Just do it!," we will encourage you to "Just think it!"

HOW DO YOU BECOME FUTURE-ORIENTED?

No one is born with a future time perspective. No gene pushes people into a future time zone. You become future-oriented by being born in the right place at the right time, where environmental conditions help transform little present-oriented babies into restrained, successful, future-oriented adults. These conditions include:

- Living in a temperate zone
- Living in a stable family, society, nation
- Being Protestant (or Jewish)
- Becoming educated
- Being a young or middle-aged adult
- Having a job
- Using technology regularly
- Being successful
- Having future-oriented role models
- Recovering from childhood illness

Living in a Temperate Zone

Preparing for seasonal change involves planning and modifying behavior to fit the changing weather. For that reason, people become used to anticipating worse weather in winter and summer than in the usually glorious fall and spring. In contrast, living in a mildly tropical climate is being in paradise with an extended lease. It is always the same season, only with more or less rain.

Living in a Stable Family, Society, Nation

When you focus on the future, you make decisions that anticipate consequences. In predicting the pluses and minuses that will result from a given action, you assume there is sufficient stability for you to make that judgment possible. A stable government and family allow you to predict what actions will generate desired rewards or, indeed, if there will ever be the promised reward for chores you do now. In general, stable, reliable environments are likely to be the best breeding grounds for budding futures.

Being Protestant (or Jewish)

The concept of original sin in Christian doctrine is based on Eve's succumbing to her present-oriented appetite when the serpent tempted her to eat the fruit of the Tree of Knowledge of Good and Evil. All Christians have been paying for her moment of "weakness" ever since, and are often reminded that "Idle hands are the devil's workshop." After the Protestant Reformation, Calvinists in particular came to believe in predestination—the idea that God had predestined some people to be saved and others to be damned. The worldly sign of this destiny was apparent in one's worldly success and accumulation of wealth. The Protestant work ethic generated a new hardworking class of entrepreneurs. In general, even today the gross national product per capita of primarily Protestant nations is greater than that of Catholic nations.[1]

Being Jewish is likely to push one toward future orientation, because Jewish tradition honors scholarship and education as a means of personal and community advancement. Education in academic settings is all about goal-setting, planning, delaying gratification, and anticipating rewards for progress, the building blocks of a solid future-oriented foundation.

Becoming Educated

Education makes a student more future-oriented. Schools teach delay of gratification, goal-setting, cost-benefit analysis, and abstract thought. Cynics would argue that the subtext of a program for success is learning to respect authority: staying in one's seat, knowing one's place in the hierarchic ranking of intelligence, and learning to tolerate boring lectures, all in the promise of securing boring jobs. Nevertheless, education is the boot camp that trains presents to become futures.

Being a Young or Middle-aged Adult

The time of life for adopting, rehearsing, and refining a future orientation is from your late teens through your late fifties. In your teens and young adulthood, the childhood play and indulgence (in affluent societies) that generated present hedonism come under assault as grown-ups demand that you make something of yourself. This is the time when educational and work opportunities challenge you; the expectations of marriage, a family, and generally settling down entice you; and planning your legacy begins. Beyond this golden age, some become more past-oriented and begin to develop a new kind of present orientation in which selected small bites of social life dominate.

Having a Job

Having a meaningful job imparts a sense of self-identity, generates pride in your achievements, and enables you to form social contacts beyond the boundaries of "the neighborhood." Most important, having a job provides temporal structure to each workday and cultivates self-discipline. Ideally, a job also enhances the opportunity for personal development, realizing ambitions, and gaining economic security and independence. All of these experiences develop a strong future time perspective. Of course, being future-oriented can help you get a job in the first place.

Using Technology Regularly

Technology is a time saver and enhances efficiency. We accomplish more in less time than we would without it because it allows multitasking. Moreover, the Internet has created social and intellectual worlds without physical boundaries. We are "there" instantly, with only milliseconds to wait. It is virtually impossible to be a successful future in this age without also being a master of some relevant technology. Technology also creates compelling virtual video game alternate realities that attract young present hedonists, who live in that alternate space endlessly.

Being Successful

Nothing succeeds like success. Early success rewards effort, practice, and discipline. It also reinforces the notion that your actions can yield desirable consequences. Early repeated failure breeds a sense of helplessness and makes you shun that arena of performance where you failed, be it school, work, or sports. Future orientation accrues over time through little wins and moral victories and is cemented into place by larger attainments. It is not how you win the game but whether or not you win that matters to futures.

Having Future-Oriented Role Models

You are influenced by others around you, as well as by others in the media whom you emulate. Parents, teachers, and friends can help push you toward future orientation through their suggestions, instructions, and even modeling key features of that attitude toward time. A future is usually fortunate enough to have one or more such influential people in her or his life. Learning that a hero or heroine became successful through hard work, effort, practice, and self-denial in order to pursue a dream inspires emulation of that person.

Recovering from Childhood Illness

Though not supported by hard evidence, anecdote supports the notion that an extended illness or injury during childhood or young adulthood can orient youngsters toward more introspection than extroversion. The inability to act makes them live imagined scenarios of action as well as imagined self-sufficiency. These mental activities become substitutes for the ability to run and play outside with friends. They become the cornerstones on which to build a solid future time perspective. The cyclist Lance Armstrong, who overcame cancer to win the Tour de France seven times, provides an excellent example of how hardship can be transformed into future orientation.

Obviously, none of this set of ten attributes is necessary or sufficient for making you future-oriented. Each one simply makes it more likely that you will develop that attitude. Many factors are involved in the creation and maintenance of a given time perspective. Some are broad geographical, cultural, economic, and social factors. Others are psychological. Added to these are interpersonal dynamics and personal experiences. One of the reasons that few of us are consciously aware of wearing the time-binding lenses through which we see is that they are crafted slowly over time from a variety of sources.

Time-out One: Relationships Between Attitudes Toward the Future and Psychological and Behavioral Characteristics

Behavioral Characteristic	People High in Future TP Are
Aggression	Less aggressive
Depression	Less depressed
Energy	More energy
Wear watch	More likely
Balance checkbook	More likely
Use day planner	More likely
Floss teeth	More likely
Drug use	Less drug use
Alcohol consumption	Less alcohol
Friendliness	Not different
Conscientiousness	More conscientious
Emotional stability	Not different
Openness	More open
Consideration of future consequences	More concern for future consequences
Ego under control	More ego control
Impulse control	More impulsive
Novelty-seeking	More novelty-seeking
Preference for consistency	More preference for consistency
Reward dependence	More reward dependence
Self-esteem	More self-esteem
Sensation-seeking	Less sensation-seeking
Anxiety	Less anxiety
Grade point average	Higher grade point average
Hours studied per week	Study more
Creativity	More creative
Happiness	Not different
Frequency of lying	Lie less
Frequency of stealing	Not different
Shyness	Not different
Temper	Not different

Futures do not seek novelty but are generally not depressed. They also are reluctant to lie, unlike their hedonistic, fatalistic, and past-negative peers, who are significantly given to lying. For example, you do not have to lie if you are faithful in delivering on your promises. On the other hand, futures are very reluctant to take chances, unlikely to be adventuresome or to rush in where fools and presents do. They live by Mama's golden rule, "Better safe than sorry." On the positive side, they tend to be more emotionally stable and predictable than those who score low in future time perspective.

WHAT'S GOOD AND BAD ABOUT A FUTURE TIME PERSPECTIVE?

First, let us see what good can come from developing a future time perspective. Phil and John have a stake in uncovering the good in a future time perspective, because both score a high: 4.5.

Health and Well-being

Futures get regular medical and dental checkups. Future-oriented women arrange for breast cancer checkups and Pap tests. In an Italian study, future-oriented women took advantage of free breast cancer screenings significantly more often than comparable present hedonists and a comparable control sample of women did.[2] Because futures prefer good nutrition to tasty but unhealthy food, they are more likely to buy organic foods despite the expense; they are also likely to be weight-conscious and therefore less likely to become obese or diabetic as adults. They are also not likely to smoke, drink heavily, engage in binge eating, or take drugs. They plan to have fewer children, and they accumulate greater disposable income when they are married. Futures have health and retirement plans, but they devote less time to recreation and vacation. All this suggests that they will attain their ambition to live long and successful lives—if they do not die prematurely from excessive stress.

Futures may be less depressed than others because they do not spend time ruminating on negative past experiences. They focus on tomorrow, not yesterday. In the general population, the higher rates of depression among women than men appears to be due in part to their greater tendency to ruminate about unpleasant and traumatic past experiences. Work by researcher Susan Nolen-Hoeksema and her colleagues indicates that there is also a greater likelihood of women sharing their emotions with other women, which may keep bad memories recycling rather than fading. Neither would seem typical in future-oriented women—neither ruminating about the past nor engaging in emotional sharing with others. New research should find lower depression rates among future-oriented women (and, of course, past-positive women).

Futures, like everyone else, experience varying degrees of everyday stresses, as well as occasional major ones. But futures reported high levels of support, especially from significant others, when under stress. To put this finding in perspective, consider that present hedonists get support from friends and acquaintances, and past positives get it from family. Past-negative people get less social support from anyone and are more likely to associate with family members who are full of conflict. Stress is likely to escalate without positive social support, so futures, presents, and past-positives are going to be healthier in resisting stress, but futures will be healthiest of all.[3]

From our surveys of hundreds of high school students, we found yet other reasons that futures thrive compared with presents, who are likely to confront danger daily—and to create danger for themselves. Future-oriented high school students are *less* likely to take bike risks, skateboard risks, or car risks; to race cars, drive drunk, or use alcohol; to engage in unsafe sex or get into physical fights. One key to the longevity of futures is that they look before they leap. Moreover, because substance is more important than style, futures will take time to have their cars serviced regularly rather than keep them polished and shiny. Therefore, they have fewer accidents from worn tires, defective transmissions, or worn brakes. Because they are free from the addictive temptations that plague many people who have low or no future focus, it is unlikely that they will get lung cancer from smoking. Futures are more likely to survive the hazards of adolescence and live longer as adults.

Futures Get the Job Done

As we said in the last chapter, the highest grades in our large introductory psychology course at Stanford were earned by students who were most future-oriented. Present hedonists and present fatalists brought up the rear. This could be because future-oriented students are just smarter, but we don't buy that. Being future-oriented goes hand in hand with doing appropriate planning, scheduling one's time wisely, and anticipating detours and traps that might appear on the path to success. Futures almost never get incompletes in their courses, or require extensions to complete their work. That means they don't have to double their burden of work as they simultaneously finish the old work and begin the new.

Imagine that you have an important presentation or test on Monday. When do you start preparing? Presents will begin on Sunday night, so the material will be fresh in their minds. Futures, on the other hand, will prepare on Friday, to have sufficient time to review all the material and clear up any confusion in their minds.

In many general psychology courses, students are required to participate as subjects in a number of psychological experiments. The rationale behind this procedure is that students get firsthand experience of the research process. We tracked the times that students first signed up to start their required six hours of participation for our courses, when they completed each hour, and when they finally finished. Lo and behold, future-oriented students began a full week earlier on average than their present-oriented classmates. They kept signing up regularly until they had completed the assignment a week on average before their present peers. Present-oriented students often had to do makeup experiments until the final week of school, when they should have been finishing papers and preparing for finals. Getting the job done on time also means not having to lie and make excuses, for which future-oriented students thereby earn credibility from teachers and, later, their bosses.[4]

Futures Are Mindful of Mortality

On a sundial at eighteenth-century Castle Howard in England, this inscription is etched: TIME BY MOMENTS STEALS AWAY, FIRST THE HOUR, THEN THE DAY. ON THINE EYELIDS IS THE SHADOW OF DEATH. Early clocks and watches often had engravings of skulls and cross-bones on them as a reminder to the wearer of his mortality.[5] Recognizing that death is inevitable at some unknowable time, futures seek to delay their end by making wise decisions now. They arrange for retirement while they are still young, establish trusts and write wills, and put hard-earned cash into insurance policies.

A sundial at Castle Howard, England

Futures Are Problem Solvers

When challenged to solve puzzles as quickly as they could, the presents and futures responded very differently.[6] The presents jumped out to a lead and moved their pencils through the mazes this way and that, trying to find the elusive goal. Surprisingly, the futures did not move at all at first, just observed, looking for the goal and then working backward to the starting point. They checked out cul-de-sacs en route. Guess who won the match?

Futures use what are known as backtracking algorithms and future checking, subprocedures in problem solving that attempt to foresee and evaluate alternate strategies for attaining goals. No one taught them these fancily named techniques. They developed them by naturally dealing with the world through trial and error.

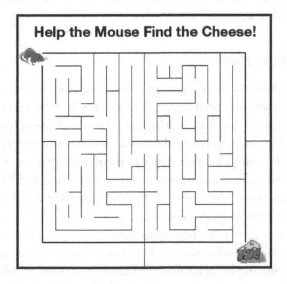

The futures won. Over 80 percent of them solved the mazes, in contrast to under 60 percent of the presents. Many of the presents who failed got frustrated at not finding the right path and ended up making a straight line to the goal, bursting through the cul-de-sac barriers.

You are probably thinking that there must be an explanation for this considerable difference in performance. Maybe future-oriented students play with puzzles, mazes, and other similar games often, while presents seldom play such games. If that were true, the future-oriented students would solve more puzzles because they had more practice, not because of their future orientation. How could we put that reasonable assumption to rest? Hypnosis came to the rescue.

A follow-up study used exactly the same procedures with one exception. All the students were initially future-oriented, but when half of them were hypnotized and given the instruction (described in the previous chapter) to expand the present, they mirrored what the true present-oriented students had done in the first study. Thirty percent more of them failed to solve the maze, compared to the continuing superior performance of the future-oriented students. A future's approach to solving life's everyday mazes is more effective than a present orientation.

Futures Make Money

For many reasons, futures end up making more money than people with any other time perspective. Because they have more education, they get better jobs. Because they save more and spend less on frivolity and socializing, they compound their investments; they have better credit ratings because they pay their credit cards on time and don't run up debt. Most important, they work long and hard, take shorter vacations, and realize in the end that they are exchanging their investment in work for money.

A recent interesting study sheds new light on one way in which futures come to value saving their hard-earned wages. Attitudes toward economic behavior held by Dutch household members ages sixteen to twenty-one were compared with those of their parents. The results show that parents who discuss financial matters with their children influence the children's financial behavior, teaching them the importance of saving money. The effects of such early socialization extend into adulthood, and key predictors of children's financial success are their fathers' conscientiousness and their parents' future orientation. Children observe a wide variety of future-oriented behaviors of their parents, so they have plenty of opportunities for learning. We suspect that future-oriented parents use whatever circumstances arise to instill mindfulness of consequences, for instance those of not brushing one's teeth, not studying for examinations, spending pocket money too quickly, or putting homework off to the last minute.

Parents also use proverbs and folk wisdom to encourage children to think of the future.[7] A Sicilian student told us of an interesting lesson on the importance of thinking about future consequences. She recalled her grandmother telling the story of Cinderella, but instead of the happy-ending conclusion, Grandma had another. She shrugged and said sadly, "That happens to *them;* for *us,* nothing changes. We go back to being the poor servant." Her present fatalism showed her granddaughter the need for realism by stripping away illusions and fantasies of a better life. The student learned that she had better plan if she wanted to avoid suffering her grandmother's fate.

Futures Persevere and Make the Best of Failure

Even futures may fail in their quest for a good life. Once-solid middle-class people can end up out on the streets through the unexpected consequences of an unexpected divorce, illness, or loss of employment. Yet futures in homeless shelters in San Francisco fared better than those who were present-oriented. Our survey and interviews with nearly fifty homeless people revealed that the more present-oriented they were, the more time they wasted watching TV or just passing time and eating. These presents also worked less. The opposite was true for futures living in the same shelters: They were less likely to waste time, spent significantly less time depressed, and spent more time working. Not surprising, the duration of stay was shorter for futures.[8]

Similarly, futures persevere in the face of other difficulties. Teach First is a new program in Britain in which extremely bright graduates from Cambridge University teach for two years in schools that are challenging and underprivileged. Such jobs are quite stressful, and the lack of resources, bored students, and challenges from ethnic and linguistic diversity cause many young teachers to quit. The novice teachers who stick it out despite the stress are largely future-oriented. Investigative interviews with teachers revealed two interesting motivations for signing on and sticking to it: "The vast majority of Teach First teachers were motivated by factors related to the future. Most of all, they were sold on adding value to their CV's, making business contacts to use in the future, gaining experience and skills and 'getting on the job ladder.' Virtually *all* motivations and considerations fit your notion of the 'future-oriented.' "[9]

Current societal forces may be creating ever more competition, which, in turn, is making future orientation the new norm for educated young people. High future orientation may be more likely today than ever.

For Futures, a Realistic Hope Springs Eternal

Hope is the expectation of positive outcomes of one's present actions at some time in the future. Being hopeful is part of being future-oriented.[10] But futures' hope is tempered with realism, not inflated with fantasy. They know they have to work to make hopes come true and that discipline and sometimes righteous suffering are necessary for getting from here to where they want to be.[11]

You can see the difference in hope and time perspectives in the patients who start in physical rehabilitation programs. As many as half quit before completing the regimen. When people discontinue treatment prematurely, they can lose the use of their limbs and suffer a lasting loss of mobility. But many do so simply because it hurts more to complete the regimen than to quit it. Rehab exercises do hurt, sometimes excruciatingly, because they stretch sore muscles and reposition bones. Patients with low pain tolerance opt out as soon as they reach their pain threshold, but those with a well-defined future orientation are more likely to persevere and endure the pain for the short term because of the long-term gains it provides.

In practical terms, rehab centers can use these findings to administer strategies that fit a patient's time perspective. Present- and past-oriented people may need extra attention and support. Less painful initial exercises and intermediate rewards may keep them on track to healing. Regular infusions of hope and encouragement can keep them going. Anticipating the likelihood of their quitting, their need for more personal attention, and their need for appointment reminders may cut down on the high failure rates that plague rehabilitation efforts.[12]

Futures Avoid Social Traps

Futures are competitive go-getters, their eyes always on the prize. Present- and past-oriented people are no match for them when negotiating deals or arguing. However, when futures realize that ultimate long-term gains are better than short-term quick fixes and profits, they will be the first to cooperate with others for a common win-win. They avoid or escape "social traps" that ensnare present-oriented competitors.

A social trap is a conflict over what is the best use of any given resource for the interest of the individual, as opposed to the common or collective good. It was once in the best economic interests of fishermen, herdsmen, farmers, loggers, and manufacturers to catch all the fish they could from the oceans, to graze as many cattle, to plant as many crops, to cut down as much timber and dump as much toxic waste as they could get away with. Yet when individuals act independently to maximize profit, they ultimately all lose because every resource is limited and at some point no longer renewable. Then the yield for the individual as well as for society diminishes and may even vanish. This was the case with the overfishing of sardines in Monterey Bay, California, for instance, and salmon in the Columbia River, Oregon. Many fishing companies and individual fishermen hauled in huge catches of these fish until one day virtually none was left.

Social traps also are called commons dilemmas, or the tragedy of the commons, a term coined by nineteenth-century British economist William Forster Lloyd. Consider a common pasture used for cattle grazing. Each owner gains most by having as many cattle as possible graze there, but that economic model clashes with the cost to the community; if everyone were to adopt that same selfish orientation, overgraze, and deplete the resource, all would suffer—a tragedy. Garrett Hardin popularized this idea in 1968, concluding that if policing the commons were left to the individual conscience, then the selfish would prevail over the farsighted because shorter-term individual yields would be greater than communal, longer-term gain. Hardin believed further that there could be no technical solution to this problem—for instance, no additional energy from fertilizer to boost grass production, or technique to minimize waste and toxicity from building up, could be found that would not ultimately be harmful to others within and around the commons. Only a moral solution that addressed a change in values and individual expectations would help.[13] The relevance of this model to our natural resources in today's world are obvious—latter-day commons include clean air and water in oceans, lakes, and rivers; birds, bees, whales, and food stocks; national parks; oil, coal, and other energy sources.

We believe that the common good is not a moral matter but a time-perspective matter. Adopting a narrowly focused present orientation for immediate gain is not selfish; it is simply the way presents everywhere think. Future-oriented workers also want to earn as much as they can, but their time perspective leads them to value long-term over short-term gain, because they can foresee that in the future, attempts to maximize short-term gain will have negative consequences. Therefore, they seek long-term returns and advance cooperative strategies rather than quick big hits. Futures are generally the environmental activists who encourage sustainable farming, fishing, and water use, and promote energy-efficient cars and homes. They are in the vanguard sounding a warning about the long-term consequences of global warming and overpopulation, the stockholders who force boards of directors to look beyond quarterly profits and ahead to sustained long-term yield on their investments. They promote recycling programs, invent new ways to profit through green services.

One of the few studies to address the association among time perspective, basic values, and environmental attitudes was conducted recently with several hundred Brazilian college students who completed our ZTPI (in Portuguese).[14] The data show that environmental preservation and concern for the biosphere were significantly related to future orientation and altruism. Positive attitudes toward exploiting natural resources correlated with tendencies of self-enhancement. As with other beneficial characteristics associated with a future time perspective, positive, balanced attitudes toward environmental sustainability can be promoted through education.

REHEARSING FOR A SUCCESSFUL FUTURE

As we have done in the two preceding chapters, we would like you to complete a version of the Who Am I? test now. This time we would like you to answer the question Who Will I Be? Think of the person you want to become and what the evidence of your accomplishment might be once you have reached your goals. Spend time answering the question thoughtfully as many times as you can.

Time-out Two: The Who Will I Be? Test

1. I will be: _____

2. I will be: _____

3. I will be: _____

4. I will be: _____

5. I will be: _____

6. I will be: _____

7. I will be: _____

8. I will be: _____

9. I will be: _____

10. I will be: _____

11. I will be: _____

12. I will be: _____

13. I will be: _____

14. I will be: _____

Concrete *Future Goal*	*When Will the Goal* *Be Accomplished?*
1. _____	_____
2. _____	_____
3. _____	_____
4. _____	_____
5. _____	_____

Once you have finished the Who Will I Be? test, go through your answers and identify five or so concrete goals that you hope to reach in the future. These goals may involve getting a better job, retiring, having children, getting out of debt, traveling, or finishing school. Once you've identified five concrete goals, arrange them in order from the one that you hope to reach soonest to the one that you hope to accomplish last. After you've indicated how long you think it will take to reach them, we want you to mentally rehearse reaching them. Professional athletes improve their performance by visualizing themselves successfully completing an action before it occurs. Basketball players visualize themselves making free throws with perfect form before each attempt, and baseball batters visualize themselves taking the perfect swing before every pitch. It turns out that when we practice succeeding at a task mentally, our performance actually does improve. Moreover, *how* you practice matters as well.

In research examining students studying for midterms and coping with stressful events, psychologist Shelley Taylor and her research team found that those who practiced mental rehearsal and focused on what they needed to do to succeed enhanced their performance more often than those whose mental rehearsal focused strictly on the outcome they desired. People who rehearsed the steps that they needed to take in order to get good grades and to deal with stressful experiences did better than people who imagined themselves getting good grades and alleviating stress.[15] When you focus on the *process* of achieving your goal rather than imagining the end *product* of your efforts, your chance of success will increase.

Starting with the first goal on your list, visualize step by step the actions that you need to take to reach it. What is the first step that you must take? Where does it lead? Also pay attention to the thoughts and feelings you are likely to experience on the way to achieving your goal. Mental rehearsal is not magic. It works to clarify your path to your goal and your steps toward it. As the old saying goes, "A journey of a thousand miles begins with one step." Once you are mentally on the path toward your first goal or have reached it, move on to the second. Once you've completed the second, move on to the third, and so forth. Before you know it, you will have run out of the goals you have listed and will be developing new goals to achieve and new plans to rehearse them.

AND NOW FOR THE BAD STUFF

It is possible that too great a future focus can cancel out its many benefits. Again, this is a paradox of time. Are you so busy that you dress your kids the night before school so they will be on time? Do you brush your teeth in the shower, talk on your cell phone while pedaling your bike and reading the business section? If you answered yes, you may be a member of the time-press generation.

Time Press and Time Crunch

The questions above led off a *USA Today* weeklong series on the pressures that many Americans feel. Most feel they do not have enough time to do all they want.[16] Nearly half of those questioned reported being busier than they were last year. The majority used a host of devices and services to save time: microwaves rather than ovens, catalogs and televisions rather than stores for shopping; they

banked by phone, employed laundry services, and listened more
often to answering machines than to human voices. Nevertheless,
their savings of time ended up letting them devote more time to
work. Wasting time became sinful, a source of emotional distress.
The majority reported becoming angry, impatient, ticked off when
they were forced to wait for late people (85 percent); when stuck in
traffic (63 percent); when they had to stand in any line (61 percent);
when they were kept waiting in a doctor's office (59 percent); or
when restaurant service was slow (51 percent). Nearly as many
added other forms of waiting that were toxic to their mental health:
government slowness to act; repairpersons who failed to keep scheduled appointments; finding parking places; waiting for delayed
flights, or buses.

You can bet that marketers are well informed of this time crunch
and how to exploit it. Take, for example, an advertisement that
proudly promotes oatmeal as the ideal for today's supermoms: "Instant Quaker oatmeal. For moms who have a lot of love but not a
lot of time." It apparently appeals to Sherri Greenberg of New York
City, who is shown hugging little Nicky: "I can give him a terrific
breakfast in just ninety seconds." And, Mom explains, the second-
ary time-saving benefit, "I don't have to spend any time coaxing
him to eat it."

Besides using the time they saved to work longer hours, over half
also reported making other personal sacrifices: cutting back on
household chores, recreation, hobbies, and watching television.
Almost as many felt they had to sacrifice going to church or engaging in charitable activities. What was most unexpected and alarm-
ing was that over 40 percent of all those surveyed said they had to
sacrifice time with friends and family!

More remarkable is that the *USA Today* data are probably under-
estimations, because they were collected "way back" in 1989. Today
we engage in what author Jeremy Rifkin calls "time wars"[17]—our
hyperefficient, nanosecond world disturbs the organization of our
social time and creates havoc with our orientation to the rhythms of
the natural world. Our excessively future-oriented high-tech lives
subjugate us to a new simulated environment.

In Chapter Eleven, we will propose ways to temper extreme time perspectives and achieve a balanced focus that is healthier for individuals and society.

The two most powerful warriors are patience and time.
—Leo Tolstoy

Sacrificing Family, Friends, and Sex for Success

In their quest for success, businesspeople try to do it all, but they can't. In the end, they trade off social pleasures, like spending time with family and friends, and enjoying personal pleasures, like smelling the roses or even noticing that they are in blossom. Many even give up on sex with their partners.

MALE BUSINESSMEN SAY LIVES "EMPTY" was the headline story based on a survey of more than four thousand successful, middle-aged businessmen. These company managers reported that despite their status and financial success, their lives were empty, unfulfilling, and contained little pleasure. Like survivors of near-death experiences, some decided to start their lives over again: working less, playing more, and taking time to enjoy their spouses, children, and friends. For others, it was too late to make up for lost time, which would have required a major overhaul in priorities and making amends to all those they had "time-slighted."[18]

The birds do it. The bees do it. But educated futures do not do it. Recent polls reveal that a large number of marriages qualify as low-sex marriages in which couples engage in sexual intercourse less than once a week. Men are surprisingly less interested in sex than are their wives. Marital therapists report that their female clients in such marriages feel hurt, rejected, and angry; some even express "rage and despair."[19]

Without firm time-perspective data in hand, we hypothesize that these men are probably like those senior executives whose lives are empty—for the most part, future-oriented workaholics who do not cultivate sensuality and sexuality and have little interest in making friends or "wasting" time in playful activities—a recipe for sexual deprivation. Another reason, we suspect, for infrequent sexual encounters among future-oriented men is their tendency toward perfectionism. Sex becomes performance and thus induces evaluation apprehension and the expectation of receiving gold stars for getting erections, sustaining them, and achieving orgasms. But performance concerns breed anticipatory anxiety, which, in turn, makes sexuality a cognitive jungle instead of an oasis of pleasure.

As more women move up the executive ladder, we suspect that they, too, will stop wasting time on that birds-and-bees thing. Ladies, don't let that happen to you. Hold out for balancing career in the office and sensual pleasure in the bedroom (or wherever).

six

THE TRANSCENDENTAL FUTURE

New Time After Death

11. And I saw a great white throne, and him that sat on it, from whose face the earth and the heaven fled away; and there was found no place for them.

12. And I saw the dead, small and great, stand before God; and the books were opened: and another book was opened, which is the book of life: and the dead were judged out of those things which were written in the books, according to their works.

13. And the sea gave up the dead which were in it; and death and hell delivered up the dead which were in them: and they were judged every man according to their works.

—The Bible, Revelations 20:11–13[1]

(24) And they say: There is naught but our life of the world; we die and we live, and naught destroyeth us save time; when they have no knowledge whatsoever of (all) that; they do but guess. (26) Say (unto them, O Muhammad): Allah giveth life to you, then causeth you to die, then gathereth you unto the Day of Resurrection whereof there is no doubt. But most of mankind know not.

—The Koran, 45:24 and 26[2]

Naturally, most of us would like to die a peaceful death, but it is also clear we cannot hope to die peacefully if our lives have been full of violence, or if our minds have mostly been agitated by emotions like anger, attachment, or fear. So if we wish to die well, we must learn to live well.

—The fourteenth Dalai Lama[3]

God is, or He is not. But to which side shall we incline. . . . Let us weigh the gain and the loss in wagering that God is. . . . If you gain, you gain all; if you lose, you lose nothing. Wager, then, without hesitation that He is.

—Blaise Pascal[4]

Believing as I do that man in the distant future will be a far more perfect creature than he now is, it is an intolerable thought that he and all other sentient beings are doomed to complete annihilation after such long-continued slow progress. To those who fully admit the immortality of the human soul, the destruction of our world will not appear so dreadful.

—Charles Darwin[5]

All that pleases is but for a moment.
All that troubles is but for a moment.
That only is important which is eternal.

—Inscriptions over the triple doorways of
the Cathedral of Milan, Italy

Somewhere in the Middle East, a young man—let's call him Omar—stands on an overturned milk crate with his arms outstretched. Close friends circle around him in the center of the room as a tailor tugs at his clothing.[6] Others stand back and admire him from a distance. A radiant smile of contentment stretches across his face. Tears well up in his father's eyes as he beams with pride: "I am very happy and proud of what my son is about to do, and I hope that all of the men of our faith do the same."[7] One by one, they congratulate Omar, kiss him on the cheek, and say a heartfelt good-bye. Omar accepts their affection and walks out onto the street to face this world—and the next world—alone.

After this informal ceremony, Omar's life will change. For the event about to take place, he wears not a suit and tie, but a loose jacket fitted over a suicide belt that contains about ten pounds of plastic explosive. Omar is about to take his own life and, in so doing, hopes to take as many other's lives as he can.

Omar calmly walks to the middle of a crowded open-air market, pauses to reflect on his decision, and then detonates the belt. Wooden stalls splinter, produce scatters, small fires break out, and lives are destroyed. Smoke and screams fill the air. Omar and twelve others are killed instantly. Thirty innocent bystanders are wounded. Their lives as well as their families' lives and Omar's family's lives have been changed forever.

For most Westerners, if we knew that we were going to die in a violent explosion in fifteen minutes, terror and despair would grip and convulse us. Yet Omar displayed none of these emotions. He walked calmly and coolly, even pausing to admire the quality of the figs in the market stalls. He acted not as a "brainwashed" religious fanatic but as though his willful actions made perfect sense. To most Western religious and nonreligious people, however, Omar's actions don't make sense at all. What could motivate such an extraordinarily evil act? How could he justify killing innocent civilians, even children? What cause, what ideology, could induce people to follow in Omar's footsteps?

SOME TRADITIONAL EXPLANATIONS OF SUICIDE TERRORISM

The Abnormal Psychology Explanation

A common explanation for suicide bombings such as Omar's is that the bomber must be crazy. Senator John Warner advocated this position, arguing that, "Those who would commit suicide in their assaults on the free world are not rational and are not deterred by rational concepts."[8] Explaining suicide bombing as the work of the mentally ill allows us emotional distance from the acts and reassures us that we are different from these terrorists: We are sane. Suicide bombers are not. We could never do something so terrible. To some Western mind-sets, this explanation also relieves suicide bombers of guilt for their actions. After all, if they are crazy, they cannot make rational decisions, for by definition, crazy people think, feel, and do abnormal things that do not make sense to the rest of us.

The "crazy" explanation does not predict who will become a suicide bomber. It places their actions squarely outside the explanatory power of "normal" psychological theories. If suicide bombers are mentally ill, then we can only hope to predict who will become a suicide bomber as well as we can currently predict who will ultimately suffer from clinical depression, personality disorders, or schizophrenia. But for all of these abnormal mental states, although we can sometimes predict them, preventing them is still years in the future.

Some mental disorders are linked to violent behavior. Depression is a risk factor for suicide. Antisocial personality disorder and schizophrenia are associated with the acts of violence, and even murder, infamously perpetrated by Ted Bundy, Jeffrey Dahmer, and Ted Kaczynski. Despite their infamy, these well-known cases are vivid exceptions to the rule. Mental disorders are clearly unnecessary to motivate violence against self or others. Most people with mental disorders never harm anyone.

By all informed accounts, suicide bombers are exceptional only in their normality. Most suicide bombers are not mentally ill. United Nations director of information service Nasra Hassan concluded from her study of Palestinian suicide bombers that:

> None of the suicide bombers—they ranged in age from eighteen to thirty-eight—conformed to the typical profile of the suicidal personality. None of them was uneducated, desperately poor, simple-minded, or depressed. Many were middle class and, unless they were fugitives, held paying jobs. More than half of them were refugees from what is now Israel. Two were the sons of millionaires. They all seemed to be entirely normal members of their families. They were polite and serious, and in their communities they were considered to be model youths.[9]

According to the results of a recent study of four hundred al-Qaeda members, three quarters came from the upper or middle class. This study by the forensic psychiatrist Marc Sageman also found evidence of the normality and even intellectual superiority of these youths turned suicide bombers. The majority, 90 percent, came from caring, intact families. Two thirds had gone to college. Two thirds were married, most of them with children, and most had jobs in science and engineering. "These are the best and brightest of their society in many ways," Sageman concluded.[10]

Although it may threaten our views of what constitutes normality and, more significant, what threatens us, the data are clear. Suicide bombers are no crazier than the rest of us. The percentage of "crazy" suicide bombers should therefore reflect the same low percentage of people who are mentally ill in the society from which they come.

The Brainwashed Explanation

A second common explanation for suicide bombers is that they are normal, but—through unfortunate circumstances and personal vulnerabilities—they fall victim to brainwashing by cultlike religious leaders. William Safire set forth this explanation:

> Such fanatic indoctrination takes time and isolation; it takes teachers of terror skilled in evoking visions of a martyrdom and requires recruits from vulnerably infuriated families who are known to other cells. The brainwashing is reinforced with official broadcasts of films of a dead boy beckoning potential suicide killers to join him in paradise.[11]

The brainwashing explanation can be seen as absolving individual bombers of responsibility, placing it squarely on the shoulders of religious leaders. The training by religious leaders, however, does not meet the classical definition of brainwashing. Brainwashing is the "intensive, forcible indoctrination, usually political or religious, aimed at destroying a person's basic convictions and attitudes and replacing them with an alternative set of fixed beliefs."[12] It involves separating individuals from family and friends, "washing" away their existing beliefs, and replacing them with new beliefs. Classic examples of brainwashing include Patty Hearst's abduction by the Symbionese Liberation Army and the Jim Jones Peoples' Temple suicide. These groups systematically modified the conventional beliefs of captives or members and replaced them with radical beliefs. In the case of suicide bombers, existing beliefs do not need to be washed away and replaced by new beliefs. Society inculcates some of the beliefs during the course of the youths' normal development.

Many Middle Eastern societies embrace the beliefs, values, and actions espoused by terrorist groups. Immediately after 9/11, 95 percent of Saudis supported al-Qaeda, 73 percent of Lebanese Muslims believed suicide bombing to be justifiable, and only 6 percent of Egyptians supported America's War on Terror.[13] Because suicide bombers do not break from the extremist beliefs they and their community hold, the term "brainwashed" does not apply to them.

Although there may be a cultural readiness to accept their violent orientation, some essential training is necessary before an angry person, seeking revenge against his nation's "enemy," decides to blow himself and others apart for the cause. The Israeli psychologist Ariel Merari has studied this phenomenon over many years and outlines the common steps on the path to these explosive deaths in Israel. First, senior members of an extremist group identify young people who appear to have an intense patriotic fervor, usually from their declarations at a public rally against Israel or their support of some Islamic cause or Palestinian action. Next, potential recruits are invited to discuss how much they love their country and hate Israel. They are then asked to commit themselves to training. Those who do make that commitment become part of a small secret cell of three to five youths. They learn the trade from their elders: bomb-making, disguise, and selection and timing of targets.

Finally, they make public their private commitment by making videotapes in which they declare themselves to be "the living martyr" for Islam (al-shahid-al-hai). In one hand they hold the Koran, in the other a rifle; the insignia on their headband declares their new status. This video binds them to committing the final deed because it is sent to their families. The recruits are told that not only will they earn a place beside Allah in the afterlife but their relatives will also be entitled to a high place in heaven because of their martyrdom. Their families' reward is sometimes sweetened with a sizable financial payment or monthly pension.

The bombers' photos are emblazoned on posters that are put on walls everywhere in the community the moment they succeed in their mission, thereby inspiring the next round of suicide bombers. To alleviate any concern about the pain they'll feel from the wounds they will be self-inflicting, recruits are assured that before the first drop of their blood touches the ground, they will be seated at the side of Allah, feeling only pleasure. Their minds are carefully prepared to do what is ordinarily unthinkable.

In these systematic ways, a host of normal young men and women are transformed into heroes and heroines for their culture, their lethal actions evidence of self-sacrifice and total commitment to the cause of the oppressed. That message is sent loud and clear to the next cadre of young suicide bombers in waiting.[14]

The Unbearable Present Explanation

A third common explanation for suicide bombers is that they have lost hope and therefore feel they have nothing to lose in taking their own lives. We would describe such individuals as being high in present fatalism, low in future, and low in present hedonism time perspectives. They do not enjoy the present; they do not look forward to the future; and they do not believe their acts can have any effect upon the future. Having a high past-negative time perspective—which is strongly associated with anger, perceived victimization, and aggression—they may be likely to attempt escaping their unpleasant present through violent means.

Economic comparisons between the United States and the Middle East suggest that there may be something to this explanation. Compared with the United States, the Middle East is vastly underprivileged. And the region's people frequently express a feeling of being culturally victimized by the West. That this disparity in wealth should produce anger makes sense from a Western perspective, since in the West we tend to equate wealth with happiness. Middle Easterners, however, are less likely to use money as a measure of happiness.

Research on suicide bombers supports this Middle Eastern perspective and suggests that they are neither hopeless nor despairing. A white paper published by the Singapore government containing interviews with members of Jemaah Islamiyah—a Muslim terrorist group—concluded that "They do not vent fear of enemies or express 'hopelessness' or a sense of having 'nothing to lose' for a lack of life alternatives that would be consistent with economic rationality." [15] Among the people interviewed by Nasra Hassan was a suicide bomber who had survived his mission: Israeli security forces apprehended him before he could detonate his bomb. When Hassan asked him what attracted him to martyrdom, the man replied, "The power of the spirit pulls us upward, while the power of material things pulls us downward. Someone bent on martyrdom becomes immune to the material pull." [16]

In comparison to the United States, the Middle Eastern region is poor, but being poor does not preclude hope. If it did, we would have seen a decline in suicide bombings worldwide as levels of prosperity increased. Here we're trying to make the case that poverty alone does not cause suicide bombings. Poverty has decreased even in areas from which suicide bombers frequently originate, while suicide bombings have increased. Therefore, poverty cannot be the sole cause of suicide bombings. Suicide bombers are typically normal, healthy, upstanding members of the communities from which they originate. They are not poor, disenfranchised, or crazy—at least no more so than everyone else in their communities, which do tend to be relatively impoverished by Western standards.

The primary point that we want to make is that the issue of suicide bombing is not going to be stopped by eliminating poverty. The people who become suicide bombers typically do not value money that highly, although they are not poor relative to their peers. Suicide bombing is a complex issue that necessitates a complex solution, which must factor in the motivational power of the belief in a future that transcends their earthly life.

The Religious Explanation

The religious explanation asserts that suicide bombers are fanatics who have taken religion too far. Suicide bombers do tend to be religious, but some data indicate that typically, they are no more religious than other members of their societies. Robert Pape, a professor of political science at the University of Chicago, analyzed all 315 suicide bombings that occurred between 1980 and 2003. One of his primary conclusions was that suicide bombing is a secular issue that is often obscured by religious rhetoric. He writes:

> Pundits have painted Al Qaeda as a fearless enemy motivated by insatiable religious hatred. Amid prognostications of doom, we lost sight of the truth: Suicide terrorism is a tactic, not an enemy, and beneath the religious rhetoric with which it is perpetrated, it occurs largely in the service of secular aims.[17]

Nonetheless, in identifying potential Islamic terrorists in Western governments since 9/11, authorities do look into highly religious enclaves and mosques for young people who have become newly strict in their observations and practices. Suicide bombing is not only a Muslim phenomenon, especially when viewed with a longer time perspective. Right now it largely is. But other groups conducted suicide attacks in the past, and there is no doubt that other groups will conduct suicide attacks in the future.

Probably the best-known suicide bombers are the Japanese kamikazes of World War II. Russian and German pilots also engaged in suicide missions during World War II, although to a much lesser extent. Thousands of Japanese participated in these attacks. For Christian and Jewish examples, we would have to go back further in time to the Knights Templar to find organized suicide attacks, but that doesn't invalidate the examples. Part of the reason why suicide bombing is largely a contemporary problem is that the technology to conduct effective suicide attacks is a relatively recent innovation.

There is not something unique about Muslim people that causes them to become suicide bombers. There is something about the situation in which some of them currently find themselves (of which beliefs about a heavenly future are a large part) that motivates them to become suicide bombers.

The Rational Strategy Explanation

Finally, the rational strategy explanation suggests that suicide bombing is the one available option that provides sponsors of the groups with the most bang for their buck. Advocates of this explanation point to the fact that suicide bombing has often been an effective strategy in achieving desired political objectives, that the "body count" ratio is "better" than that of alternatives to achieving success, and that it requires no escape plan. Consider one terrorist group leader's description of the ingredients necessary for a successful suicide bombing:

> Apart from a willing young man, all that is needed is such items as nails, gunpowder, a battery, a light switch and a short cable, mercury (readily obtainable from thermometers), acetone, and the cost of tailoring a belt wide enough to hold six or eight pockets of explosives. The most expensive item is transportation to a distant Israeli town. The total cost of a typical operation is about a hundred and fifty dollars.[18]

There is a cold logic to the prescription. When you run the numbers, the rational strategy explanation makes sense. Nevertheless, it runs counter to the paramount value of human life that most people around the world—including Muslims—hold.

SUICIDE TERRORISM: TIME AS AN EXPLANATION

In the late 1990s, we authors began to suspect that time perspective might partially explain suicide bombing. We believed that if we could explain complex behaviors like suicide bombing through time, understanding normal behavior would be simple by comparison. We started with the hypothesis that having a specific time-perspective profile might predispose individuals to suicide bombing. Initially, our prototypical suicide bomber was a person who was:

- High in past-negative time perspective: The person may be aggressive and may seek substantial change motivated by a desire for revenge.

- Low in past-positive time perspective: The person may place little value on tradition and stability.

- High in present-fatalistic time perspective: The person may believe that his life is in the hands of fate.

- Low in present-hedonistic time perspective: The person may not enjoy his present circumstances and feel that he has little to lose.

- Low in future-time perspective: The person may not look forward to the future.

We felt that we were on the right track, but were still missing something. These time perspectives might predispose someone to become a suicide bomber, but they are not deciding factors. Our search for an explanation led us to a topic that is still taboo in the field of academic psychology: the topic of life after death. However, our ideas do not suppose the *reality* of life *after* death, but rather, the influence that a belief in life after death can exert on the way people behave *before* they die. From our objective views as social psychologists, it does not matter what actually happens after we die. We are interested in how belief about life after death affects the behavior of the living.

According to conservative estimates, 80 to 95 percent of Westerners believe in God and in a life after death. But such self-reports probably minimize the belief. Freud said that even when people imagine their own death, they survive it as spectators,[19] and insisted that "In the unconscious every one of us is convinced of his [or her] own immortality. . . . Our unconscious . . . does not believe in its own death; it behaves as if it were immortal." From a secular point of view, if we believe that we are immortal, there is little reason to plan for our lives in the future. Serious errors that we might make would be insignificant. We could live for today and risk our lives with careless abandon. Tomorrow would be guaranteed. Some religious dogma declares that immortality brings additional responsibility. Our bodies die, but our souls live forever. Because souls are immortal, people are responsible for their actions on earth, which determine our fate for eternity. The "wages of sin" are not only death but a fate even worse: eternal damnation.

At the turn of the last century, 77 percent of Americans believed in life after death, and that percentage has increased since 1944.[20] Because most people believe in life after death, most have goals that are beyond life: staying out of hell, going to heaven, or being reincarnated in a higher life form.[21] The reward or punishment that we anticipate after death may influence present behavior just as pre-death goals do. After all, the psychologist's conception of the future is no more real than the conception of an existence after death. Visions of the future and of life after death are psychological constructs, imaginative inventions of the human mind.

THE TRANSCENDENTAL-FUTURE TIME PERSPECTIVE

To test whether beliefs about the goals, rewards, and punishments that await us after we die foster a unique time perspective, we added questions to the Zimbardo Time Perspective Inventory that presuppose a life after death. Several hundred people completed the combined inventory, and when we reanalyzed the results, we found that a distinct and meaningful new time perspective, which we called the transcendental future, had emerged. (Phil's score on the transcendental-future time perspective is 1.5. John's score is 1.8.)

For many people, pre- and post-death periods partition the psychological future into two segments.[22] The traditional or mundane future begins in the present and extends to the point of imagined death, with its lifetime goals, such as graduating from college, becoming a parent, owning a home, and marrying. This is the future that is traditionally studied by psychologists. The transcendental-future time perspective extends from the death of the physical body to eternity. The transcendental future encompasses different events that include divine judgment, reunion with dead loved ones, eternal life, achieving oneness with nature, reincarnation, and the end of poverty, pain, and suffering. It is this undocumentable "future" that is usually ignored or minimized by most psychologists.

As one might expect, the transcendental-future time perspective is related to self-reported religion, spirituality, and a belief in life after death. Transcendentals, people who score high on the transcendental-future time perspective, attend religious services and perform religious rituals at home more frequently than people who score lower on the scale. While the transcendental-future time perspective is generally related to religious belief, there are substantial differences among religions in the extent to which believers adopt this time perspective. Christians and Muslims score above average on the transcendental-future scale, while Jews, Buddhists, and those with no religious affiliation score below average.[23]

Table 1: The Transcendental-future Time Perspective and World Religions

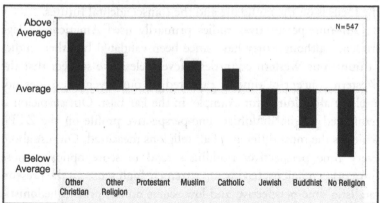

Each religion approaches the transcendental-future and other time perspectives differently. Each has its own time-perspective profile. As the chapter introductory quotations indicate, Christians and Muslims strongly believe in a transcendental future. Indeed, both religions view the mundane future as a preparation for judgment.

Protestants tend to be extreme on every time perspective and score extremely low on the past-negative and extremely high on the future time perspectives. Protestants take the positive from their pasts and work assiduously toward the "good" future. The Jewish profile is similar but less extreme. The past-positive is the only time perspective on which Protestants and Jews differ. While Protestants tend to be high on the past-positive time perspective, Jews tend to be slightly below average, with low past-negative and low present-fatalistic time perspectives. In other words, Jews do not dwell on the negative elements in their past and believe that their actions determine their fate. The unique characteristic of Catholics is their moderation. They are neither high nor low on any time perspective.

Like Protestants, Muslims tend to be low on the past-negative, low on the present-fatalistic, and high on the future time perspective. But the Muslim profile is also extremely low on past-positive and present-hedonistic time perspectives. The Muslims in our sample tended not to bring positive elements from their past into the present, and they tended not to focus on pleasure. For Muslims, the focus is on the mundane and the transcendental futures.

Our time-perspective studies primarily used American college students, although they have since been validated by other studies in numerous Western countries. Nevertheless, we suspect that the Western concept of time as captured by our inventories does not apply in all cultures, for example, in the Far East. Our suspicion is reinforced by the Buddhist time-perspective profile on the ZTPI, which is the most different of all religions measured. On just about every time perspective, Buddhists tend to score opposite those from other religions, having an extremely high score on the present-fatalistic time perspective and low scores on the present-hedonistic and future time perspectives. Buddhists tend not to focus on the future or on pleasure in the present. This fascinating profile suggests that the Buddhists concept of time is very different from the Western concept of time, more along the lines of the holistic-present orientation that we described in Chapter Four. We look forward to exploring these differences further in future studies.

Table 2: The Past-negative Time Perspective and World Religions

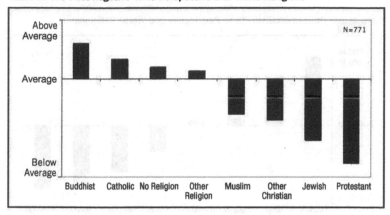

Table 3: The Past-positive Time Perspective and World Religions

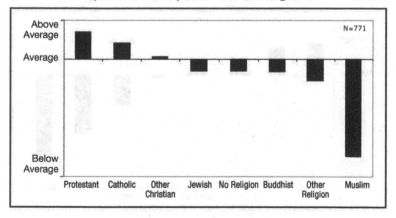

Table 4: The Present-fatalistic Time Perspective and World Religions

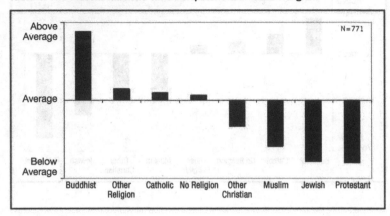

Table 5: The Present-hedonistic Time Perspective and World Religions

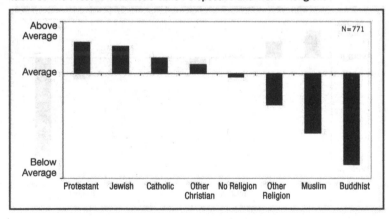

Table 6: The Future Time Perspective and World Religions

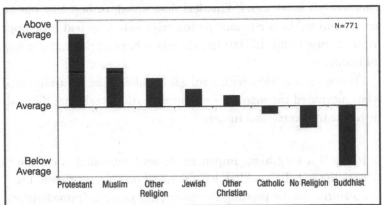

Transcendental-future scores also differ in important demographic characteristics. Women and girls score higher than men and boys. The young and the old score higher than young adults and the middle-aged. African-Americans and Hispanics score higher than Asians or Caucasians. The typical Transcendental is an older Protestant woman of Hispanic or African-American origin who believes in salvation, attends religious services, and performs religious rituals at home. She seldom watches R-rated movies; she believes in future rewards; she has great empathy for the feelings of others; and she is happier than are people with lower scores.

How Belief in the Transcendental Future Motivates Behavior

As we saw in Chapter Five, the future is our primary motivational space.[24] Our goals, hopes, and fears live in the future, and belief in the transcendental future is psychologically equivalent to belief in the mundane future. Neither of them is real. The transcendental-future time perspective therefore allows theories of motivation to be extended past the point of imagined death and can be used to explain what is often thought to be incomprehensible behavior. Seemingly irrational behavior can be understood as culturally acceptable attempts to secure reward or avoid punishment in the transcendental future. Seen from a transcendental-future perspective, a suicide bomber's act is not crazy, fanatical, hate-filled, or hopeless, but an act committed by a religious person who may have had little hope for his future in this life but has abundant hope in the transcendental future.

During an interview with a suicide bomber, Nasra Hassan asked what motivated the man. His response clearly reveals that his goals lie in the transcendental future:

> It's as if a very high, impenetrable wall separated you from paradise or hell. . . . Allah has promised one or the other to his creatures. So, by pressing the detonator, you can immediately open the door to paradise—it is the shortest path to heaven.[25]

Other time perspectives may also contribute to the decision to become a suicide bomber. For example, it is easy to understand why a young Palestinian boy would be high on past-negative, high on present-fatalistic, and low on future time perspectives: His past is filled with violence, pain, and loss; he has little control over his life; and he has little hope for a peaceful prosperity tomorrow. Each of these factors has been discussed as a potential cause of suicide bombing. Time perspective helps to unify these disparate explanations conceptually, and it also adds the explicative power of the transcendental future. The transcendental-future time perspective is the "secret" ingredient for understanding this phenomenon. In the end, suicide bombers are fighting for time.

People with goals in the transcendental future have a map of a distant land that they cannot visit in this lifetime.

> *Strange, is it not? That of the myriads who*
> *Before us pass'd the door of Darkness through,*
> *Not one returns to tell us of the Road,*
> *Which to discover we must travel too.*
> —Omar Khayyám, *The Rubaiyat*, Verse 64

Believers must have faith that their map of the transcendental future will prove accurate, but there is no way to check the accuracy of the map because there can be no reliable feedback. All events in life are open to interpretation as road signs on the path to enlightenment. Positive events can be interpreted as signs of "good" behavior, while negative events can be interpreted as divine tests, like those that Job endured in the Old Testament. Because there is no possibility of contradictory evidence, belief in the transcendental future may be especially resistant to change.

In the mundane future, nothing lasts forever. Careers end, health declines, and people die. As rewards are exhausted, the motivational power fades. Goals that once provided motivation recede into oblivion. But transcendental-future goals do last forever. The reward achieved after death—eternal life, for instance—lasts for eternity. Because the reward does not fade, in the transcendental future, goals may generate infinite motivation. Once people expect to exist after death, they are accountable for their behavior forever. Positive acts lead to eternal bliss, while negative acts lead to eternal damnation.

THE TRANSCENDENTAL FUTURE AND COPING

Coping with the Present

Karl Marx argued that religion numbed people to the injustices of the world and kept the masses from rising against their oppressors. He wrote, "Religion is the sigh of the oppressed creature, the heart of a heartless world and the soul of soulless conditions. It is the opium of the people." [26] Consistent with Marx's sentiment, groups that have been oppressed—the young, the old, women, and minorities—score highest on the transcendental-future scale. For the oppressed, the promise of rewards in the transcendental future far exceeds anything that is obtainable in this lifetime. That promise can make life among the proletariat, in the ghetto, in the dysfunctional home, or in the trailer park easier to bear. Doris Kearns Goodwin gives a similar rationale for the suffering endured by early immigrants to America. She writes:

The degradation endured for generations by the poor peasants in the Old World combined with a Catholic value system in which the preparations for one's death and rebirth eclipsed the affairs of the immediate present to produce an acceptance of conditions in the New World which few other people would have tolerated.[27]

A firm belief in the transcendental future may make present inequities less painful to endure and rebellion less imperative. Spilling blood in a revolution is not an attractive option when it may result in an eternity of punishment. People may tolerate mistreatment and subjugation if they believe they will be eternally punished for violence and eternally rewarded for turning the other cheek.

Coping with Death

Two days after Omar's attack, family and friends bury his mortal remains. They mourn their loss but take comfort in the belief that their loved one is not gone forever. Their loved one's physical body has been destroyed, but his soul lives on in the transcendental future, a better place where they will one day join him. Transcendental-future beliefs thus can transform an eternal loss into a momentary separation. The very time perspective that caused them anguish now eases their sorrow. By minimizing the period of loss, transcendental-future beliefs reduce psychological pain.

SECULAR TRANSCENDENTAL-FUTURE BELIEFS

A Native American belief

Not all transcendental-future beliefs are related to religion or even to the expectation of life after death. Some transcendental futures are concerned about generations into the future. For example, the Great Law of Peace of the Iroquois—a confederacy of Native American Indian tribes that lived near Lake Ontario in northeastern North America—reads:

In every deliberation, we must consider the impact on the seventh generation . . . even if it requires having skin as thick as the bark of a pine.

According to this law, we must think seven generations into the future not because our souls depend upon it but because our progeny do. To project one's attention to an imagined heir seven generations in the future is not easy, which is why the Iroquois wrote the law. They would need a thick skin to think and act for those seven generations to come, and to protect themselves from the sniping of less transcendental peers and from the present needs of the decision-makers themselves.

The Iroquois treat present and transcendental-future time perspectives as equal. The transcendental future is a partner in the present, and seventh-generation descendents have a seat at the table where present decisions are made. This perspective creates a vicarious representative democracy comprised of those living today and all of those who will live in the next seven generations. People living today cast votes for those who will live in the future, benefitting those who will live in the seven generations to come, as well as those who are living now. So expansive a distribution of power leaves little room for self-interest.

Sustainability

Groups of private citizens in the United States and in other nations have united under the banner of "sustainability."[28] The sustainability movement promotes the use of resources in a manner that "meets the needs of the present without compromising the ability of future generations to meet their own needs." Like the Iroquois, those in the movement seek to protect the transcendental future not because they fear for their souls but because it is the right thing to do. Unlike the Iroquois, these activists do not stop at seven generations in the future. Protecting the world's natural resources is a project without a time limit.

The Long Now Foundation

Established in 1996, the Long Now Foundation[29] promotes thinking about the future on a grand scale. The foundation seeks to counterbalance the present orientation in vogue today with a future time perspective that promotes very long-term social, economic, and environmental responsibility. The foundation took its name from the longest period of time that the founders believe people can reasonably grasp. For the foundation, the long now is ten thousand years. Who knows? In ten thousand years, people may be looking hundreds of thousands of years into the future, and the foundation may be renamed the Short Now Foundation. For now ten thousand years is the long now.

Among the foundation's activities are creating a ten-thousand-year clock and working to reformat contemporary dating measurements. The ten-thousand-year clock will be mechanically powered and will keep time relatively accurately for the next ten thousand years. The foundation has built working prototypes; they plan to entomb a full-size version in a mountaintop in Nevada. In regard to dating, the foundation encourages the use of five digits for years. In their calendar, the year 2008 becomes 02008, a format that suggests a great vista of time ahead of us and avoids the dreaded Y10K computer bug, a descendent of the Y2K millennium computer bug that occurred in the year 2000. We will encounter the bug in a mere eight thousand years, when the four digits of the year 9999 roll over to the five digits of the year 10,000. From the perspective of the transcendental future, it is never too early to plan ahead.

Deathswitch.com

While the Long Now Foundation worries about a decamillennium bug, others worry about personal transcendental-future issues. As with other time perspectives, one person's worry is another person's business opportunity. Deathswitch.com is a website dedicated to helping people communicate important information after they die. Deathswitch.com members first store important information, such as account numbers, passwords, insurance policy numbers, and last words on deathswitch.com. Members then receive periodic e-mails from deathswitch.com, asking for confirmation that they are still alive. If members fail to respond to a series of such e-mails, death-switch assumes that they are dead and sends all of the stored information to the appropriate people.

THE FUTURE OF THE TRANSCENDENTAL-FUTURE TIME PERSPECTIVE

The War on Terrorism: A War of Time Perspectives

Since the future is our primary motivational space, destroying a person's expectations of the future can substantially undermine motivation. If a teenager who wanted to play professional basketball loses a leg in a car accident, his motivation to work toward perfection in basketball is destroyed. Destruction of future goals appears to reduce the motivation of countries as well as individuals. For example, in World War II, Germany and Japan had well-articulated visions of world domination with goals that lay squarely in the mundane future. Japan was largely Buddhist—a religion related to below-average scores on the transcendental future. Germany was a fascist state officially opposed to religion. Germany and Japan had similar mundane future goals but minimal transcendental-future goals. As the countries and their expectation of future success were destroyed, Germany and Japan lost the motivation to fight and agreed to surrender. It could be argued that the Allies won World War II not by destroying people but by destroying people's plans for the future.

That will not be the case with the current war on terror. We now face an enemy whose visions of the mundane future lie smoldering in the ruins of Palestine, Afghanistan, and Iraq. This enemy's remaining hopes lie squarely in the transcendental future. As we have seen, there is no way to prove, disprove, or destroy belief in the transcendental future. Fighting an adversary with strong transcendental-future goals by destroying its mundane future goals ensures that transcendental-future goals alone are obtainable. We will win the war on terror not by destroying our enemy's future but by nurturing it. The motivational power of the mundane future must be restored if mundane future goals are to compete with transcendental-future goals. Only by building a mundane future full of hope, optimism, respect, health, and prosperity can the motivational power of the transcendental future be balanced. Without mundane future goals, Muslims have little desire left to preserve this life and, understandably, look to the transcendental future to realize their dreams. Restoring the motivational power of mundane future goals will prevent the transcendental future from being the lone oasis in an otherwise desiccated life.

While the West looks to new strategies that can turn the tide of the war next week, next month, or next year, this adversary plans for the distant future. Retired general and past-presidential candidate Wesley Clarke said, "I think al-Qaeda and its affiliated organizations take a very long view, not a four-year view but a forty-year view, a hundred-year view." The West worries about troop levels next year. Al-Qaeda worries about the next century. Times have changed, but our political and military strategies have not. The war on terror is a battle between the United States government's vision of the mundane future and the vision of the transcendental future held by those who are its enemies. Short-term victory is unlikely when the adversary is planning for eternity. Employing World War II–era tactics is likely to make eternity more appealing to the enemy. The mismatch of strategies in conducting asymmetrical war in Iraq are reminiscent of the static line tactics that English troops employed during the American Revolution, or Pickett's charge into repeating weapons during the American Civil War. It is bloody folly, and, unfortunately, it is humanity's blood.

THE TRANSCENDENTAL FUTURE: A TOOL FOR GOOD OR EVIL

Like most motivational devices, the transcendental future can be a tool for good or for evil. We have seen how transcendental-future beliefs motivate the evils deeds of a very small minority of believers. That transcendental-future beliefs are untestable makes them especially powerful and unstable. The Stanford University philosopher

Sam Harris says that conflicting and untestable beliefs about the transcendental future are a recipe for disaster. In *The End of Faith*, he writes:

> Give people divergent, irreconcilable, and untestable notions about what happens after death, and then oblige them to live together with limited resources. The result is just what we see: an unending cycle of murder and cease-fire. If history reveals any categorical truth, it is that an insufficient taste for evidence regularly brings out the worst in us. Add weapons of mass destruction to this diabolical clockwork, and you have found a recipe for the fall of civilization.[30]

If the recipe does not change, Harris may be right. But Harris does not have to be right. We can reset this clock. Doing so requires replacing past-negative and present-fatalistic time perspectives with past-positive and present-hedonistic ones. We have to respect people for their pasts and allow them to enjoy the present. The first step toward such a change must entail providing adequate resources and opportunities to those who lack them: food, shelter, and money, as well as opportunities for education, employment, recreation, relaxation, and community celebration—the basic human needs in any civilized society.

A second step requires instilling a sense of personal responsibility for seizing a desirable opportunity. Individual initiative must be encouraged and rewarded. The embers of intrinsic motivation must be carefully tended and fanned. Fatalistic passivity must be replaced by an "I can do it!" stance.

The third step entails moderating transcendental-future time perspectives and supplementing them with more practical future time perspectives. Expecting people to change their transcendental-future beliefs is insulting, naive, and may exacerbate conflict. A more reasonable approach is to offer hope, opportunity, and fulfillment in the future *on the way to* the Promised Land. The development of a mundane future time perspective requires stable political, economic, and family conditions. People must believe that their actions today will lead to predictable and desirable rewards in the future. Without stable environments, accurate prediction is impossible. Creating political, economic, social, and familial stability may require creating structures that guide and protect, stabilizing those structures, and eliminating the external forces that threaten them.

The transcendental-future perspective can be a potent source of motivation—and has been for centuries. It is of value to both individuals and their societies. For people without hope of material success, existence is made more bearable and even meaningful by the transcendental future. For society, transcendental-future goals encourage civil behavior out of concern for the living and for generations into the future. Governments can be made to better serve their citizens when leaders realize that their decisions have enduring consequences. Their failure to enact legislation "to protect and serve" will bear bitter fruit in the future. Whether transcendental-future beliefs are true or illusory—mere figments of our imagination—cannot be known until we die. Until then they soften harsh reality, enhance self-worth, and infuse lives with meaning.[31] Those with secular transcendental-future views can be motivated by them to do the right thing for future generations. Those with religious transcendental-future beliefs are motivated to do the right thing for the sake of their souls, even at the expense of their current selves. They do not value money, fame, or pleasure in this life, but are willing to die to secure rewards in the next. The statute of limitations never expires for them, and they expect to reap the fruits of their present behavior from here to eternity.

part two

MAKING TIME WORK FOR YOU

seven

TIME, YOUR BODY, AND YOUR HEALTH
More Than Your Biological Clock Is Ticking

TIME HEALS ALL WOUNDS—MORE OR LESS

Over two hundred years ago, the renowned botanist Carolus Linnaeus built—or rather, planted—a living clock, carefully selecting varieties of plants that open and close their flowers at predictable times, arranging them in a circular pattern, each segment corresponding to the number of an hour. His flower clock told time accurately to about thirty minutes, which was not bad by eighteenth-century standards.[1]

As Linnaeus and others recognized, even plants synchronize their functions to the world around them, tracking the movement of the sun across the sky by opening and closing their flowers or leaves in harmony with it and with the cycles of insects that pollinate them. We live embedded in time, but time also lives within us, as it lives within all living things.

Natural clocks are all around you—the migration of animals, the passing of the seasons, the phases of the moon, and your own bodily processes all mark the passage of time. You can use the beats of your heart to count seconds and menstrual cycles to count months. Even the family pet helps us keep time: God help the cat owner who is late for a feeding.

The physiologist, physician, and Nobel Prize winner Ivan Pavlov was more of a dog person. He noticed that dogs in his research laboratory began to salivate in *expectation* of being fed.[2] His observation began in a curious way. One morning the notoriously punctual and demanding Pavlov was excoriating a research assistant for being ten minutes late for work. The year was 1917, and the assistant had run into a roadblock set up by revolutionaries who had barricaded his usual thoroughfare, forcing him to detour. That was not a sufficient excuse for Dr. Pavlov, who was furious when the assistant finally arrived. But he noticed that the laboratory dogs they were studying had begun to salivate when they heard the regular, consistent sound of the assistant's footsteps coming into the laboratory, even before they saw him preparing their meal. Pavlov seized on this observation of "psychic secretions," as he called them, as evidence of a new behavioral law: conditioned reflexes. The dogs had learned to respond "conditionally" to neutral or irrelevant events that signaled the approach of the real thing, tasty food in the mouth. Timing had led them to associate certain events with other events. Virtually all animals—single-celled organisms as well as humans—are conditioned to react in predictable ways, some of which we can modify and some of which are more difficult to change.

Rats and pigeons, too, can be conditioned to keep time. In now classic studies, the psychologists John Watson[3] and B. F. Skinner[4] trained rats and pigeons to press a lever in order to release food pellets. Some animal subjects were given a food pellet every time they pressed the lever, while others were given a pellet after a fixed amount of time had passed since they had received the last pellet. For example, if a rat pressed the lever and received a pellet of food, the rat might have to wait ten minutes before his pressing would release another food pellet. When they were first placed in such a situation, the rats pressed the lever almost continuously, expecting a food pellet to be delivered with every press. Over time, however, the rats learned that they would have to wait a fixed period before another pellet would be released. Therefore, instead of continuing to press the lever to receive a pellet, the rats left off pressing to do other rat things. Interestingly, when the ten-minute interval neared expiration, the rat returned to press the lever again and again, as though an internal alarm clock had gone off, telling the rat that the ten-minute waiting period was about to end and he must get to work pressing to ensure that he would get the desired reward.

In some ways, you, too, are conditioned by life to react to time's pressures and passing. But some of the ways you sense time are innate—unconditioned—and live deep in your body and mind.

TIME IN YOUR BRAIN

Our Internal Clock and Circadian Rhythms

Plants, animals, and humans can all keep time, but where do they keep it? In people, while every cell of the human body contains a simple clock,[5] the master internal clock is located in the suprachiasmatic nucleus (SCN),[6] a small cluster of about ten thousand brain cells located at the base of the brain, in the hypothalamus near where two main nerves from the eyes intersect. The optic nerves give the SCN a window to the external world, and its location at the base of the brain gives it an internal door through which to secrete neurohormones that control other brain and body functions.

The primary function of the SCN is to control our internal circadian rhythms. The term "circadian" comes from the Latin *circa,* "around," and *dies,* "day," meaning "about a day."[7] Over fifty circadian rhythms—including those of blood pressure, digestive enzymes, fertility cycles, mood, and sleep/wake cycles—are regulated by the SCN.[8] Our internal clock runs a little slow, so each circadian day lasts a little longer than twenty-four hours. How, then, do people avoid becoming a bit more out of sync each day? Well, although our internal clock is less accurate than a spring-wound wristwatch, it is reset more frequently. Natural environmental cues—or zeitgebers (literally, "time givers" in German)—reset our internal clock each day so that our bodily processes continue to be in harmony with the world around us.

For people and animals, light is the most important zeitgeber. Light passes directly through our eyes and is signalled to the SCN by the optic nerves. Once it reaches the SCN, light resets the internal clock and, among other functions, inhibits the production of a hormone called melatonin, which makes you sleepy. Synthesized from the amino acid tryptophan, melatonin is produced in the pineal gland (which Descartes thought was the seat of the human soul) and starts to flow when it gets dark, making you tired, and making you go to sleep.

For years scientists thought that our natural "free-running" circadian rhythm lasted about twenty-five hours. Although that is what the data from sleep studies showed, it didn't make sense, because we live in a twenty-four-hour world. Then a brilliant Harvard researcher named Charles Czeisler began to wonder whether there wasn't something about the experiments that made the participants' body clocks run for that length of time. In the studies upon which the supposed twenty-five-hour day was based, participants were kept in windowless lab rooms and were not permitted to know the time. When research participants awakened, they turned on the lights in the lab. When they were sleepy,[9] they turned out the lights, melatonin began to flow, and they drifted off to sleep. Czeisler found that the participants' manipulation of the lab lights—in effect creating an artificial "sun"—lengthened the hours of light to which they were exposed. The intensity of the lab lights did not automatically wax and wane as the sun does, but like the sun, the light did inhibit melatonin production. Consequently, participants had longer exposure to light than they would have had they been exposed to daylight. The room lights in the laboratory had artificially extended the human circadian rhythm by almost an hour.

To measure the actual free-running rhythm of the internal clock, Czeisler and his colleagues kept lab lights at a constantly low level that did not affect the internal body clock and found that our internal body clock has about a twenty-four-hour-and-eleven-minute day.[10] So the next time you are feeling pressured to get a lot done in a single day, remember that you have an extra eleven minutes in which to do it.

You might not think that having your internal clock off by one hour is important, but it can be. If you have ever pulled an all-nighter or taken an international flight, you have experienced the negative physiological and psychological effects of jet lag—when your internal biological clock is out of sync with the external clock. You become mentally dull, irritable, clumsy; you may sleep excessively or not at all. But jet lag happens to people other than travelers. It can also happen at home: For instance, when we set our clocks forward one hour in the spring, for daylight savings time, the effect is the same as if all Americans took a flight one time zone east. Car accidents increase by about 10 percent the day after clocks are set forward in the spring, and decrease by a smaller amount the day after clocks are set back one hour to standard time in the fall.[11]

Jet Lag and Shift Workers

Even though your internal clock does not need winding, you can use a host of strategies to help adjust it to the 24/7 world. The Internet, TV, TiVo, twenty-four-hour stores, international travel, and ordinary hundred-watt lightbulbs constantly push and pull at the hands of your internal body clock. Psychologist Mark Rosekind— former director of the Center for Human Sleep Research at the Stanford University Sleep Disorder Clinic and of the NASA Jet Lag and Fatigue Countermeasures Group—has made a career of teaching people how to push back. Rosekind teaches frequent fliers how to reduce the effects of circadian disruption, with recommendations for how to manage naps and sleep; how to moderate food, medication, and beverage consumption to affect sleep; how to calibrate your caffeine intake for alertness and so that it doesn't impede sleep. Smart pilots, doctors, drivers, military personnel, and shift workers routinely employ such strategies to help them cope with the demands of their 24/7 schedules.[12] You can improve your own alertness and performance with them, too. For surgeons, pilots, and others for whom safety is critical, naps can mean the difference between life and death. Rosekind's work with NASA showed that cockpit napping can dramatically increase pilots' performance. Short twenty-minute naps can improve alertness by 50 percent and performance by 34 percent. Nevertheless, in its bureaucratic wisdom, the FAA forbids one of two United States pilots from sleeping in the cockpit, fearing that the public would respond negatively to having pilots sleeping on duty. The science clearly shows, however, that an intentional nap by one pilot at a time is much safer than two extremely tired pilots landing a plane—or both pilots falling asleep spontaneously. Uncontrolled cockpit sleep does happen, which is what the FAA and the public really should fear. In one terrifying case, a flight from the East Coast to Los Angeles continued hundreds of miles past Los Angeles and *out to sea* before one of the two sleeping pilots awakened.

Meet Your Prefrontal Cortex

While the SCN keeps basic biological processes in harmony with the external environment, other parts of the brain have important functions associated with time. For example, the cerebellum—a large protrusion at the back of the brain—plays a role in timing intricate physical behaviors, such as walking. Complex physical movements require precise timing and choreography. Throwing a baseball, for example, requires that the thrower's arm be cocked before he steps forward, and he must step forward before he begins to bring his arm forward: Bend arm—step out—move arm forward—set foot down—hand releases ball. It's difficult to describe the complex timing involved in throwing a baseball, but the cerebellum coordinates these movements automatically, without forcing us to think about them, so that the motion becomes a fluid bendstepmovesetrelease.

When it comes to thinking about time, the prefrontal cortex (PFC) is where the action is. In evolutionary terms the prefrontal cortex is a relatively new addition at the top front of the brain, and it is responsible for performing "executive" functions, such as identifying goals, predicting the future consequence of actions, delaying gratification, and balancing future rewards against present desires.[13]

When the prefrontal cortex does its job, we stay on track, steer clear of temptation, and avoid embarrassing social situations.[14] When it doesn't, our lives fall apart.

Performing these executive functions can be stressful for some brains: Planning activities, meeting deadlines, and resisting temptation are hard work for most people; for some people, they are overwhelming and can result in disabling levels of anxiety and depression. In 1949 Antonio Caetano de Abreu Freire Egas Moniz won a Nobel Prize in medicine for a radical procedure he had designed to treat disabling anxiety disorders, depression, and even schizophrenia.[15] The procedure used tools similar to ice picks to destroy a patient's prefrontal cortex. Once the prefrontal cortex was destroyed, the person experienced a marked reduction in stress and anxiety and other profound personality changes. Unfortunately, the changes were not all for the better. People who underwent the procedure were no longer anxious, but they became apathetic, lethargic, and, in extreme cases, profoundly indifferent to doing anything. An inability to enjoy life replaced their excessive worrying about it. Doctors performed approximately forty thousand lobotomies in the United States before medications replaced lobotomies as the treatment of choice.[16] In effect, the lobotomy eliminated the mental structures that are essential for having a future time perspective. If it were possible to take back a Nobel Prize, this is one that should have been rescinded.

WHAT GOOD IS THINKING ABOUT TIME, ANYWAY?

What Will Surely Kill You Now Versus What Will Probably Kill You Later

In one sense, all threats to your life are equivalent, since ultimately, such dangers lead to death, which is an absolute. One can be dead but not "deader." Threats differ, however, in determining the length of time to death: Some kill immediately—asphyxiation, accident, predators, falling from heights, and the ingestion of toxic substances. Others take time, accruing slowly and surely, posing a less immediate danger but one that is lethal in the long run: starvation, drought, chronic diseases, environmental pollution, and, of course, smoking tobacco. Although you can be killed only in the present, you can be threatened from the future. Death from starvation is as real a threat as death by stroke. It just takes longer to kill. Most threats fall somewhere in between.

Clearly, the most important threats to avoid are those that exist in the present. You can put off responding to threats that loom in the future, but you must deal with present threats today or you may not reach tomorrow. Consequently, older brain structures that evolved earliest must have been passed on because they allowed our ancestors to adapt to the most pressing threats. Had the most primitive brain systems not allowed humankind to overcome most immediate threats, our forebears would not have survived and produced descendents to develop further additions to the brain.

How Emotions Save Us

Emotion helps us avoid immediate threats and move toward future goals. Aristotle[17] believed that some emotions are responses to immediate threats, such as fear, a basic emotion[18] he defined as:

> A kind of pain or disturbance resulting from the imagination of impending danger, either destructive or painful: . . . For things at a great remove are not feared. All men, for instance, know that they will die, but because it is not near, they think nothing of it. . . . For that is what danger is—the proximity of the frightening.[19]

Not only are we afraid of things that threaten us in the present, these threatening things make us more present-oriented. Morton Beiser, a psychiatrist at the University of Toronto, demonstrates in his interviews with more than a thousand refugees from Southeast Asia that dangerous events often restrict time perspective to the present. When they were under acute stress, refugees narrowed their view to a highly focused present.[20,21,22] Refugees were significantly more present-oriented than were a matched group of residents of Vancouver with whom the refugees were compared. With displaced people from Darfur to Iraq facing basic threats to their survival from lack of food and shelter to repeated attacks by outlaw and military forces, it is not surprising that they would have difficulty creating a vision of a positive future for themselves. Under great present stress, these refugees are being robbed of both their present lives and their future.

The increase in present orientation happens whether fear is natural or self-induced. Houston researcher David Eagleman designed an ingenious test of present orientation by asking people to read digital numbers that flashed rapidly on a small display. He found that when they are relaxed, most people cannot read the numbers because they flash by too quickly. When people are in free fall during a bungee jump, they can read the numbers. The free fall— which elicits strong emotion—focuses all our mental resources squarely on the present. The ensuing extra mental power allows people to read numbers that were previously undecipherable.[23] Fear and excitement heighten our present awareness, sharpen our instincts, and help us survive. The stories of soldiers, fighter pilots, firemen, and policemen—as well as mothers facing threats to their children—attest to this.

How Thinking Saves Us

> *What win I, if I gain the thing I seek?*
> *A dream, a breath, a froth of fleeting joy.*
> *Who buys a minute's mirth to wail a week?*
> *Or sells eternity to get a toy?*
> *For one sweet grape who will the vine destroy?*
> —*William Shakespeare,*
> The Rape of Lucrece[24]

Emotions deal with the present. Thinking prepares for the future. The Nobel Prize–winning biologist Jacques Monod[25] argues that a primary function of thought is "To imagine, that is to say, *represent* and *simulate* external events and programs of action" [italics his]. Thought allows us to rehearse events, imagine outcomes, form expectations, and make predictions with a certain degree of accuracy. The predicted outcomes then guide behavior.[26] Antonio Damasio, a neurologist at the University of Southern California, tells us that fruit-eating monkeys who must predict where they can find edible fruit have larger neocortices—and thus more thinking capacity—than their leaf-eating relatives, who have no need to figure out where to find food and predict its location.[27]

Along with emotions, thinking about the future also helps us to avoid threats and reach goals. We attempt to predict future events and environments and control them and our behavior so that, when the future arrives, it yields the outcome we desired. Emotion is a weather report; thought is a weather forecast, an internal representation of possible future circumstances. Like actual weather forecasts, our predictions are often wrong. Predicting the future challenges both you and the meteorologist.

TIME AND MENTAL HEALTH

> *A disorder of time consciousness . . . is a primary alteration of consciousness and may be found as often as it is looked for in mental illness.*
> —Aubrey Lewis[28]

> *The time is out of joint: O cursed spite,*
> *That ever I was born to set it right!*
> —William Shakespeare, Hamlet[29]

Disrupted Internal Clocks

A host of psychological and physiological problems can ensue when you are not living in harmony with time. Jet lag is a mild problem, but a more serious one is seasonal affective disorder (SAD), which occurs frequently at latitudes above 30 degrees, where winter sunlight is short, dim, and too weak to reset and entrain some people's internal body clocks. As a result, the signals that direct the brain to wake and to sleep are weak or nonexistent.[30] People who suffer from SAD report profound lethargy, a depression of mood, and a loss of interest in activities that they previously enjoyed. They feel sad and depressed but often do not know why, because none of the obvious external causes of stress is present. Fortunately, there is a simple, effective treatment for people with SAD: to sit in front of a special light box for thirty minutes each morning. The intense light resets the biological clock and often provides a complete cure.

Sometimes the disruption between internal and external clocks is not caused by external things or events but by changes within the body, such as disease. The ways in which people relate to time can illuminate underlying medical conditions. For example, a clock-drawing test is used to help diagnose people who suffer from cognitive impairment such as Alzheimer's disease. The patient is given a blank piece of paper and asked to draw the face of a clock. People with cognitive impairment typically produce drawings that resemble the clocks children draw, with the numbers bunched closely together in one area of the clock face, or out of sequence, or simply wrong.[31]

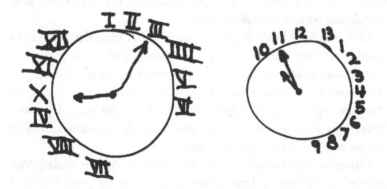

Examples of how people suffering from dementia may draw a clock showing 11:10.

Speed of the Passage of Time

The future looks cold and bleak, and I seem frozen in time.
—A depressed patient[32]

At about the time when Phil conducted his Stanford prison experiment, a young psychiatrist named Frederick Melges began to investigate the relationship between time and mental illness on the same campus. Melges had observed that time is a frequent topic of conversation in therapy sessions, and had identified the time perspectives inherent in popular psychotherapy, distinguishing various psychological disorders' relation to time. Melges believed that people with mental disorders have consistent misconceptions about time.[33]

One consistent misconception relates to the speed with which time passes. Some people feel that time passes more quickly than it does; to others, it passes more slowly. People for whom time is passing too quickly tend to feel that they need to do everything all at once. People for whom time passes too slowly tend to feel that they are stuck in the present; they are likely to suffer from depression and believe that things will never get better. For them, the present is painful, and they feel that no better future will ever arrive to relieve their pain. In a given year, approximately 7 percent of the adult population suffers from depression.

Melges believed that depressed people suffer from destructive "vicious cycles" or "vicious spirals." The thought of a past experience pains them; this rekindles other bad memories, which in turn produce more pain. Their thoughts snowball out of control and derail them from pursuing their goals. People who suffer from depression have downward spirals, in contrast with the upward spirals of people who are acting to fulfill their goals.

Princeton psychologist Susan Nolen-Hoeksema extended Melges's work on time and depression in studying the ways in which preoccupation with the past reinforces depression.[34] Depressed people look not to the future but to the past to relieve their depression; they feel that rehashing and rehearsing the causes of their symptoms will somehow help to solve their problems. Nolen-Hoeksema's research clearly shows that this kind of thinking—which she calls depressive rumination—quickly deteriorates into a vicious downward spiral that aggravates and prolongs depression.

Time-out One: Problems with Time and Corresponding Psychological Disorders

Problem with Time	Description	Psychological Disorder
Order of passage	Confusion among past, present, and future	Schizophrenia
Speed of passage		
	Time passes too quickly	Mania
	Time passes too slowly	Depression
Bias		
	Bias toward future	Paranoia
	Bias toward present	Personality disorders
	Bias toward past	Anxiety disorders
Social coordination	Mistimed or inappropriately timed interactions with others	Adjustment disorders

Why does ruminating about the past make depression worse? Nolen-Hoeksema and her colleagues believe that an obsessive focus on the past makes people less able to think about the future. As a result, ruminators are less able to plan for the future than others and less able to follow through on plans. The key to relieving depression lies not in untangling the Gordian knot of the past but in accepting and planning for the uncertain future.[35] Maintaining past-negative attitudes by thinking and talking about them repeatedly is not a good strategy. Put the past to rest and build on it the vision of a better future.

When Relieving the Past Is Bad for Your Well-being

The prevalence of chronic mental health disorders among people who survive acts of terror, natural disaster, and other traumatic experiences is substantial. Psychological debriefing, in which survivors are helped to express and vent their feelings openly soon after an event, has become the standard of care for mitigating the consequences of traumatic experience. It is a compulsory therapy for emergency services professionals and other first responders. This emotional catharsis supposedly allows survivors and servicepeople to get painful experiences off their chests, and a great many anecdotal reports both by participants and by those who administer the treatments describe beneficial outcomes.

But after over twenty years of research, the benefits of emotion-based debriefing appear to be totally unsupported. Controlled trials demonstrate that debriefing failed to relieve psychological disorders, including post-traumatic stress, and in some cases, found that this method embedded painful emotions more deeply in memory, ready to be recalled and relived.

Some research suggests it is better to carefully screen individuals to determine their needs, and to apply emotional first aid in the wake of trauma only where appropriate, rather than mandate a single treatment for all survivors and emergency workers. Cognitive behavioral treatment that is provided to individuals with traumatic symptoms some months after the critical incident appears to be the best of all options.[36]

As with depression, trauma survivors who dwell on the past tend to stay in past-negative or -fatalistic mind-sets that impede their lives in the present as well as their ability to look toward a positive future.

DISORDERED PASSAGE OF TIME

My body is an hourglass, and my mind is like sand pouring through it.
—*A schizophrenic client*[37]

Time has stopped; there is no time. . . . The past and the future have collapsed into the present, and I can't tell them apart.
—*A schizophrenic client*[38]

Some people have difficulty distinguishing among the past, the present, and the future. They confuse memories with future events and mistake future events with past ones. Such confusion is closely associated with schizophrenia, which also involves a loss of contact with reality. Schizophrenia is less common than depression, but in any given year, approximately 1 percent of the adult population suffers from schizophrenia—a percentage that prevails around the world.

A friendly paranoid schizophrenic lived on the Stanford campus during the 1990s and was a frequent visitor to the psychology department. Joe Euclid, as the students called him, was homeless and poor, but he remained resolutely focused on the future. Joe's mission in life was to rid the world of senseless crimes and bizarre disasters. Whenever he was asked how he was doing, Joe invariably replied, "Some progress!"—his perceived level of success.

★★★·   MONDAY, AUGUST 19, 1996

Joe Jonah Euclid
96.aug.19

I did Recieve a Heavenly
Premonition of this plane crash
It was more than a week before
the Plane Crash. It had a forumat
that it was not simple.

Specifically, the Angel
of God/Goddess Told me to
write-up a List of Women who
would do well to go out to
the Interstate Highway and
put out her Thumb and hitchhike
out here to Palo Alto, Calif
to work on the New Dispensation
from Goddess/God. And Number
One on that List is:

of ▮ackson Hole, Wym.

Also the Angels told me
to Write to ▮▮▮▮▮▮
and to tell her that she is
fully compatable with
▮▮▮▮▮ and ▮▮▮▮▮.
And that ▮▮▮▮▮ has
Heard Angelic Voices all her
Life and they tell her that
I am a good man.

Clinton Cargo Plane Crashes in Wyoming

Los Angeles Times

Washington

Air Force authorities began an investigation yesterday into why a U.S. military C-130 cargo plane providing support for President Clinton crashed into a mountainside near Jackson, Wyo.

The plane had been assigned to bring equipment from Jackson, where the president had been vacationing, to New York City. But shortly after takeoff from the Jackson airport Saturday morning, the plane slammed into the side of Sheep Mountain, about 15 miles southeast of Jackson, in the remote Gros Ventre Wilderness. The crash site was less than 1,000 feet from the mountain's 11,300-foot summit.

Authorities said nine people were on board the plane, a crew of eight plus one U.S. Secret Service agent. Government officials said the crash victims were Air Force Captain Kevin N. Earnest; Captain

ASSOCIATED PRESS GRAPHIC

Jackson yesterday afternoon to begin looking into the cause of the crash.

Clinton was not in Wyoming at the time of the crash. He had re-

Time-out Two: Joe Euclid's Writing on Time

Joe promoted his cause by posting typewritten treatises on bulletin boards, telephone poles, and walls around campus. Typically, his posting consisted of a newspaper clipping that described a recent tragic event—the death of a celebrity or a plane crash—along with a description of his premonitions of the event. His prescient visions of the future probably resulted from his confusion of the present with the past and the future, given that his visions were always documented *after* the occurrence of the tragic event.

Beliefs About Mental Health and Time

You may recall that people's belief in a transcendental future motivates them to act in ways that do not make sense to others who don't share their perspective. Yet people who blow themselves up believing that they earn eternal reward in the transcendental future are not necessarily crazy. Similarly, understanding the divergent beliefs that people hold about the order and speed with which time passes may help to make sense of their behavior. For example, you can understand how someone who confuses the past, present, and future can believe that he can predict the future. When you understand his confusion, you can appreciate that his bizarre belief appears to be a reasonable response to an organic inability to keep track of time. For people who believe that time passes too quickly, it makes sense that they feel they must accomplish everything today, because by tomorrow all of their time might have passed, and it will be too late.

Most people agree about the order and speed of passage of time. This agreement makes it tempting to label people who hold different attitudes toward time as weird, wrong, and even crazy. But we need to be careful not to mistake conventional consensus for an underlying truth, for at the core of time are riddles that the most brilliant among us have not completely answered. Therefore, we judge others' beliefs about time at our own peril. We recommend keeping an open mind and a compassionate attitude about people with seemingly aberrant views toward time.

> *For us convinced physicists, the distinction between past, present, and future is an illusion, although a persistent one.*
> —Albert Einstein

OPENING AND CLOSING THE DOORS OF PERCEPTION: DRUGS AND ALCOHOL

Marijuana is well known for its ability to alter the perception of time, by slowing sight and hearing and encouraging reflection and introspection. More powerful drugs, such as mescaline, alter time in different ways. In *The Doors of Perception*, Aldous Huxley reported that his interest in time fell "almost to zero" when he was under the effects of mescaline. When asked to describe his altered perception of time, he replied, "There seems to be plenty of it. . . . Plenty of it, but exactly how much [is] entirely irrelevant." [39]

Drinking alcohol and using drugs are particularly dangerous for present hedonists, because drugs and alcohol numb the higher thought centers in the brain and lead to an increased present orientation. For example, "alcohol myopia" refers to the cognitive nearsightedness and constriction of perspective to the present that accompanies alcohol consumption.[40] For futures, alcohol myopia can be a welcome temporary respite from worry about the future, but for presents, alcohol myopia leads to drinking more alcohol or using drugs, which further amplifies their present orientation. The result is a vicious cycle—much like that which Melges identified in the mentally ill—that keeps people chained to the present. In moderation, the present is a wonderful place to be, but in excess, it robs you of your ability to learn from the past and plan for the future.

TIME AND YOUR PHYSICAL HEALTH

Eating and Weight

Dr. Phil McGraw tells a story about a time when Oprah Winfrey urgently summoned him to meet with "the girls" at her home. They needed his help in solving a problem, and Oprah's private jet was waiting. Dr. Phil arrived at Oprah's home some hours later and found the women seated in the living room engaged in earnest conversation. Quickly introducing Dr. Phil to the group, Oprah revealed their predicament to him. According to Dr. Phil, the dialogue went something like this:[41]

> Oprah: Dr. Phil, we need you to tell us why we're fat.
> Dr. Phil: You interrupted my dinner with my family and flew me hundreds of miles to ask me that?
> Oprah: Yes, it troubles us all deeply.
> Dr. Phil: Hmm, I see. Well, there's a quick answer. I can probably make it home for dessert. You're fat because you want to be.
> The girls: We've been talking about it all weekend, and we can't figure it out ourselves. So we really need you to tell us.
> Dr. Phil: Oh, so you want the honest answer?
> The girls: Yes, we are ready for it.
> Dr. Phil: Okay, you're fat because you want to be.

Oprah: No, really. You can tell us. We can take it.

Dr. Phil: Oh, now I see. You want the whole truth. . . . Okay, you're fat because you want to be.

Then Dr. Phil patiently explained that each of the women had made choices in the past that had caused her to gain weight. No one had forced her to make those choices; she had made them because she wanted to. The small choices that each had made regarding food and exercise ultimately had led her to being fat and sitting in Oprah's living room that evening.

From the girls' perspective, they had never chosen to be fat. But from Dr. Phil's perspective, the choices that they had made in the past clearly had led to their present weight. When the women chose their actions, they chose the consequences. They wanted to be slim, but they made choices as though they wanted to be fat.

We authors think that both the girls and Dr. Phil are right. The women never consciously chose to be fat, but they had chosen what they ate from a purely present-oriented perspective, without regard for consequences. From the girlfriends' perspective, the choice was not skinny or fat but to enjoy what they were eating, so based on their present desire, not the future result, they chose potato chips over a carrot stick, a doughnut over a bran muffin, a chocolate bar over a granola bar. They thought, I'm hungry. What should I eat? Potato chips or a doughnut? They did not think, I am hungry and must eat. Do I want to be skinny or fat? From a present-oriented perspective, their choices to eat fatty foods made sense. But good-tasting food is often not good for you in the long run, and from a future-oriented perspective—the perspective that Dr. Phil took—their choices did not make sense. Food that tasted good months ago had the unintended but predictable consequence of making them fat now.

Did you identify with Oprah and her friends? Have you ever gone grocery shopping when you were really hungry? We don't recommend it, because if you do, you are likely to come home with bags full of junk food. Rationally, you know that you want to eat healthy food—at least we hope you do—but the hungry conductors in your brain make you present-oriented. Your stomach says, "I need food now! And the only thing I care about is that it tastes good!" Everything looks good, and sweets top the list. When you are full, your stomach backs off and lets you think about the future. Your brain says, "I'm going to eat wisely the next time I'm hungry, because I want to be skinny."

But we should warn you that the strategy of grocery shopping when you are full can backfire. If you are too full and feel fat, you may buy only things that are exceptionally good for you, and when you get hungry again, the tofu and bean sprouts that you bought don't look good. You bought them because you cared about the future when you were shopping, but now that you're hungry again, you care only about present taste. So you decide to order a pizza. Again, you need both a present-hedonistic and future time perspective to stay healthy. (This may be why grazing is an effective diet strategy—eat small meals five times a day. You never get too hungry or too full.)

GAMBLING [42]

When we are focused on the present, we tend to make different choices from those we make when we are focused on the future. No industry is better at exploiting this fact than the gambling industry. From the moment you enter a Las Vegas casino, you enter a timeless world of present hedonism in which the future does not exist. The temperature, lighting, and noise level remain constant twenty-four hours a day. There are no clocks and no last calls by bartenders. Flashing lights, lively music, and the partial nudity of the hostesses encourage men to immerse themselves in a world of pleasure. None of this occurs by chance. The gaming industry is one of the world's largest employers of statisticians. They compute the odds of your winning at any game with the cost of the free drinks you will consume and the amount of money you are likely to lose so that no one ever beats the house over time (unless you run some scam, which, when detected, will leave you without kneecaps).

Free drinks serve at least two purposes. First, they allow you to stay firmly planted in place, with your time perspective myopically constricted to the present. You are more likely to lose money while you are gambling than while you are waiting in line for a drink. The longer you gamble, the more the odds favor the house. Second, the alcohol in the drinks causes you to become further present-oriented, which decreases the likelihood that you will carefully consider the consequences of betting your mortgage money. The casinos would serve mescaline instead of alcohol if it helped the bottom line.[43] Also, when you accept drinks gratis, you become a guest who feels obliged to your host to hang around for an anticipated dessert.

The statisticians also calculate how the physical layout of a casino affects profits. If they are not making enough money, they change the decor and measure the results. If profit goes up, they keep the change. If it goes down, they try something else. After years of constant experimentation, the standard guidelines are relatively well known—such as the "no clocks" rule—so that all casinos today look pretty much the same on the inside.

We can imagine that the world's least profitable casino would have none of these present-directing features and instead contain numerous reminders of the future. It would have clocks on every wall, would dim the lights at night in accordance with the movement of the sun, and would have no sound other than that produced spontaneously by gamblers, who would be given small digital screens that blinked their running tab of winnings or losses. ATM withdrawals would require parental or spousal consent. There would be a two-drink maximum instead of a two-drink minimum. The restaurants would serve primarily health foods, and servers would point out unhealthy selections. Smoking would be strongly discouraged, and the smoking area would be fully stocked with brochures from the American Lung Association and the American Cancer Society. Children would be welcome, and guidance counselors would sit at each table explaining the benefits of private college education. Condoms would be distributed freely by women dressed in surgical scrubs and masks to discourage promiscuity as a sober warning that we are all one small, careless act away from destroying ourselves. Upon checking in to the casino hotel, guests would sign a nonbinding consent form releasing the casino from liability for their possible financial ruin. Imagine the fun!

Okay, so too much future-orientation is as bad as too much present orientation. This is yet another paradox of time. Our point is not that you should have no fun but that you should have only as much fun as you can afford. Fun in excess is mania that harms ourselves and others.

TIME—STRESS AND HEALTH

Not all behaviors associated with the future time perspective promote health. Planning for the future, which in moderation is healthy, can, in excess, lead to a lack of enjoyment in the present and to anxiety about the future. Many futures are control freaks who sweat over insignificant setbacks and worry that negative events will occur or that positive events will not.

The Stanford sociobiologist Robert Sapolsky claims that our human ability to prepare for and worry about the future is both a blessing and a curse.[44] The blessings are all the preventive and preparatory behaviors we've discussed. The curse is that our propensity to worry about the future causes constant stress. To illustrate the dramatic effects such worry can have on our health, Sapolsky contrasts the stress that a zebra on the veldt in Africa experiences with the stress that a businessperson, student, nurse, or modern worker experiences during a typical day.

Healthy zebras in Africa spend most of the day sleeping and eating grass. They have few enemies, and on the flat African plain, they can see their enemies coming from great distances. When lions approach, the zebra has an acute stress response as it prepares to run for its life: Its heart rate increases; its breathing deepens; and blood is directed to its muscles. Any biological activity that requires energy and is not necessary to escape the stalking lions—the immediate threat—is shut down. Within a few minutes, however, the threat is over. The lions have made their kill. Our zebra escaped being dinner on this day and can relax. Nonetheless, there are physiological consequences of avoiding the lions: Long-term biological processes, such as digestion, growth, and the immune systems that were turned off because they were not needed to escape the lion, have to be restarted. Hormones released into the bloodstream placed tremendous stress on the heart and lungs. Fifteen minutes of terror followed by twenty-three hours and forty-five minutes of relaxed grazing—that's the life of a zebra on the veldt. The nice thing about this life is that he has to fire up his stress response for only a short time each day, when the lions approach. The zebra's stress response is idle for the rest of the day while its biological processes can concentrate on less pressing tasks like disease prevention, digestion, and growth.

It turns out that we humans evolved to avoid threats, just as the zebra does, and we should be kicking back for most of the day, running like hell only when danger approaches. But instead of periodic *physical* threats, like predators, we humans are faced with continual *psychological* threats, like those involved in getting a job, getting in to the right college, making the house payment, dealing with problem kids, paying for college, and maxed-out credit cards. Although the types of threats that we face have changed, our biological responses to them remain the same. Unlike brief physical threats, psychological threats hit us in the deepest recess of our brains. No matter how much we would like them to go away so we can concentrate on eating grass, they persist in tormenting us.

Here is the good news and the bad news. Our stress response does not shoot through the roof when we think about losing our jobs, as the zebra's does when a lion approaches, but neither does our stress response drop into the basement, as the zebra's does when the lion departs. The zebras have an *acute* stress response every now and then. We, in contrast, have a *chronic* stress response that is seldom as extreme as the zebra's but never goes away. Sapolsky has shown that persistent stress of this present kind can actually shrink areas of the brain involved in past memory.[45]

Pick your poison. Zebras tend to die quickly from predators, but we humans tend to die from the accumulation of less exciting but just as deadly causes: coronary heart disease, cancer, and other diseases of chronic stress responses that stem from unhealthy time perspectives. For example, medical researchers believed for many years that the Type A personality—typical of the impatient, sometimes hostile, goal-driven, future-oriented high achiever who does not like to waste time—was related to coronary heart disease. It turns out that only the hostility component of the Type A is linked to heart disease, and that link is not very strong.[46] Stress causes heart disease for all personality types, not just Type A's, but only when that stress is unpredictable and you have no control over how to respond to it. When stress is predictable and you can control how to respond to it, stress does not have a significant effect in causing heart disease. The two big stress factors to be aware of are: predictability and control.[47] Personality characteristics form only part of the picture. The social situation matters as well. Recall that our colleague Robert Levine described a social factor that he called "pace of life" and consistently found higher rates of coronary heart disease in people who lived in countries driven by a fast pace of life.[48] Live too fast, die too young.

There is more to Frederick Melges's story. Deeply interested in how his clients' relationship with time influenced their thoughts, feelings, and behaviors, he sought to document his findings for the benefit of others in his only book, *Time and the Inner Future*. As Melges wrote, he was in a race with time himself. Melges suffered from worsening Type I diabetes and at times wondered whether he would live to see his life's work completed. In his book's epilogue, Melges explains:

> While I was writing this book, my own future was under almost constant threat. The specter of death made time ever so precious.
>
> Since I had been conducting studies on time and the mind for 18 years, and since I had come to realize the importance of time and the personal future in clinical work with my patients, I had a great desire to complete this book before I died.
>
> The year that I started the first draft was the very year that the long-term complications of my juvenile diabetes began to take their greatest toll.

During his battle with diabetes, Melges's kidneys failed, and he faced certain death unless he received a transplant. Melges was forty-three. Possible donors were identified but had to be excluded for various reasons. He raced to finish a first draft of the book and arranged to have it published posthumously, if necessary. Green jolts of light began to shoot across his vision signaling that the end was near. In the search for a new kidney, his doctors considered cadavers, which offered only a 25 to 50 percent survival rate. Desperate, they ultimately identified a possible living donor: his seventy-five-year-old mother,[49] who had been ruled out as a donor the first time around because of her age. Melges felt guilty even asking her for a kidney, but he did, and his mother unhesitatingly agreed. Melges writes, "My mother's love felt like the most timeless element ever known."[50] The kidney transplant was a success, and both Melges and his mother recovered fully. In a final postscript to his book, Melges writes:

And life goes on. My mother is fine, and my health is good. Looking back, except for the physical hardships, I wish that somehow I had had an experience like that of the transplant much earlier in life. It has helped me to live more fully in the present toward the future regardless of what might happen in the future.

Melges died years later, in 1988. The message within his life's work is that time is related not just to mental and physical heath but that every life—healthy or sick, normal or abnormal—is a race with and a battle against time. If we run the race not as a solitary runner, but as part of a relay team, the social presence of others on our side can make us all run better and longer.

A life well lived is the best antidote to that fatal truth. Be active, not a passive worrywart. Find magic in the moment, joy in making someone smile. Listen to a lover's sigh; look into the dancing eyes of a child you made feel special. Most of all, marvel at the wonder that eons of evolutionary time and all your unique experiences have joined to comprise the symphony that is YOU.

eight

THE COURSE OF TIME
Life Choices and Money
in Balancing the Present
and the Future

As we mature and retire, Time ripens all things.
No man is born wise.
> —*Miguel de Cervantes,* Don Quixote

Be ruled by time, the wisest counselor of all.
> —*Plutarch,* Life of Pericles

Age is a case of mind over matter.
If you don't mind, it don't matter.
> —*Satchel Paige*

Imagine that you are a four-year-old nursery school student. Your teacher explains that you'll be playing a new game today. He offers you a single tasty marshmallow that you can eat immediately. However, if you don't eat it right away, he will give you two marshmallows when he returns from an errand. What do you do? Do you take the sure thing and gobble the goodie in front of you? Or do you fight temptation, delay gratification, and reap the double pleasure of two marshmallows?

Most four-year-olds and virtually all younger children choose the immediate over the delayed reward and eat the single marshmallow within seconds of being left alone with it. Psychologist Walter Mischel conducted this simple study at Stanford University's Bing Nursery School. In other research, Mischel replaced the marshmallows as a reward with one or two Oreo cookies or one or two bags of jelly beans. The type of goodies did not matter. Some youngsters resisted, and others yielded to the lure of immediate gratification.

So what? A big what! When they were interviewed years later, as eighteen-year-olds, the children who had delayed gratification had developed a range of superior emotional and social competencies compared with the children who had eaten the treat immediately. They were better able to deal with adversity and stress, and they were more self-confident, diligent, and self-reliant. Mischel and his team also discovered that the intellectual ability of children who controlled their impulses was markedly higher than those who did not. The third of the children who were able to control their impulses at age four scored 210 total points higher on verbal and math SAT scores than the impulsive four-year-olds! How big a difference is that? It is as large as the average difference recorded between the abilities of economically advantaged and disadvantaged children. It is larger than the difference between the abilities of children from families whose parents have graduate degrees and children whose parents did not finish high school. The ability to delay gratification at age four is twice as good a predictor of later SAT scores as IQ.[1] Poor impulse control is also a better predictor of juvenile delinquency than IQ.[2]

Time-out One: Characteristics of Preschoolers Who Controlled the Impulse to Eat One Marshmallow and Those Who Did Not

Children Who Demonstrated Impulse Control	Children Who Were Impulsive
Delayed gratification	Could not delay gratification
Were assertive	Were indecisive
Coped well with frustration	Overreacted to frustration
Were trustworthy	Were stubborn
Worked well under pressure	Were overwhelmed by stress
Were self-reliant and confident	Had a lower self-image
Were dependable	Were not reliable
Responded to reason	Were prone to jealousy and envy
Could concentrate	Provoked arguments
Were eager to learn	Had sharp tempers
Were academically competent	Were poorer students
Persevered on plans	Gave up in face of failure
Scored 610 on the SAT verbal section	Scored 524 on the SAT verbal section
Scored 652 on the SAT math section	Scored 528 on the SAT math section

SENSE OF TIME INFLUENCES HUMAN DEVELOPMENT

How people change over the course of their lives is central to developmental psychology. The obvious key marker for this study is chronological age. Calendar time is a good predictor of the development of cognitive ability, language comprehension and use, and the coordination of sense and motor response. After adolescence, however, chronological age becomes a less reliable predictor of motivation, thought process, and emotional response. Recently, leading psychologists have begun to explore whether your chronological age—time passed since birth—is as relevant as your sense of the time remaining until your death.

In an impressive series of studies, Stanford psychologist Laura Carstensen found that anything that constrains our sense of an unlimited future shifts our motivations and priorities away from future goals and toward present emotional satisfaction. A limited future encourages us to make choices that enhance our positive emotional state rather than, for instance, to pursue an education or other future-oriented activity. Because older people anticipate a limited future, they are more apt to do what feels good—from speaking their minds to traveling to making dramatic changes in their lives. The same may be said for anyone who is in a situation that portends an uncertain future or clearly defined end, such as having a terminal disease or losing a job.

We regulate our emotions to try to maintain a sense of overall well-being. When you imagine that you have a lot of time left, you use it to learn more about the world, meet new people, and experience novelty. When a life's time is short, its goals become short-term. The mantra of those who anticipate a long-term future is "More is better," and they generally look to spend time with a lot of different people and new acquaintances. The mantra of those who anticipate a short future is "Quality, not quantity," and they choose to spend quality time with fewer people.

Earlier research suggested that the elderly are caught in the paradox of aging. They have smaller social networks and reduced spheres of interest, and they are less drawn to novelty than younger people. Once considered to be disengaged from life, or lacking social opportunities, they are nevertheless as happy, or even happier, than young people are. Carstensen's theory and new research reveal that reducing their social activity and novel experiences show the elderly to be discriminating among choices that allow them to live more emotionally satisfying lives.[3,4,5,6,7,8,9]

Most people move through life among a group of people from whom they derive support, self-definition, and a sense of stability and continuity.[10] From childhood through late adolescence, we expand our range of social contacts, exploring new relationships and engaging with different "convoys" to determine which best fits our needs. By our early thirties, we tend to select one favorable, reliable group with whom to identify. (Men who have not established such a convoy by early adulthood may never do so and may go through life with few or no close friends.) Ideally, over time, we maintain those convoys that are most satisfying and discard or relegate to the periphery of our circle many, perhaps most, of our acquaintances. Interaction with mere acquaintances steadily declines as significant relationships increase and contact with a core group of friends and partners who provide emotional satisfaction and support becomes more frequent. Interaction with close friends may ebb and flow, but the quality of the emotional closeness they provide remains stable.

Interviews of people at ages eighteen, thirty, forty, and fifty-two showed the highest rate of interaction and satisfaction with acquaintances in the youngest group. Interaction and satisfaction with acquaintances dropped off sharply in the older groups. One possible life strategy is to seek knowledge about yourself and your world and to look for help doing so from a range of experts and a variety of acquaintances. A second strategy is to seek emotional gratification and derive emotional meaning from life by deepening intimate relationships. In a study of U.S. Caucasians and African-Americans ages eighteen to eighty-eight, older people placed more importance on the emotional qualities offered by social partners than on the informational value that might be derived from future relationships. However, young gay men who were HIV-positive and had disease symptoms responded as the elderly did in desiring deeper, more meaningful emotional relationships. Their comparison group was gays of the same average age who were HIV-negative. The HIV-negative gay men chose knowledge contacts over emotional ones. A German sample also found that the elderly have fewer peripheral social contacts than the young, but they have just as many close social partners.

Let's make you a participant in one of these studies. With whom would you prefer to spend thirty minutes: A) a member of your immediate family, B) a recent acquaintance, or C) the author of a book you just read? If you are older, you will probably choose A. If you are younger, you are likely to choose B or C. Now imagine that a new medical procedure can confer an unexpected twenty more years of longevity. Would your answer change? Research showed that imagining an extra twenty years of life expectancy made the elderly respond like youngsters. They no longer preferred the company of familiar social partners over someone from whom they might learn something new. The finding is the same for older people, whether they are American or Chinese. When Chinese youths were asked to imagine emigrating out of Hong Kong, however, they all preferred familiar over new social contacts. Their responses were comparable to those of Stanford seniors shortly before graduation who narrowed their social choices to those people who were most likely to be emotionally supporting rather than those who would be intellectually stimulating.

From these studies, we can see that constraints on time change the value we place on emotional goals. With a constrained sense of the future, older people are more likely to prefer familiar social partners who satisfy their emotional needs. But when anyone gains an expanded sense of time, his or her priorities become more like those of the young.

The Power of Impulse Suppression

In the marshmallow research by Mischel, many of the children were from middle-class white academic families with future-oriented parents who were more likely to encourage their naturally present-hedonistic children to engage in planning, saving, toothbrushing, and other actions that would yield delayed rewards and avoid future regrets.[11]

Learning to control impulses and make better choices is inextricably connected with being aware of one's internal states and with managing feelings rather than acting them out. Emotions rather than reason tend to drive the behavior of people who have poor impulse control. Impulsivity is the hallmark of present-hedonistic adolescents, but many carry it over into adulthood, which makes them susceptible to various addictions that feel good now but are not worth the negative future consequences. Since emotions trump reason, knowledge about the dangers of drugs, alcohol, smoking, overeating, or excessive gambling does not inform and curtail current behavior. Thrill wins over will.

Because future time perspective has to be learned, teaching people to balance their desire for thrills can release them from destructive hedonistic cycles and extreme susceptibility to temptation to allow them to pursue more positive dreams. New Year's resolutions to stop smoking, lose weight, quit gambling, reduce credit card debt, or stop compulsive shopping are all useless unless you can delay gratification and reject short-term gain for anticipated bigger later gain, a key aspect of emotional intelligence (EQ).[12]

CONSCIOUS AND UNCONSCIOUS CHOICES

In 1993 John Boyd worked part-time at the California Board of Equalization while preparing for graduate school in psychology. From the top floor, the twenty-fourth, he could see all the way to his hometown, fifty miles away. One crystal-clear November morning, John was in the eighteenth-floor file room of the new board office building in downtown Sacramento, California. This is the rest of the story in John's words:

> Suddenly, a frantic woman rushed into the file room and exclaimed, "You need to follow me." It was an odd request, so I asked, "Why?"
> "There's a man around the corner with a gun," she replied. That's

all she needed to say. Later, I learned that a gunman had shot his way past security and was holding several coworkers hostage around the corner on an otherwise open floor.[13]

I quickly moved to the east stairwell, where I found several women and a man lowering a wheelchair-bound coworker one excruciating step at a time. The paraplegic man had been abandoned by his "buddy," who was supposed to look after him in case of an emergency. I picked up the handicapped man and carried him down to the eleventh floor, where I called 911.[14] News helicopters flying around the building at eye level soon confirmed that the story was out and was big local news.

The office building is just blocks from the state capital, so a SWAT team responded within minutes, confronted the gunman on the eighteenth floor, and ordered him to drop his weapons. He refused and was shot repeatedly. He was probably dead even as paramedics performed CPR on him while he was wheeled from the building to a waiting ambulance.

Ironically, the gunman had been a California highway patrol officer earlier in his career. Job stress, drinking, and a bad relationship had led to his involuntary retirement from the CHP some years earlier. The end of his career spiraled down into more drinking, depression, and, ultimately, the tax problems that had brought him to the Board of Equalization that November morning. In addition to the rifle, shotgun, pistol, and paper bag of ammunition that the gunman had brought with him, he had a list of tax collectors with whom he intended to settle scores. Only one of them actually worked at the board, but fortunately, he was out of town that day.

Claiming that he wanted to speak with board members was just a pretense for his visit, of course. The real reason the gunman appeared that day was because he no longer wanted to live. He was there for an "officer-assisted suicide," a permanent solution to what many people would consider temporary problems. This is a tragic example of time perspective gone awry. He no longer wanted to repair the past or enjoy the present. He wanted only to avoid the future. For him, time was not a valuable resource but a burden that he no longer wanted to bear.

Imagine that we could have sat this man down the week before this tragedy to ask him why his life had turned out the way it did. Would he understand what had led him to this point? Or would he fail to see that a sequence of small choices had resulted in the big problems that dominated his life?

Recall the case of Oprah's overweight friends, who had followed a series of seemingly inconsequential decisions down a path that led further and further away from their desired destination—to be slim and trim. Like them, the gunman had made bad decisions: He had put off working and neglected his responsibility to his family until he reached the point where he lost his job, his wife, and, finally, his life.

As Dr. Phil McGraw is fond of saying, "When you choose the behavior, you choose the consequence." For Dr. Phil and many others, future consequences govern every decision. From this perspective, everything that happens presents a choice, including the feelings you experience.

This Dr. Phil (Zimbardo) and Dr. Boyd, your authors, also recognize the power of personal choice—and the basic need for choice, or at least the illusion of choice—and the effect that choice has on our lives. But we diverge from the other Dr. Phil's point of view on personal choice in recognizing that choice is not always made consciously or in accordance with a rational process that considers future consequences. For instance, our friends, colleagues, and community—our social environment—can influence the decisions that we make, often without our being aware of their power. Phil's Stanford prison experiment dramatically demonstrates the power of situation to influence personal beliefs and actions (for more information see www.lucifereffect.com).

A Stanford colleague and mentor, Robert Zajonc, has shown that people can feel and act without thinking of future consequences. In fact, people can feel and act without thinking at all. In a series of brilliant experiments, Zajonc projected an image onto a screen in front of subjects for fifty milliseconds, which is just long enough for a person to notice that there is something there, but not long enough for him to recognize what it is. In comparison, a typical eye blink takes about three hundred milliseconds. In some experiments, the images projected were abstract drawings; in some, they were Chinese characters; and in others, they were human faces.

After participants saw a group of images for fifty milliseconds each, Zajonc put two images on the screen and left them there for people to study. One of the two images had been seen before for fifty milliseconds. The second had not been seen before. He then asked, "Which of these two images have you seen before?" People could identify which image they had seen only about 50 percent of the time, which is not above the level of chance. Zajonc also asked, "Which image do you like more?" Subjects chose the image that they had seen for fifty milliseconds—but which they could not recognize—about 60 percent of the time. In other words, they developed a preference for things that they had seen before, even though they could not remember seeing them.

After they had chosen the image they preferred, Zajonc asked why they liked the image they had chosen. The subjects came up with creative reasons—symmetry, thickness, shape—but no one said that it was because he had seen the image before. In other words, their preferences had changed without conscious thought or awareness. In Zajonc's view, a decision, for instance, to drink Coke or Pepsi does not involve thought. You simply like Coke, and you drink it. No thought required. In his words,

> We sometimes delude ourselves that we proceed in a rational manner and weigh all of the pros and cons of various alternatives. But this is seldom the actual case. Quite often "I decided in favor of X" is no more than "I liked X." . . . We buy the cars we "like," choose the jobs and houses we find "attractive," and then justify these choices by various reasons.[15]

Zajonc's work shows that we do not always consciously make our choices. Sometimes we are merely making automatic responses to the world around us.[16] Sometimes when we choose, we are not thinking about the future and our actions are based completely on the present. If we make choices without conscious thought, whom do we hold responsible for them? That's a good question, and as we'll see, the answer is not simple.

The psychologist John Bargh extended Zajonc's work in profoundly provocative—even disturbing—ways. Bargh's work demonstrates that the unconscious decisions we make can be influenced by subtle elements in our present environment. In Bargh's words, there is a trend toward "automaticity" for most behaviors.[17] For example, when we first learn to drive a manual transmission car, the actions we take are very consciously considered. Our thoughts run something like this: "Foot off gas," "Depress clutch," "Move shift lever—no, that's reverse—okay," "Release clutch," and "Depress gas pedal." With time and practice, driving a car becomes so automatic that we are scarcely aware of what we are doing. You may find yourself pulling into your driveway and realize that you don't remember the route you took to get there or even how you made the last turn down your street.

In one of Bargh's studies, participants formed thirty four-word sentences using four of the five words provided. For example, the words "they her bother see usually" could be arranged to read "They usually bother her." One group of participants received lists that contained words chosen to elicit the idea of rudeness. These words were: aggressively, bold, rude, bother, disturb, intrude, annoyingly, interrupt, audaciously, brazen, impolitely, infringe, obnoxious, aggravating, and bluntly. A second group of participants received lists that contained words chosen to denote politeness. These words were: respect, honor, considerate, appreciate, patiently, cordially, yield, polite, cautiously, courteous, graciously, sensitively, discreetly, behaved, and unobtrusively. A third group of participants received lists of neutral words chosen to suggest neither politeness nor rudeness. Bargh and his colleagues were interested in how priming the concept of rudeness or politeness would alter the participants' behavior in a second part of the study.

After forming all thirty sentences, participants were told to meet the experimenter down the hall for instructions on the second half of the experiment. Participants found the experimenter engaged in a nonstop conversation with what appeared to be a participant in another study but who was actually a confederate. Bargh was interested in whether participants who had been primed with politeness would wait longer before interrupting the experimenter than participants primed with rudeness or indifference would. He capped the amount of time they would wait to interrupt at ten minutes. Over two thirds (67 percent) of those in the rudeness condition interrupted before the ten minutes were up, compared to about a fourth (28 percent) of those in the neutral condition, and only 6 percent of the people in the polite condition. Bargh then asked participants to describe why they had waited or why they had interrupted. As Zajonc's participants had done, they came up with creative answers, but none identified the scrambled-sentence task as having had any influence on his or her behavior.

In another experiment, Bargh again had participants unscramble sentences. This time one group of participants got lists of words that primed the conception of being elderly. Another group got lists of words that were unrelated to age. Once they had unscrambled the sentences, the experimenter told participants that the experiment was over. As the participants left the room, the experimenter timed the speed at which they walked down the hall. Bargh found that participants primed with being elderly walked down the hall much more slowly than those people who were not so primed. Again, when asked for an explanation about why they had walked down the hallway as they did, no one connected the scrambled-sentence task with their subsequent speed in walking. A simple language test had affected their speed—thinking about elderly matters made them act as though they were elderly—but participants were completely unaware of this effect.

Zajonc's and Bargh's work stresses the automatic influence of our immediate environment. We can like things and do things automatically without thinking about the future—without thinking at all. Yet when we are asked to explain our preferences and behavior, we deny the effect of the present circumstances and expertly rationalize alternative explanations, coming up with creative and plausible explanations for our behavior that have no basis in truth. We automatically feel and act, and then we automatically rationalize our feelings and behaviors.

If either the personal choice perspective espoused by Dr. Phil—which stresses future consequences—or the automatic choice perspective espoused by Zajonc and Bargh—which stresses the impact of the present environment—were right all of the time, there would not be a problem. If we always chose the consequences of our actions when we chose those actions, none of us would be fat, drink, smoke to excess, or fail examinations by not studying. Future-oriented people believe that when you choose a behavior, you choose its future consequences, but Zajonc, Bargh, and many others in social psychology have demonstrated that sometimes you do not choose a behavior. Sometimes a behavior chooses you based upon the environment in which you find yourself.

We live our lives swimming in an ocean of time, tossed and turned by the currents around us, swimming toward goals and away from danger, heads down. Every now and then, we pop up our heads out of our present-oriented, unconsciously perceived world and look at where we have been and where we are going. Occasionally illuminated by brief periods of consciousness, we reflect on the past and plan for the future. Then the head goes back down, and we swim like mad toward the next life raft or land mass.

MAKING MONEY MAKING YOU

Remember that time is money.
—Benjamin Franklin[18]

In one respect, Ben Franklin was right. Time can be money, but time can be much more. Franklin could have said just as easily that time is health, time is happiness, time is fun, or time is love. However, he didn't. For Franklin, time was money. This simple statement contains three nuggets of wisdom. The first is that time is valuable. How valuable? Time is so valuable that although time is money, money is not always time. When Queen Elizabeth proposed to trade "all my possessions for a moment of time," there were no takers. The second is that time can be converted into money through hard work. Time spent laboring can bring money. Industry pays. The third is that over time, the value of investments appreciates by means of compound interest.

Time influences the job that you choose, and it influences how successful you are in that job. Time also influences what you do with the money that you make from your work. This is especially true in regard to your disposable income—the money that you have left after you have paid fixed expenses such as housing, food, clothing, and transportation. Do you use it to pay off debt? Do you spend it on new houses, cars, and jewelry? Do you put in the bank for a rainy day? How you think and feel about time will affect your financial decisions.

Pasts and Money

Pasts are less concerned with enjoying today or saving for tomorrow. They are more interested in preserving money that they made in the past. Promises of high-investment returns hold little allure for them. They tend to have little debt, and when they do, they repay it promptly. They learn from the past and thereby hope to avoid repeating past mistakes. People who lived through the Great Depression, for example, can be extremely frugal and may prefer the security of hiding money under their mattresses to putting it in banks or investing it in stocks and bonds. Their "investments" are usually designed to avoid losing money rather than making more of it. They are more risk-averse than those who have other time orientations. They want to keep what they have. Their purchases tend to be need-based, not want-based. They buy the least expensive item that will meet their needs. Their pasts taught them to suffice, not to optimize, so they get by with things that will do, not with things that will do best. They cherish and preserve both time and money.

Their conservative views suggest that they are comfortable with the present and desire the future to be no better than the past. Most of all, they want to ensure that the present and future are no worse than the past. An exception might be people who are high on past-negative time perspective. While people high on the past-positive time perspective want to keep what they have, people high on the past-negative time perspective want to avoid the past, because the strategies they employed in the past did not produce positive experiences. As a result, they may be inclined to gamble on new strategies in an attempt to change the past.

Presents and Money

Presents have one of two attitudes toward money. Present fatalists treat money as though it doesn't matter. To them, the lessons of the past are irrelevant, and investments are unlikely to pay off in the future. Consequently, their environment strongly influences them. If they see something interesting, they buy it not because the purchase gives them pleasure but because they cannot think of anything better to do with their money. Their spending and investment habits tend to be variable and random. When what you do with your money does not matter, all possible use of it appears equally appealing and unappealing. They don't want to preserve what they had yesterday, enjoy what they have today, or save for tomorrow. It just does not matter. For them, money is not special. Money does not hold the key to the past or to the future, and they believe that how much or little they have is largely beyond their control.

Hedonists use their money to create fun and excitement. Money is to be enjoyed right now, unencumbered by memories of the past or expectations of the future. A dollar in hand is worth two in the bank. If they do save, it is for a faster car, fancier clothes, and a bigger ring. They never expect it to rain, so they don't save for a rainy day. When it does rain, they think, they will deal with it then. When the rain stops, they dry out quickly and return to their prodigal ways. They journey from rags to riches and back again repeatedly, max out credit cards, overdraw bank accounts, and lose their homes to foreclosure.

Futures and Money

Futures balance their checkbooks more frequently than people lower on the future perspective scale. They pay their bills on time, have savings accounts, and carefully consider their investments. For them, time and money denote possibilities for the future, which may provide things that they did not have yesterday and probably do not have today. Time and money are forces that can bring them things to have and to do.

Considered by itself, each time perspective is problematic. Pasts tend to be overly cautious or overly reckless, presents tend to save too little, and futures tend to enjoy the present too little. Clearly, a balanced time perspective that combines elements of past-positive, present-hedonism, and future time perspectives will allow people to learn from the past, enjoy the present, and plan for the future.

FIVE SIMPLE STEPS TO FINANCIAL FREEDOM

Given that wise people like Ben Franklin have linked time and money, it follows that we might be able to exploit that link to our financial advantage. How can you convert time into money? Fortunately, it is not much work, and little luck is involved. It does, however, take time. You have to take time to make time work for you.

1. The present is the best time to start investing.

Albert Einstein was an expert on time, and he is rumored to have said that compound interest "is the most powerful force in the universe." We doubt the authenticity of the quotation, but we do not doubt its veracity. The only better time to start investing was yesterday. If you started investing yesterday, good for you. If you did not, today is the next best day. Do not let it pass you by.

With enough time, a glacier can shape mountains. With enough time, money, too, will create mountains of cash. As long as your investments are reasonably secure, you are much better off starting sooner rather than later.

2. Time in the market is more important than timing the market.

So you started investing yesterday. Congratulations! That is a good first step, but investing does not end there. The more time you put between the time you begin investing and the time you harvest the yield, the better off you will be. Financial writer Jonathan Burton claims "It's time, not timing" that matters to financial success.

One way to put time in the market systematically is dollar-cost-averaging, the practice of putting a fixed amount of money in an investment at constant intervals. For example, you might invest a hundred dollars in a stock automatically on the first of every month. By buying a fixed dollar amount of shares, you buy more shares when the stock is priced lower and buy fewer shares when the stock is priced higher. As multiple monthly investments accrue, the average purchase price of your stock will converge around the average price for the stock of the same period. As a result, you are protected against buying high and selling low—and against buying low and selling high. Your long-term return, therefore, will closely match the overall rate of return of your stock, which, history has shown, is likely to be up.

3. Know when your time will be up.

People with long investment horizons—those who have a long time until retirement or until they need their money back—can afford much more risky investments than people with short investment horizons. People with short investment horizons may need the yield on their investments to pay the mortgage in a few months and cannot afford to put their money into investments that are likely to go up or to go down sub-stantially over the short term. In contrast, people with longer investment horizons—typically, younger people—can afford to have their investments fluctuate in value, because they have time enough before they need their money to recoup their losses. Higher returns are typically associated with higher risk. Younger people may be able to afford to take risks, but older people may not. Before you start investing, you must consider for how long you will invest your money.

4. You can't time the market.[19]

Here's an investing secret: No one *ever* buys low and sells high all the time. It's just too difficult to do, even for the pros. Most people who invest in stocks, mutual funds, or bonds can iden-tify a point at which they could have bought the stock or bond more cheaply. Those few people who have never identified a point when they could have bought more cheaply have un-doubtedly identified a time when they could have profitably sold for more than they did. As the markets are fond of re-minding us, perfection is difficult to obtain. The wisest don't bother to try. The best that you can realistically hope for is to take advantage of a general upward trend in the markets. Don't try to time the market; instead, let time work for you. If you do try to time the market, you are just as likely to miss good days as bad ones.

5. A hedonistic time perspective is an expensive habit.

A present-hedonistic motto is "If it feels good, buy it!" Their enthusiasm for living is expensive, and it gets in the way of boring activities like paying bills. As a result, people high in present hedonism often get stuck paying for a thing twice. They pay for it once the first time, and then they pay for it again and again in credit card interest payments and late fees. Spend some money on fun, but plan your purchases so that you can afford them and don't end up paying for them twice.

There you have it: five simple steps to financial freedom. Unfortunately, when you add these five simple steps to the hundreds of other simple steps to financial freedom you've heard about over the years, matters are not so simple anymore. The complexity increases exponentially. On top of this complexity is another factor that we have ignored until now: Our five steps focus on *when* you should invest, but we have sidestepped the issue of *where* to invest. Which stock(s) should you buy? Are bonds a better investment than stocks for people your age? Mutual funds are an easy way out of the investment jungle, but there are thousands to choose from. And what about derivatives and hedge funds? Where you invest is as important as when you invest, and determining where to invest takes intelligence and skill.

In some retirement funds, advisers counsel workers to blend conservative bond investments with more risky stock investments. Sounds reasonable, but one of our future-oriented colleagues checked the long-term data for us and found that stocks always outperform other investments. For the past forty years, his teachers' retirement fund was 100 percent equity. His accumulation is now five times greater—and $5 million greater—than that of his sensible, short-term future-oriented colleagues.

THE SMART MONEY

Smarter people have higher annual incomes but are no wealthier than average people are.[20] On average, each extra IQ point leads to an increase of about $425 in annual income. Possible explanations for why this is true include that smarter people get better grades in high school, go to better colleges, and get better, higher-paying jobs upon graduation. Because of their higher annual income, we would expect smarter people to end up wealthier than people of average intelligence. Even if their investment decisions are only as good as the average person's decisions, they should still end up wealthier.

Yet each additional IQ point adds little if anything to a person's net worth. On the surface, this doesn't make sense: Smarter people make more money every year, and we would expect their investment decisions to be at least as good as those of average people. So what happens to the extra money that smarter people make each year? Many of them spend it all. Some of them spend more than all.

In some cases, higher intelligence is related to an increased likelihood for maxed-out credit cards, missed payments, and bankruptcy. This high probability reeks of present hedonism. Smarter people make more money, but they don't keep it because they spend too much, often more than they have. They obviously do not make wiser investment decisions than average people. Planning for a rainy day is characteristic of a future time perspective. Spending all of your money is not.

The moral of this story is that you don't have to be smart to end up wealthy. You don't have to be an econometrician to gain wealth. To become wealthy, you cannot spend more money than you make, and you must invest wisely. As for where to invest, index mutual funds are a great place to start for anyone.[21] Index mutual funds protect both the below-average and above-average investor from him- or herself. The bottom line is that *where* you invest turns out to be less important than *when* you invest.

> *An unhurried sense of time is in itself a form of wealth.*
> —Bonnie Friedman

RETIREMENT: IS TRADING MONEY FOR TIME WORTH THE PRICE?

Jill is a sixty-year-old recently retired business executive. At eight A.M. each weekday for the last twenty years, Jill reviewed her day's schedule with her assistant. By nine A.M. Jill was moving quickly between meetings and didn't stop moving until nearly seven P.M. Jill was good at her job and earned enough money to send her children to the best schools. Even as a single parent, Jill was able to save so much money that she could afford never to work another day in her life.

But today is different. Today is Monday, the first day of her retirement. The alarm clock sounds as usual at six A.M. Jill had automatically set it the night before. She sits up in bed, ready to start her workday. But there is no office to go to today—or on any future day. What will she do?

When we retire, we give up a job and gain new time. The trade-off presents us with opportunities and unique challenges. Now that the largest segment of our population, the baby boomers, are reaching retirement age, these issues are particularly pertinent to our country's present and future state. In the earlier stages of their lives, Baby Boomers had well-defined social roles and obligations, and they either conformed to them or rebelled against them.

Four point three million babies were born in the U.S. in 1957, a record that still stands.[22] For the last thirty or so years, many have led lives much like Jill's: rising early, scanning the news over coffee, getting the kids dressed, hustling them off to school, and then rushing off to jobs that kept them busy nonstop until their kids' soccer games and dinnertime. Then dinner was made and served. Dishes had to be cleared, the next day's agenda laid out. Then it was time to check on parents or to congratulate friends about some milestone reached. Then it was time for a late-night comedy show before collapsing into bed in a dead heap.

Jobs, careers, and family roles define who we are. They confer identity and purpose on us. In retirement, these roles break down. With no jobs to occupy their minds for most of their time awake, retirees must find meaning in themselves. When the identity a job confers is gone, they can no longer rely on work as their major descriptor. How will they choose to be identified when the comfort of a job-labeling title is no longer theirs? What is lost on retirement, and what can be gained from it? Will the sudden advent of free time make them feel useless or worthless? Retirement may also be a period of regret—for all the goals that were not reached, the youthful ambitions left unrealized, and the promises not kept. A retired person can become sharply aware of all the sacrifices he has made for a successful career—giving up time with family and friends and enjoying hobbies, sports, travel, and culture. Remember the survey cited in Chapter Five in which the majority of middle-aged men who were successful managers described their lives as "empty," despite their wealth.

Consider this real-life example of an extremely successful businessperson who recently realized that he was a failure as a father and husband. This realization came to him in response to reading Phil's book *The Lucifer Effect*, which described the ways in which people get caught up playing roles within systems that enable and reward dominance over others.

My life has been so enmeshed in "the System" that I might as well have been living on automatic pilot. I thought that I had been doing all of the "right" things. I had made my stockholders happy, received a good annual bonus, joined the most visible service clubs, had my name in the business section of the newspaper on occasion, attended church on Sundays and at Christmas and Easter, and had been a good provider for my family. But I have been more than a scoundrel. I have been an outright bully.

First of all, I spent forty married years telling my wife and children how lucky they were to have me for a husband and father. Didn't I provide well for them? Hadn't I worked my butt off to give them everything they wanted? Didn't they belong to the best clubs, go to the best schools, have the nicest cars? In my eyes I was the chest-thumping Tarzan, king of the jungle who came home every night bringing food for the table. In their eyes, I am afraid that I was an absent father, an egotistical jerk, and, as my Texan friend tells me, I "was all hat and no cattle."

When my wife left me two years ago, that was my wake-up call. She was done and I didn't understand why. So for the past two years I have been looking for the answers and I don't like what I have been seeing. I thought that the marriage ended because we had grown apart over the years. When I started reading about the Stanford prison experiment, I began to realize that for forty years I had been the prison guard in our house, and my wife and kids were the prisoners. I had even lined my children up against the wall, just like the videotape of the Stanford prisoners. I would pace back and forth, yelling at my four beautiful children, telling them how hard I worked to buy things for them and what a disappointment they were turning out to be. Something inside of me wanted to break them, to break their spirits. And I didn't know why.

Your book *The Lucifer Effect* explained the role I was playing during those many years, and with that understanding, I think that I can take off my dark glasses and my uniform now. Maybe I can even set things right with my kids and my ex.[23]

The good news is that this man has been able to establish a more wholesome relationship with his children by apologizing and asking their forgiveness. He plans to do the same with his former wife. He has not yet retired, but having cleaned up his act before he does is likely to give him a more fulfilling retirement than he would have had if he'd continued to be the guardian of a now empty prison/home. By liberating himself from the constraints of that oppressive role, he opened new channels of communication that will pay him spiritual dividends for the rest of his life.

In retirement, we must refocus and reorient ourselves, toning down the future-oriented perspective while ramping up present hedonism along with a richer past-positive view. We have to fill new disposable time with meaning and purpose and create sources of identity and self-worth that lie beyond job description. A common solution to the problem of retirement is to do what you love; then you will be fulfilled no matter how much money you make. Finding pleasure in what you do is the quest toward which we want to direct you. Many retirees wish they had realized sooner the cost of working for material gain alone. How time perspective influences the choices that we make in retirement has implications for both retired people and those who are still years away from achieving it.

Trading Old Money for New Time: A Retirement Primer

Successful retirement requires money, good health, and a plan. You have earned free time. Now you must use it well. That means you have saved enough money in pension funds and reliable investments to compensate for your loss of income. These days men can expect to live until eighty and many women until ninety, so between retirement at sixty-five or seventy and death is a long time that requires a great deal of money to thrive as one survives.

It is equally important to practice a good health regimen before and during your retirement. All the usual recommendations bear repeating—and should now constitute a daily routine—exercise regularly, walk as much as you can, eat less but eat more healthy foods, drink a lot of water (up to a gallon a day), enjoy good wine in moderation, and get regular medical, dental, and vision checkups. Retirement is a good time to rearrange your body mass: to slim down, get rid of flab, and tone up. Don't make a simple commitment to lose weight, because then the present-oriented child within will try to find where you lost it and get it all back. Obesity is a curse and an epidemic in many developed countries. It increases the risk of diabetes, heart disease, and other chronic illnesses that impair your quality of life—and you can prevent it with the system outlined above. A variety of studies has shown that establishing a buddy system is the best way to exercise regularly and manage weight. So find a reliable partner, and become one for a friend or family member.

Successful aging works best for the young at heart. As the wear and tear of time takes its toll on our bodies, it is imperative to think young, to retain a youthful outlook. That, of course, is easier said than done, but you can achieve flexibility of mind if you adopt these suggestions. Read more, now that you have time to do so. Join or form a book club. Do crossword puzzles if you find them pleasurable. Listen to music on your iPod. Develop a new skill, such as photography. Watch good television programs, but do not allow yourself to be a couch potato. Have an at-home movie night when you watch past Oscar winners. If possible, give sexual pleasure a higher priority than you did when you were younger. Practice variations in sexual behavior that substitute style for stamina.

Without the regimen of work to organize your days and nights, it is crucial to have a plan to get the most out of retirement. In a sense, retirement is like the first day of summer break from school, eagerly awaited until the second day, when you realize there is a long quiet time ahead. Past-positive-oriented folks can rely on continuing to do what they always did or what their folks and friends did. Presents may find leisure time harder because, without the external constraints of a work schedule, their days can become scattered. Hit-or-miss activities promise fun but can quickly become boring, and presents are also susceptible to get-rich-quick schemes and to gambling savings for a big hit. Futures will fare best because their whole lives have been organized around plans, lists, and goal setting. However, they, too, must moderate their future time perspective when today is all they can count on.

A retirement activity plan sets out things you want to do but do not have to do. That is the major blessing of retirement—trading must-dos for want-to-dos. Start with a yearlong calendar on which you fill in plans for travel to the exotic places you have always wanted to visit: Bali or Florence, Rio or Las Vegas. Consider cruises and elder hostels that do not involve too much solitude. Add travel to visit kids or grandchildren, favorite friends, and relatives. Delete obligatory visits to anyone who is likely to be a drag. Every month, program in a combination of health maintenance and self-indulgent activities: Visit a spa for saunas, hot tubs, facials, and massages. Add treatments by a good chiropractor, go to a beauty salon for a manicure and pedicure (men as well as women). A carefully designed plan forces you to consider what you really want out of the remaining years of your life, and what you must do sooner rather than later while you are healthy and independently mobile. How about making reservations at top-rated restaurants for lunch—usually cheaper than dinner but just as good. Expose yourself to cultural activities; buy annual subscriptions to theater, symphony, ballet, and opera. Become a member of your local museum and public library, which always stage special events for members.

As important as feeding your mind and body wisely and well is feeding your spirit. Become more active in your church or temple, or find a religion that fits your current orientation. You now have time for something you may have wanted to do but had no time for—volunteering. Donate your services to local and national organizations. Volunteering not only serves the social good but, as research has shown, improves the health of those who perform it.[23] One of the most important things for seniors is to stay engaged with their juniors. Being around the young makes people feel younger. Volunteer to work in a local school as a teacher's aide, in a local public library, or at a nursery school. Babysit for neighbors, a two-way gift for them and you.

Say No to Retirement Homes

What should you *not* do? Resist being put into a home for the elderly. Unless you are incapacitated and incompetent—in which case you would not be one of our readers—resist pressure to move out of your home into those alien places. Research shows that all too many of the elderly who are sent to standard-care homes for the aged die within a relatively short time after entering[24,25]—short like a year or less! Among the reasons for this is the stress of moving to a new place, of giving up familiar surroundings, furniture, photos, art, your bed, and familiar acquaintances, then being forced to make new ones. Moreover, most of these places offer little opportunity for exercise. All these stresses negatively influence physical health and well-being.

Patients/clients are too often confined to bed to avoid falls and insurance claims and restricted to fixed regimens that determine mealtimes, lights-out, and a schedule of activities that allows little freedom of choice. Because in even the most benign of these institutions, things are done to you and for you, you lose personal initiative. Everyone there is old. Some are very sick and dying. Usually, no one touches you except to administer medical or caregiving procedures. We need the human touch to survive: handshakes, pats on the back, strokes across the forehead, even kisses on the cheek. Our observations of geriatric centers in expensive rehabilitation units revealed that no one ever touched the elderly. Rather, they were put in wheelchairs or propped up in bed before TV sets. When we confronted the director of one facility with our observation, he explained that avoiding touching patients was a standard policy designed to avoid claims of sexual harassment.

If you must enter a home for the elderly, use some simple psychological tactics to ensure your survival. Two Yale University researchers, Judith Rodin and Ellen Langer, did an unusual study at a home for the elderly near New Haven, Connecticut. On one floor, every patient was given the gift of a plant and told that the nurses would care for it. They were also told of a new program of evening movies that would take place on a given night of the week. The patients were all happy to receive the good news. On a different floor filled with comparable patients, the plant came with the proviso that the recipients had to care for it themselves. Movies would be shown at two different times of the week, but residents had to choose the night on when they preferred to watch them. These seemingly simple differences had a huge effect on the subsequent health of the residents, mostly elderly women. Follow-ups by the researchers revealed that those residents who were given the minimal personal responsibility and freedom of choice were healthier on many measures. More interesting, when the researchers returned a year later, significantly more whose sense of control had been enhanced were still alive! Many of the elderly in the no-responsibility/no-choice condition had died during that relatively short interval.[26] Caring for the plant and deciding what night to watch movies had instilled in residents a change for the better in time perspective. The power to decide which night to watch a movie staved off the advance of fatalism. Simply caring for a plant gave residents a stake in the future, because the plant's survival depended on them.

The message here is that small changes in the environment can affect mental states, which in turn affect physical states. It is vital to sustain a sense of personal agency in which you make meaningful choices about all aspects of your life. Do not yield responsibility or freedom of choice to others as long as you have the capacity to act rationally. Finally, let no one take away your personhood and sense of human dignity by categorizing you as a patient who is cared for without really being cared about.

Case Study of a Successful Time-centered Retirement

Upon his recent retirement from university teaching, Phil—like all retirees—was forced to make his time matter. He discovered new value in having "free" time. Here is the rest of the story in Phil's words:

Reluctant to give up the love of my life, undergraduate teaching, which I had done for fifty years, I gave in at age seventy-one in order to gain access to my teacher's retirement funds. Doing so required severing my academic affiliation. After the farewell party and good-bye gift, I had a feeling of emptiness and some obvious sadness. Having been obsessively future-oriented, one key to my academic success, I didn't know what I would do without my daily and hourly planner. What would substitute for the excitement of lecturing to large, enthusiastic student audiences? What would substitute for making and grading examinations, reading and correcting term papers, holding office hours, attending long and boring faculty meetings, performing tedious work on seemingly endless committees, and driving the two-hour daily commute to work? Hold on. Living life more fully would be a great substitute for these less than wonderful correlates of teaching.

Laying out the positives lost and the negatives gladly relinquished, I made a simple plan to get back some of the good and reallocate the time that had been drained by some of the bad aspects of being a university professor. I agreed to teach part-time, only a day a week, to a new graduate student cohort, building on the best of my oldie-but-goodie lectures that would take little time to prepare. I also agreed to give more invited lectures that involved travel to interesting venues, coupled with mini-vacations.

I spent my newly freed-up time in many ways, starting with writing articles and books about topics that were personally interesting but had not been necessary for career advancement. More central to my lifelong struggle with competing time perspectives was my decision to integrate seriously a fuller present hedonism with a reduced future focus. Coming from a family and a tradition that has always been more present- and past- than future-oriented, I had always resisted the lure of play over work. To use my newfound time to best advantage, I planned regular self-indulgence rather than leaving it to the whim of the moment. In other words, I used my future-oriented focus to put more pleasure in my life.

I now get weekly two-hour intense massages, supplemented by occasional ones that are more sensuous. Soaking in a Jacuzzi and heating up in a newly installed home sauna are treats I enjoy at random intervals throughout the week. Work breaks (from the pleasure of working with John on this book) include cappuccino runs down the street to a local café or across town for java with one of my three children. I enjoy preparing dinners by shopping at the farmers' market for fresh fruit, vegetables, and flowers. Cooking dinners for my hardworking wife, Christina, setting the table, lighting candles, playing soft jazz, and eating full meals in the Italian slow-food tradition all cultivate romance. Trips to the wonderful wine regions of Napa/Sonoma/Mendocino are now more frequently on our agenda.

I also regularly prepare surprise treats of fruits or pasta for next-door neighbors and candies for their children. I regularly attend the late show at a local jazz club, a time when it is easy to street-park, and I don't have to worry about getting up early the next day to teach. My future fun list includes learning to dance salsa, writing the memoirs of my childhood, and hopefully soon becoming an overindulgent grandfather.

My family perceives me as less controlling than I have been all of my life, more relaxed, and surely less stressed than ever before. This good new life is a healthier one; my blood sugar levels (diabetes checks) and weight are now within more normal ranges. I read the morning news while riding a recumbent bike for half an hour each day, while sipping the warm potassium soup I make out of fifteen different vegetables. I still spend too much time answering hundreds of daily e-mails from around the world, but I spend more quality time with close friends and family that complements those virtual connections and acquaintances. Researcher and Stanford colleague Laura Carstensen could now use me as a model of an old-timer productively enjoying each day's gift of life, having a newly balanced orientation that blends the best of past, future, and present time perspectives.

nine

LOVE AND HAPPINESS

Time flies when you're having fun!
—*Samuel Beckett,* Waiting for Godot

Sigmund Freud felt that when we are in love, we suffer from a very special case of mental illness: We become present-oriented imbeciles deaf to the language of the future. We do things that don't make sense in the context of our long-term goals. And that is the polite way to put it. Love makes blissful and willing idiots of us all. Tomorrow can wait, for I am in love today. Falling in love enshrines us in an expanded present state of mind, returning us to the magic and miracles of our childhood. Feelings dominate reason, and emotions become actions without reflection. In the extreme, love is a lot like an addiction in which the pleasure of the moment dominates all thoughts of future costs and possible negative consequences.

Freud's view that the intoxication of love resembled mental illness borrows from a long medical tradition in which the state of love has been medicalized into "love sickness," or "love melancholy." Robert Burton's *The Anatomy of Melancholy* (1621) offered a medicalized account of the varied effects on the mind and body of contracting "love sickness." Consider some of the author's views on how states of mind and circumstance alter one's sense of time.*

---

* When I go musing all alone,
Thinking of divers things
When I build castles in the air,
Void of sorrow and void of fear,
Pleasing myself with phantasms sweet
Methinks the time runs very fleet.

Freud also felt that love held the key to curing mental illness. According to Freud, individuals undergoing psychoanalysis—the form of psychotherapy that he pioneered—invariably fall in love with their therapists. The love that clients feel for their therapists is complex and somewhat misplaced. Clients really fall in love with what the therapist represents to them, not with who the therapist really is. This misplaced—or transferred—love gives therapists tremendous power in the therapeutic relationship, which can be used both for good and bad. When used for bad, clients are exploited. When used for good, clients are led toward health. Clients' love for their therapists motivates them to change in positive ways that will please the therapists. Freud wrote, "Psychoanalysis is in essence a cure through love."[1] Of course, love that is more genuine flourishes outside of the therapist's office, where it reveals the best and the worst of each of us. It does so without regard to title, class, prudence, good taste, and shame. We should all be so lucky to suffer from the sickness and to endure the best of its cure.

You might think that love's power and centrality to our lives would guarantee it a central place within the field of psychology. It has not. Psychology followed the path set by medicine in which the primary present-oriented focus is on curing the current ill and only secondarily on enhancing the future happiness and love of those already well. On the one hand, this approach makes sense, as it is difficult to be happy when one is in pain. One the other hand, this approach denies the complexity of human life. Happiness is not only the absence of pain. As Freud perspicuously noted, the line separating psychological health and psychological illness is hazy,

---

All my joys to this are folly,
Naught so sweet as melancholy.

When I lie waking all alone,
Recounting what I have ill done,
My thoughts on me then tyrannize,
Fear and sorrow me surprise,
Whether I tarry still or go,
Methinks the time moves very slow.

Readers might also want to check out a recent updating of the medical legacy of romanticism as expressed in various forms of love melancholy. See Marion A. Wells (2007). *The Secret Wound: Love-Melancholy and Early Modern Romance.* Stanford, CA: Stanford University Press.

meandering, and frequently straddled. In such a complex world, it makes sense to minimize the negative while simultaneously maximizing the positive. In addition, limiting psychology's purview to those that are far enough across the line to be labeled mentally ill excludes a far greater number of the relatively healthy from receipt of potential benefits.

From our perspective, the turn of both medicine and psychology toward health and wellness is, well, a very positive and long overdue directional shift. Curing illness should and will remain a focus of both fields, but there is more to life than the absence of pain and suffering, as anyone who has ever been in love knows well. For many it is central to the gift of life itself.

THE STAGES OF RELATIONSHIPS: PRESENT, PAST, FUTURE

Remember when you met your first love—the warm, tingly feelings, the inability to think of anything else, and the pangs of loneliness when he or she was absent? During the first weeks of your blossoming relationship, you stayed up until three A.M. talking together about nothing and then slept until noon. The rest of the world faded away in importance. You, your love, and your time together were all that mattered. Alas, time passed, the magic faded, and eating crackers in bed began to try your patience.

When you meet someone new, you do not share a common past, and a joint future is tenuous at best. You are stuck with the present, which you hope will turn out to be a good place. Nervousness, emotion, and hormonal chemistry exacerbate your present condition. Time passes; the initial passion fades; and the past and future reassert themselves. It is not that you or your partner changes. It's that together you have created a past and a future, which necessitate having new attitudes toward time.

That is if things go well. The transition to the future-oriented stage may be particularly challenging if, for example, one person is present hedonistic and the other future-oriented, which in heterosexual relationships is common. If one person is biased toward the future and the other toward the present, it may be difficult to make simple joint decisions. Deciding what to eat for dinner (McDonald's or Crock-Pot?), how to spend extra money (a new car or a new investment?), and how to spend free time (work or play?) are mine fields. Important decisions, such as whether to have children, can be even more problematic. Self-destructive, present-hedonistic behaviors like gambling one's earnings, using drugs, or having affairs won't keep your partner around for long.

There is substantial variability in time perspectives among individual men and women, but on average, men tend to be more present-hedonistic and women more future-oriented. Generations ago, this difference undoubtedly carried a survival advantage. Men and women may have balanced each other's time perspective. They may still do so today, but the difference between them can also lead to conflict.

In lesbian and gay relationships, we would expect fewer conflicting time perspectives between partners. For example, lesbian couples may be more likely to share a strong future orientation and a weak present-hedonistic orientation. In contrast, gay couples may share a present-hedonistic bias and plan insufficiently for the future. However, certain men can be high in future time perspective and particular women high on present hedonism.

We are reminded of a question posed to elementary school children by a local newspaper's Answer Man: "What is a honeymoon?" One ten-year-old girl had obviously heard stories about what went wrong with her parents' honeymoon when she asserted: "Honeymoons need reservations. You have to make reservations on a honeymoon." We bet the parent who had been charged with arranging the hotel or travel arrangements was present-oriented and simply put off that future-focused obligation. And her spouse never let it be forgotten, so it became part of the family lore.

DATING AND MATING

Ye Gods! annihilate but space and time,
And make two lovers happy.
                              —Alexander Pope

What people want from relationships differs depending on their time perspectives, as our research with couples attests. Future orientation is related strongly with wanting mates to be predictable. Futures are also most likely to consider what benefits they can gain from relationships. But—and it is a big "but"—they do not desire intense, exciting, romantic relationships. Presents enjoy passionate, physical, spontaneous relationships, which tend also to be filled with conflict. Their ideal partner is exciting and spontaneous. These partners usually table commitment because they do not spend time thinking about their future together. Pasts describe their romantic relationships as satisfying with reliable as the ideal partner trait. Past-negatives might spend time considering what other possible romantic partners they might have missed. Like the futures, pasts are less likely to value spontaneity and physicality in their romantic relationships. So our advice is: Before you hook up with someone new, and certainly before you make a commitment, try to determine the compatibility between your time perspectives. See if you can use the ZTPI to figure out his or her attitudes. Then you'll be prepared for any disagreements and better understand where your other is coming from.

DATING IN A FUTURE-ORIENTED WORLD

There's more dating in a monastery.
                                        —*A Stanford University student*

Early in relationships, presents clearly have an advantage. They are not distracted by the future; they can be fully engrossed in the present; and they enjoy relationships. They are funny, fun to be around, and creative. Present-oriented people are great at parties, but expect them to arrive late and spend the night on your couch. Your future friends, in contrast, will arrive on time but leave early. They will have important things to do the next day.

Futures do not deal with dating, relationships, and sex very well. Some colleges have the reputation for being all about sex, drugs, and rock and roll. You may even remember your college experience that way. But at Stanford University and other highly selective schools—indeed, in many careers and business today—people are future-oriented, driven by big plans for their lives. For them, present-hedonistic activities like dating and sex can wait.

No matter how young, suave, debonair, stunning, curvaceous, built, or well informed we are, relationships take time. We need to be in the present to enjoy them, and we need to tend to them over time. For this reason, we authors found ourselves in the unusual position of encouraging future-oriented Stanford students to become more present-hedonistic. The result was *The Score on Scoring: The Guidebook, Stanford Edition*. The guide to scoring is a thoroughly researched, funny, sincere, and—we hope—successful attempt to encourage driven young people to let their future down for a minute and enjoy the present. The voices of students we interviewed express a consistent desire for giving, receiving, and sharing, and a longing for time. All of us would do well to remember Holden Caulfield's euphemism for sex: "giving her the time." The foundation of emotional and physical love is giving and sharing time. Nothing is more romantic than to say, "I don't really have the time to do what you want to do, but for you I will make the time."

CONSEQUENCES OF MISMATCHED TIME PERSPECTIVES

Couples with mismatched time perspectives will be prone to miscommunication and misunderstanding. They may truly love each other but live in separate worlds, like lovers who speak different languages. Unlike lovers who speak different languages, however, couples with conflicting time perspectives may not understand why they have difficulty in communicating. There may be no apparent reason why one cannot hear the other. One person may make a statement about the future that she believes to be completely clear, but if the other person is low on future and high on present-hedonistic time perspective, he may not understand. She speaks future time perspective, and he speaks present hedonism. Consequently, their conversation is likely to be ineffective, not because they are stupid, uncaring, or unloving but because they speak different time perspectives. We have found this to be true of many family configurations. Children do their present-oriented things, Dad focuses on the future and his career, and Mom focuses on family rituals and nostalgia for former family good times. Conflicting time perspectives are often unrecognized as the cause of familial strife and misunderstanding.

So how do you bridge the gap in the languages of time? You start with the present. The present is the bridge from the past to the future, and it may be the only common ground for people who reside on opposite banks of the river of time. If two people attempt to meet in the past or the future, they are likely to be lost in a fog. The present is the only time marker that they both can recognize, the only place to touch and be touched, the only place to love and be loved.

The present is the meeting place for good as well as difficult times. When two people are arguing, they can be tempted to leave the bridge of the present and become lost in the fog of the past, or abandon the present for the comfort of an imagined future. When they do this, they lose their connection and may resort to lobbing incendiaries from their entrenchments on opposite banks of the river of time. It is difficult enough to communicate when both people are firmly planted in the present. Tone of voice, the meaning of words, and emotions can obscure what we say and hear. When two people argue, their emotions are often negative, and the argument centers on negative things that at least one of the two does not fully understand. One or the other is reconstructing the past or constructing a future; either position is unfruitful. You cannot hope to change a reconstructed past or a constructed future, but you can, with effort, connect in the present.

What is critical to couples' constructive criticism of each other is to first make evident what each thinks the other person is saying: "It seems to me that what you are saying is that you don't like X, don't want to do Y, and believe Z is true. Is that the case, or am I misunderstanding you?" You are not accusing the other, merely opening a dialogue about perceived differences of opinion. Second, it rarely helps to nag someone about past mistakes; that only makes him guilty or defensive. Rather, reframe the criticism in terms of what he might consider doing in the future to achieve his objective. "Next time when you want me to be more socially active at the office party, let me know in advance whom you would like me to talk with, and I will do my best to oblige." Rather than "You embarrassed me by acting like a princess who was too damn good for my friends." Alternatively, "If you want to impress people, don't tell sexist or racist jokes that others might find more insensitive than funny."

A healthy time perspective in a relationship looks a lot like a healthy time perspective in an individual. It's a balance of past positive, present hedonistic, and future. Depending on the ages of the couple, it may be more fully focused on the past, the present, or the future. No matter their shared time perspective, couples need to meet in the present at least occasionally.

HAPPINESS AND TIME

Thirty-four percent of Americans report that they are very happy. Most (50 percent) are just pretty happy. Of the remaining 16 percent, 15 percent are not too happy, and 1 percent don't know.[2] Perhaps more surprising, these numbers haven't changed much in the last thirty years. CDs replaced eight-track tapes; DVDs replaced videotape; cell phones replaced cordless phones; and the Internet was invented. Still, Americans are no happier. Why is this so? As we will see, happiness is difficult to obtain and even more difficult to maintain.

It is not that we do not recognize happiness when we see it. Everyone knows people who exude happiness, and recently researchers have even begun to identify the common characteristics of these people. According to our colleague, Sonja Lyubomirsky, those among us who are "happy people" tend to do the following things more than less happy people do.[3]

- Help coworkers and passersby

- Express gratitude for what they have

- Devote time to family, friends, and other social relationships

- Savor life's pleasures and try to live in the present
- Exercise habitually
- Express optimism about their future
- Set and pursue life goals
- Cope well with life's headaches

Each of these activities has a time perspective correlate. For example, in Chapter One we saw that seminarians who believed that they were late to give a sermon on the parable of the Good Samaritan were less likely to stop to help a person in need than seminarians believing they had plenty of time before their sermon. People under less time pressure are therefore more likely to help coworkers and passersby. In Chapter Two, we saw that gratitude is very similar to our psychological concept of the past-positive time perspective. People who score high on the past-positive time perspective tend to be more grateful and happier than those who score lower on the scale. Similarly, savoring pleasures in the present is clearly related to present hedonism and expressing optimism about the future is clearly related to future time perspective. Research by Lyubomirsky and many other psychologists has also shown that religious and spiritual beliefs are positively associated with happiness. These beliefs clearly lie within transcendental future.

Time offers us multiple opportunities to find happiness—in the past, in the present, in the future, and in the transcendental future. If you look to the past, the memory of good times can make you happy, and the memory of bad times can make you sad. In the present, great-tasting food, talking with friends, pleasant surprises, making love, contemplating beauty, and doing congenial work can all bring happiness. The future can hold happiness as well: Thoughts of closing a good deal, getting a promotion, getting married, having kids, and retiring bring their own kind of hopeful happiness.

Whether you look for happiness in the past, the present, or the future, you *experience* happiness only in the present. A happy event may have occurred in the past, but you call it to mind in the present.

Similarly, the expectation that you will win the lottery next Saturday night brings pleasure when you think about it now. When you ignore the present and look primarily to the past or the future for happiness, you can miss the happiness that is right in front of you. If you look solely to the past, you neglect a present that could provide you with more happy memories. If you look solely to the future, you may be unable to enjoy happy events when they arrive. By always looking through the present to the next goal, you likely do not fully appreciate the present. When lost in the past or engrossed in the future, you cannot be present, and happiness rushes by like a gourmet meal eaten in the car on the way to a dentist appointment. Thoughts of the past and the future can bring you happiness, but they do so by bringing happiness into the present state of mind.

OBSTACLES TO HAPPINESS

The Set Point Explanation of Happiness: Nothing Will Make You Happy for Long

Although you can find happiness in the past, present, and future, there are still many obstacles.[4] It is a sad fact of life that people habituate quickly to positive states, to happiness, and slowly to negative states, to pain. This means that good times do not last, but bad times endure. If you win the lottery Saturday night, you will be happy for minutes, days, weeks, and even months, but not for years.

A classic study compared the happiness of twenty-two lottery winners, twenty-nine paraplegic or quadriplegic accident victims, and twenty-two "normal" or ordinary people. The lottery winners were no more or less happy than the normal people were. Their winnings did not change their ability to derive happiness from the past or the future. Winners are no happier than you were yesterday, than you are today, or than you expect to be tomorrow.

The accident victims, in contrast, were less happy than others were but still rated their happiness well above neutral. They recalled having been happier in the past, looking to the past as a source of happiness, perhaps because their sources of happiness in the present were limited. Expectations of future happiness were not different among the groups. By a few months after hitting the lottery, winners regress to the steady state of happiness in which they existed before their win. They have gotten used to their newfound wealth, and it has ceased to make them happy.

Nothing will increase your baseline level of happiness for long, not even money. Remember that the next time you're about to shell out ten dollars for lottery tickets. All is not lost, however. There is more that you can do than blame your parents for giving you stubborn happiness genes. Recent research suggests that your genetic happiness set point accounts for only about 50 percent of your overall happiness level. In addition, life circumstance—age, sex, ethnicity, nationality, marital status, physical health, income level—account for an additional 10 percent of your overall happiness. While this suggests that 60 percent of your happiness is in the hands of genetic roulette and fate, it leaves open the possibility of increasing your level of happiness by 40 percent, which is much more than earlier researchers thought was possible. So you can work at being happy and jazz up your happiness quotient over whatever the "push from nature" level with which you were born.

We Don't Know What Will Make Us Happy Tomorrow

Years ago, a college professor was interested in how well people can predict what they will want in the future. To test this, he set up an in-class study that ran for an entire term.[5] As a cover story, he told students that he would reward attendance by giving all students a candy bar at the last class session each week. He explained further that he was worried about running out of the "best" candy bars, so he had students submit a form indicating the kind of candy bar they wanted each week. By the end of week one, a student predicted, she would want a PayDay. Week two it was a Butterfinger, week three a Baby Ruth, and week four a Kit Kat. When the last session of each week arrived, the professor told students that he had plenty of candy bars and that they could choose to have either the candy bar they had predicted they'd want or the candy bar they wanted right then. Most of the time, the students' predicted desire did not match their actual desire.

Some things—like candy bars—increase our level of happiness for very short periods of time. That's the good news. The bad news is that we are not good at identifying what will make us happy in the future. It is entirely possible to work for years to reach a goal—let's call it a PayDay—and, when you have achieved it, to find that it doesn't make you any happier. You find that you really want a Snickers. The silver lining of this bad news is that if something happens that you worked years to avoid—say you lose a leg in a traffic accident—there is a good chance that it won't decrease your happiness as much as you had expected. You will still be happy.

Happiness Is Not a Priority

Eating a candy bar is a guilty indulgence. For many of us, so is being happy. As we are indoctrinated into the ways of the future-oriented world, we are taught to undervalue pleasure and to value hard work. We learn that the right way to do things is to finish work first and then to play—if there is still time. We learn "Clean your bedroom" or "Finish your peas" and "Then you can go out to play." This sequencing is okay when you are a kid and your entire to-do list consists of 1) clean bedroom and 2) eat peas. As an adult, because you never make it more than a third of the way down your to-do list, you tend to give yourself little time for happiness.

Happiness is generally devalued in our society. Our lives are busy, and as a result, we feel pressure to use our time productively. Time spent working is considered productive, while time spent being happy is considered wasted. Industry and economic success are prized over happiness in the minds of futures. But income in excess of what is required to meet basic needs does not bring happiness.

Compared to people from other cultures, Americans today seem more obsessed with personal happiness and have been critized for having become a feel-good rather than a do-good culture. We are obsessed with looking good, with having a great tan, tight buns, and blemish-free skin. Yet what is important in life is more than skin-deep. It is a spiritual inner happiness that does not diminish over time.

Because happiness is not urgent, and an inner happiness can take time to acquire, happiness drops down on our list of priorities. Stephen Covey points out that there are two ways we make priorities: One is in order of importance; the other is in order of urgency. The urgent dimension is really a time dimension. Urgent actions are present-oriented, while actions that are not urgent are future-oriented. Covey found that when we combine these two priority lists into one, the urgent items always rise to the top of the list, whether or not they are important. Happiness is important, but it is not urgent.[6] The pursuit of happiness falls to tenth place on the to-do list, behind picking up the dry cleaning before the cleaner closes. In the end, our time is a fixed-size pie, and as we slice it more and more thinly, each slice becomes less satisfying.

> *Most folks are about as happy as they make up their minds to be.*
> —Abraham Lincoln

Finding happiness is more complicated than choosing candy bars, but is much more likely than winning the lottery. Despite the substantial obstacles to happiness, most people are remarkably happy. Accident victims are slightly less happy than lottery winners and able-bodied people, but they are still happy. If people who have suffered horrible accidents can be happy, it should be easy for the rest of us. As the Dalai Lama writes, "We don't need more money, we don't need greater success or fame, we don't need the perfect body or even the perfect mate—right now, at this very moment, we have a mind, which is all the basic equipment we need to achieve complete happiness."[7] Our ability to reconstruct the past, to interpret the present, and to construct the future gives us the power to be happy. We must just take the time to use it.

INCREASING HAPPINESS IN YOUR LIFE

The time you enjoy wasting is not wasted time.
—*Bertrand Russell*

Psychologist Sonja Lyubomirsky identified twelve strategies through which people can increase their levels of happiness. Each strategy is explicitly or implicitly associated with a general time perspective. The accompanying table clearly illustrates the limits of biased time perspectives. People who have a biased time perspective use a single time perspective regardless of the situation in which they find themselves. This is another feature of our Time Paradox—a biased future time perspective serves people well in some situations but poorly in others. For example, a future bias would lead a person to cultivate optimism, develop coping strategies, and set life goals. While these strategies can increase happiness, the future bias blinds the person to other viable strategies available to individuals who also incorporate past, present, and transcendental-future time perspectives. Only a balanced time perspective opens all paths to happiness. Given that only 40 percent of our overall happiness is under our own control, it is critical to pursue happiness along all possible paths. Biased time perspectives close potential doors to happiness, while a balanced time perspective provides mental flexibility and allows detours around the inevitable blocks to happiness, most of which are not in our control. As you examine each of the twelve steps listed below, reflect on how it applies to you. (We strongly recommend Sonja Lyubomirsky's book *The How of Happiness*[8] from which the table below is adapted.)

Time Perspective and Twelve Paths to Happiness

	General Time Perspective			
	Past	**Present**	**Future**	**Transcendental Future**
Activity	Express gratitude	Practice acts of kindness	Cultivate optimism	Practice religion or cultivate spirituality
	Avoid overthinking & rumination	Nurture relationships	Develop coping strategies	
	Learn to forgive	Increase flow experiences	Set and pursue life goals	
		Savor life's joys	Take care of your body (exercise)	
		Take care of your body (meditation)		

Other outstanding researchers have written extensively on the psychology of happiness. We strongly recommend their recent books, especially Martin Seligman's *Authentic Happiness* and Daniel Gilbert's *Stumbling into Happiness*. Our intent is not to relate their findings in detail but to point out that a balanced time perspective is a prerequisite to the application of strategies that these experts have identified as increasing happiness. Pursuing happiness without a balanced time perspective is like listening to great music in mono, drinking good wine with a plugged nose, and making love without foreplay. These things may remain pleasurable, but they lack a sensory completeness that maximizes happiness.

While we'll leave the specific happiness strategies to others, we do want to take a moment to discuss time's more general contributions to your personal happiness. As we've seen, each time perspective offers paths toward happiness, but, at the very least, you need to give yourself time to travel them.

Happiness in Time: Give Yourself Time to Be Happy

Good things take time. You've heard the saying, and in the case of happiness, it happens to be true. It even takes time to realize that you are happy. You have to stop swimming with your head down long enough to notice that the dangers you've been avoiding are past and have given way to tropical islands lush with flowers. Once you notice the islands you can choose to swim right by or stop to smell some flowers on your way. If you are not going to stop for happiness, for what are you going to stop?

Most people do give themselves time to be happy in their two weeks of vacation a year. But that is not enough. You need to integrate happiness into your daily life. Some of this time may be spontaneous: You see a beautiful flower and you smell it. But you can also plan your happiness: You can set aside an hour each day to talk with your partner, walk your dog, or listen to music. If you ask nicely, you might even be able to make an appointment to make love. It doesn't matter where the time comes from. What matters is that you make time for happiness to be a priority.

Happiness in the Past: Use Time to Relive Happy Memories and to Heal Wounds

Just as time can heal a scraped knee and add interest to your savings account, it can also heal emotional and psychological wounds. Let negative memories recede into the past and distance yourself from the pain associated with them. Actively work to keep positive memories in the front of your mind. Pictures, notes, and cards placed throughout your home bring the past with you into the present. You can reexperience happy times—and thus reinforce your happiness—whenever you have time to reflect upon them. Fill yourself with memories of happy times to inoculate yourself against the intrusion of negative thoughts and put you on a path to creating more happy memories in the future. Help your children develop scrapbooks of their Personal Developmental Histories to highlight the positives in their lives, year by year.

Happiness in the Present: Practice Mindfulness

One way to increase the amount of time that you spend in the present is to practice mindfulness. When you are mindful, you are fully aware of your surroundings and of yourself in the present. Mindfulness increases the time that you swim with your head above water, when you can see both potential dangers and pleasures. When you are mindful, you are aware of your position and your destination. You can make corrections to your path. Whenever you miss your usual freeway exit, pour orange juice on your breakfast cereal, and leave the baby on the bus, you are not being mindful.[9]

Once upon a time, a young apprentice trained in the way of the Buddha for years in a large valley. When he finally felt ready to test his progress, he ascended to a mountaintop where his master was meditating. The master kept the apprentice waiting for days before beginning the test. The master at last acknowledged the presence of his frustrated apprentice by saying, "I have only one question for you. At the beginning of the trail that leads to this mountaintop, there is a sign on one side of the trail. On which side is it?" The master tested not what the apprentice had studied but how he had applied it. Mindfulness matters more than abstract knowledge.

Increasing your mindfulness may appear deceptively simple, but as our apprentice may attest, it can be exceptionally challenging. Monks don't take years to master mindfulness because they are slow. They take years because it is extremely difficult to do. How difficult? Well, one simple mindfulness technique is to touch the doorjamb every time you walk through a door. As you touch it, concentrate on that present moment, its sights, sounds, and smells, and on the door of experience that has just opened for you. This habit can help keep you grounded in the present and open to experiencing happiness more fully. If you are like us, you will walk by more doorjambs, head down, than you will touch.[10]

Happiness in the Future: Pursue Happiness

Happiness is not a destination but a quest, a never-ending expedition to nowhere in particular. The direction in which you head matters less than that you keep moving forward and exploring. To some, this suggests that nothing will make us happy, but to us psychologists, it suggests that happiness is a moving target, not that it is unobtainable. What makes you happy today may not make you happy tomorrow.

One thing that generally makes us happy is success. With success as with happiness, however, we know it when we see it, but we are hard-pressed to describe what it is. Both happiness and success are difficult to define and extremely personal. Legendary UCLA basketball coach John Wooden [11] defines success in this way: "Success is peace of mind which is a direct result of self-satisfaction in knowing you did your best to become the best that you are capable of becoming." [12]

Wooden's definition of success contains elements of the past, the present, and the future. Peace of mind is experienced in the *present* as the result of hard work in the *past*. The obvious way to extend your success is to continue working hard in the *future*. Hard work and striving for success in the future are hallmarks of the Wooden way. After winning nine national championships, Wooden compiled a to-do list before his final season. Two of the fifteen items on the list relate to time. He wrote, "Forget the past and concentrate on each day of practice" and "Do not take anything for granted just because we have done so well in the past." For Wooden, time relates both to how we experience success today and to how we ensure that we will continue to experience it tomorrow.

According to the Dalai Lama, even the least enlightened among us can immediately apply two simple techniques to living. The first is to identify the things in your life that make you happy, and do more of them. Like mindfulness, this technique seems simple enough, but it is difficult to do. Pursuing happiness takes time, patience, and honesty. What you once liked can change, and it can take courage to admit that to yourself and others. Be prepared for dead ends and disappointment, but be sure to enjoy the swim.

The second technique is the reverse side of the first. Identify the things in your life that make you unhappy, and do fewer of them. Again, this is not easy, and you can't do it all in one sitting. You'll want to work to identify sources of your unhappiness and then work to eliminate them. Avoid the dangers, swim toward the tropical islands, and don't forget to smell some flowers along the way.

Learn to Embrace Change; Deviate for a Day

What makes you happy will change, and you'll need to change with it. An extremely effective way of encouraging you to embrace change is what we call being a deviant for a day. We've done it ourselves and often have whole classes do it.

Your task is to violate an important aspect of your self-image. Which part you violate is up to you. For instance, students who usually spend two hours putting on makeup before leaving the house in the morning must come to class straight out of bed. Others shave their heads. Many forgo clothing. Some dress in rags. Some beg. Some carry Bibles. Others carry flasks. Some use profanity. Others don't speak. For each person, the experience is different, and for all, it takes courage. But once you've done it and lived through it, it is liberating. You realize that change—even extreme change—is possible and is not fatal. Moreover, when you intentionally do things to make people laugh at you, you are in control of their laughter and do not interpret it as ridicule or failure. So be a deviant for a day, and be happy.

Choose Happiness

Not every consequence is born of a choice. Sometimes things in our environment lead us to act automatically and not even to notice the effect of the environment on our behavior. By being mindful, you may be able to detect the influence of your environment when you want to be rid of it, and to do something to eliminate it. For example, if you are behaving in ways that are counterproductive, you can realize that both choice and the environment are equally responsible. You then have the choice of changing your behavior directly and of changing it indirectly by changing your environment.

Once you recognize the effect of the environment upon you, you open new doors to changing behavior and make your life truly your own. Be mindful as you pass through each door. Realize that you can learn from your past, but you are not chained to it. You can decide that today is the first day of the rest of your life.

> From time to time we are faced with pivotal decisions that can affect the entire course or our lives. We may decide, for instance, to get married, to have children, or to embark on a course of study to become a lawyer, an artist, or an electrician. The firm resolve to become happy—to learn about the factors that lead to happiness and take positive steps to build a happier life—can be just such a decision. The turning toward happiness as a valid goal and the conscious decision to seek happiness in a systematic manner can profoundly change the rest of our lives.
>
> —*The Dalai Lama*[13]

You can choose how you reconstruct the past, interpret the present, and construct the future. You can choose to remember a wonderful glass of wine that you had yesterday, and forget the special bottle of wine that you spilled last week. Today you can choose to see the glass as half full and savor its flavor. And you can choose to expect the glass to be completely full tomorrow. In so doing, you make the most of your time by choosing happiness over despair, joy over heartbreak, and pleasure over pain.

The greatest gift that you can give to others and to yourself is time. Embrace the gift of time whether you give it or receive it. Allow yourself to be fully present and to choose happiness. The past is gone, and the future will never arrive. The present is all that you have. Give yourself permission to enjoy the present and to pursue happiness in the future.

ten

BUSINESS, POLITICS, AND YOUR TIME

In January 2000 Enron CEO and chairman Kenneth Lay went to bed the night before an earnings announcement, believing earnings per share to be $0.30. The next morning, earnings per share were $0.31, which was in line with analysts' revised expectations. But the change was not because Enron's accounting had discovered an error in previous earnings calculations. They had simply changed the $0.30 to $0.31. They had cooked the books.

In July 2000 Wall Street expected earnings of $0.32 per share from Enron. Executives went through draft after draft of an earnings report of $0.32 per share, but in the final report, earnings per share were $0.34. The Enron president and COO, Jeffrey Skilling, had ordered the change to keep the share price high.

On Tuesday, February 6, 2001, Enron Corporation was named *Fortune* magazine's Most Innovative Company in America for the sixth consecutive year.[1] Enron also ranked in *Fortune*'s top twenty for Most Admired Companies, Quality of Management, Quality of Products/Services, and Employee Talent. Clearly, Enron was doing something right (or so it seemed). Kenneth Lay attributed Enron's success to their "world-classed employees and their commitment to innovative ideas that continue to drive our success in today's fast-paced business environment." Shares then traded near their all-time high of $90 per share,[2] a phenomenal growth curve by any criterion of business success.

Later that same year, on December 2, 2001, Enron Corporation filed for bankruptcy. Share prices fell to $0.30 a share; $63 billion evaporated in bankruptcy. Thousands of people lost their life savings. Enron's demise also took down the Big Five consulting firm Arthur Andersen and its eighty-five thousand worldwide employees—including those accountants who had helped cook the books. "The Smartest Guys in the Room"[3]—as they were sarcastically dubbed in a best-selling book—had precipitated one of the largest bankruptcies in U.S. history. How could such an amazing business success story have turned into such a nightmare?

The Enron saga is the tale of very bright and probably initially well-intentioned men and women who had worked hard to build a successful company. At first they did so by making good business decisions that resulted in a string of positive quarterly reports. As they built up Enron, however, they wore down the future time perspective that had contributed to their initial success. In its place, they constructed a present time perspective by group consensus. They focused attention on and gave priority to the present at the expense of the future. At some earlier point, the Enron executives may have considered the future consequences of falsifying earning reports, but by 2001 they had lost sight of the long-term goal of building a successful business and focused myopically on generating high-flying quarterly earnings. Their time perspective had become organized into three-month chunks. According to Arthur Levitt, former chair of the Securities and Exchange Commission, "Enron grew out of a pervasive culture of 'gamesmanship' in a corporate world that has become so focused on stock prices and quarterly earnings that it has lost its moral compass."[4,5]

Enron executives built a virtual casino. Gamesmanship intensified their narrowly focused present orientation and discouraged any thought of negative future consequences of their actions. In such a culture, those who are not team players are shunted aside or dumped. As in real casinos, money poured in, and the quarterly gamble was rigged in investors' and Enron's short-term favor.

The executive group's collective time perspective encouraged others to adopt their present orientation as well. Eventually, sixteen executives pled guilty to various types of fraud. Two more—Lay and Skilling—were convicted of fraud by juries. Some of them knew that what they were doing was wrong, because other Enron employees had told them so months before the collapse. In an August 2001 letter to Lay, Sherron Watkins, Enron's vice president of corporate development, wrote, "I am incredibly nervous that we will implode in a wave of accounting scandals. My eight years of Enron work history will be worth nothing on my résumé, the business world will consider the past successes nothing but an elaborate accounting hoax." Watkins saw the danger, and she warned her superiors. They knew she was right, but they didn't believe the danger was imminent and ignored her forecast of the future.[6]

How could a group of smart people be so dumb? Well, they weren't dumb. The complex—and fraudulent—financial transactions that they used to inflate Enron earnings were extremely sophisticated and inventive. They were very clever and, initially, most likely future-oriented, or they never would have gotten as far as they did in business. Over time, though, greed dissolved their future orientation and replaced it with a present orientation that excluded the prospect of getting caught as a dirty rotten scoundrel. In the end, they saw no further than the next earnings report.

Unlike Lay, Skilling, and the rest, Watkins saw the connection between the past, present, and future. She wanted her past success to have a positive effect on her personal future, not to destroy it. Other Enron executives' perspectives prevented them from seeing the connections even when Watkins drew them a map.[7]

Vladimir Lenin famously said, "The capitalists will sell us the rope with which we will hang them." Not only are capitalists greedy, he believed, they focus myopically on the present and are willing to focus on the small profit they gain from selling rope today over the possibility of being hanged with it tomorrow. In the Enron debacle, Enron, along with Wall Street and individual investors, sold each other rope. All were so focused on the present that they failed to see the future tightening around their collective necks. It is true that the leaders of Enron were guilty of fraud, but all knowledgeable investors were complicit in its collapse.

Our culture of instant gratification put tremendous pressure on Enron and other companies to perform. In itself, it is not a bad thing for public companies to be accountable to shareholders for their performance. But pressure to perform today reduces concern for the future consequences of that performance.[8] It is as though we decided to crown winners of marathons after each hundred-yard sprint, not after they've completed the full 26 miles, 385 yards. Nor is being interested primarily in sprint times a bad thing. That is why we have hundred-meter races. But if we are interested in performance over the longer term, focusing on sprint times may cause pulled muscles, fatigue, or loss of focus before the race is completed. Business and investing are actually racing marathons, but our culture generally treats them as though they were sprints.

Adopting a short-term perspective is not in the long-term best interest of corporate health or national economic well-being. A truly successful capitalism would focus on creating profitable businesses that serve the needs of society and its members over generations, not quarters. Greed-driven capitalism is self-serving and treats everyone else and the environment as expendable. It becomes a kind of administrative evil wherein bottom-line profit projections are the ends that justify the immoral and unethical means by which they are attained; the procedure is "anything goes," if the company's legal counsel can rationalize it.[9]

As we were writing this book, a debacle similar to Enron's occurred in the U.S. housing industry. Banks and mortgage companies tempted buyers with loans that were beyond their means to repay when rates increased. Thousands of people lost their homes to foreclosure for nonpayment. Many communities around the country suffered the loss of stable homeowners, and banks lost value and autonomy. Numerous executives lost their jobs for not having had clear knowledge of what the future of subprime lending would hold for their companies. The surveillance necessary to keep mortgage lenders in line was missing, allowing get-rich-quick schemes to trump prudent investment. Again, lack of balance between present and future orientations in both business and government is a well-worn path to disaster.

A SHORT HISTORY OF TIME IN BUSINESS

The relationship between time and business has been recognized for centuries, but only a little over one hundred years ago, Frederick Winslow Taylor, an American engineer, invented scientific management.[10] In conducting time and motion studies designed to increase worker efficiency, he aimed to squeeze as much productivity out of each working moment as possible. Over time his ideas fell out of favor, as workers felt that Taylor was on management's side in an effort to wring as much profit from labor as possible. This schism between workers and management persists today in what is left of American manufacturing.

With a markedly different approach a hundred years after Taylor, the Japanese automobile industry successfully overtook the American companies that pioneered the industry. Their team-oriented approach to making cars and trucks was adopted from the work of a leading American social psychologist, Kurt Lewin, whose research demonstrated the importance of each member of a workforce believing that she or he was contributing personally to a team production effort. Such an idea probably smacked of communism to the bosses at GM and Ford, a costly miscalculation.[11]

Early in the last century, Joseph Schumpeter, a famous Harvard economist, wrote that capitalism unleashes waves of destruction comparable to those of fifty-year floods. Most of the time, Schumpeter observed, businesses plug along smoothly.[12] Then, every fifty years or so, an entrepreneur-fueled wave of innovation sweeps through society. But as innovation destroys old practices, it leaves new ones in its wake.[13] Other economists and businesspeople maintain that the business cycle's timing is different, but most agree that understanding time is the key to understanding business. For example, Max Ways, the editor of *Fortune* magazine, proclaimed that the pace of change was "fifty times as great as the average pace of previous centuries." He said that in 1959![14] Unlike the destructive, present-oriented capitalism practiced by Enron, Schumpeter's creative destruction is healthy in the long run.

In the 1960s, leadership guru Warren Bennis and sociologist-turned-playwright Philip Slater wrote *The Temporary Society,* in which they argued that the pace of change would continue to accelerate until everything was temporary.[15] Substantial change that, in the past, had occurred only every fifty years or so was suddenly occurring constantly. Today we distinguish between Internet time and real time.[16] The waves of creative destruction and change described by Schumpeter and others have become so regular that they are now normal and permanent. Everything around us changes with astonishing speed. Schumpeter's staid fifty-year business cycle now occurs in seconds. Soon it will occur in nanoseconds.

Time as problem, time as part of the team, time as adversary, and time as a universal force and catalyst for change—in all these outlooks, time, money, and business are related. Yet today old views of time continue to dominate the economy. For example, scarcity is a fundamental concept in economic theory. The classical economic model posits that there are not enough resources to go around. The role of business and economic regulations is to allocate scarce resources among competing uses. Some economists have questioned the validity of the scarcity assumption of classical economics, including the Harvard economist John Kenneth Galbraith, who suggested that scarcity is no longer the defining characteristic of the post–World War II Western economy,[17] because many nations—surely those in the G8—have enough fundamental resources such as food and shelter. Indeed, we have a surplus of so many items that we rely on making goods "fashionable" to make them more desirable and thus maintain an artificial level of demand.[18] This has actually been the case for some time. For instance, Wedgwood dinnerware was one of the first manufacturers to realize that supply was outstripping demand. Early in its history, Wedgwood produced only a single style of dinnerware. This was problematic because once a wealthy family purchased a set, their need was satiated. To artificially inflate demand—and thus increase profits—Wedgwood launched a second style of dinnerware. Today we can see this in the proliferation of name brands and their diversification from, say, handbags as their core, to clothing, shoes, scents, and bedsheets.

Defenders of the classical position argue that if Galbraith had been right—if scarcity had been eliminated—the economy would have changed substantially, but it has not. Why not? One possible answer is that as visible resources have grown plentiful, another underappreciated resource—time—has actually become more scarce. Time is the most scarce of all resources, and its availability is constantly decreasing.

Imagine that you are an entrepreneur starting a business that will sell an innovative, even revolutionary, line of paperweights. Your initial resources are limited. Your capital consists of your great idea for a new kind of paperweight—your intellectual capital—and the five hundred dollars in your savings account. Labor consists of all the hard work that you can do yourself. Resources are scarce. A great idea, five hundred dollars, and one person are a start, but you obviously need more to succeed. So, what do you do? You probably look for investors, maybe even venture capitalists, to fund your business. Imagine that they like your idea. They write you a check for a million dollars, and, suddenly, resources aren't so scarce. You now have enough of everything you need to start your business.

You use the million dollars to buy raw materials and manufacturing equipment, and to pay people to run the equipment. Things are really starting to look up. You are three months from launching your new paperweights, and you begin to dream about buying a small Caribbean island with the money that you are sure to make. Then disaster strikes. You learn that another company is making the same kind of paperweights and that they are only *one month* from launch! You panic for a moment but remember that when you previously needed more scarce resources—money, raw materials, equipment, and labor—your venture-capitalist friends made them appear out of thin air. You talk to the venture capitalists and explain that you need more time, but they laugh at you. You think, If no one will give me time, then maybe I can buy it. You imagine going to a time store that sells time in packets like prepaid calling cards. You imagine that you will walk in and ask for two one-month cards and a couple of one-week cards just to be safe. Alas, there is no such store. We can trade for any other resource except time.

Time's pricelessness makes it the great equalizer. We all have to play the hand that time deals us. We cannot buy more cards or exchange the cards that we hold no matter who we are. We can learn, however, to play the hand that we are given more effectively, which we hope we are conveying in this book.

Selling You the Future

Predicting the success of businesses like our imaginary paperweight company is extremely difficult. Despite long odds, some people, like Warren Buffett, Peter Lynch, and Bill Gross, appear to be correct in predicting business successes and business cycles more often than not. Some forecasters probably do have special expertise that allows them to predict the future performance of businesses accurately, but others are undoubtedly the beneficiaries of chance. For example, let's assume that the chance of a financial adviser predicting whether a stock will move up or down is 60 percent.[19] Let's also assume that there are five hundred thousand financial advisers in the world and that they all make two independent judgments a year for ten years. In this scenario, eighteen financial advisers would be correct in their predictions 100 percent of the time simply due to chance. All eighteen would undoubtedly be featured on the cover of *Fortune* magazine. Given their extraordinary records, you may expect that their next stock pick would have close to 100 percent chance of also being correct. You may even be willing to pay these whiz kids a lot of money for their prediction. Don't do it. You would be wrong. The chance that their next stock pick will be correct is still 60 percent, on average. Sixty percent of the eighteen would be correct, and 40 percent would be incorrect. No one—not even the lucky—can escape the clutches of probability.[20]

Predicting the future is difficult, and no one can do it consistently.[21,22] That doesn't stop people from trying and trying to convince others that they can. Financial advisers do not make money only when investors make money. They also make money when you lose money. They make money whether their predictions about the future are accurate or not. It is interesting that financial advisers sell predictions and that they've rigged the system so they make money whether their predictions are accurate or not. Maybe they want all of us to benefit from their gifts as prognosticators, but they certainly realize that there is more money to be made in selling predictions than in investing themselves on the basis of their predictions. Rest assured that if they could predict the future, they would be relaxing on their own Caribbean islands, not trying to sell you a hot stock. Having made more than enough money from acting on their predictions, they would not need to make money selling them to you.

LEADERSHIP: CHANGING THE FUTURE

When Phil Zimbardo was just beginning his teaching career in the early 1960s, he invited Malcolm X, then a young activist, to address a psychology class at New York University. Here is the rest of the story in Phil's words:

> Even in our diverse academic environment, the tension of the sixties was palpable as the class began. Malcolm X had made national news by attacking "blue-eyed devils" and absentee property owners who he claimed were destroying the black community in Harlem. Many of those property owners, he had said, were Jews.
>
> After my brief introduction, the neatly dressed Malcolm rose from his seat and walked quietly to the podium, where he opened a worn book. He explained to the class that he was a religious man, and with the class's permission, he would like to begin with a brief prayer from the Koran. Surprised by his politeness and the nature of his request, the class, composed largely of Jewish students, quickly consented, and he began with a softly spoken prayer.
>
> Over the course of the next fifty minutes, Malcolm's speech became more and more passionate as he explained where he had been, who he was, and where he was going. What initially had been a hostile audience was transformed into an impassioned force united behind the activist's vision of the future. They were melted by his words. No one left the class feeling the same way about Malcolm X or about their own place in the world as when they had arrived. They

vowed to persuade their parents to think differently about Black
Pride. In fact, some students volunteered to spend part of their
summer vacation teaching in a Head Start–style program in Harlem
that I helped organize.

What was it about Malcolm X that made him such a charismatic,
powerful leader? Our work suggests that great leaders are able to
become completely engrossed in the present and to harness the passion they generate in the service of future goals. They have a unique
ability to be fully in the moment and to make an audience feel that
they are the exclusive focus of their attention. Then they use the
energy they generate by their present focus to create a compelling
vision of the future. Good orators, including evangelical ministers,
have that skill. They use vivid immediate images, a hypnotic cadence of speech, alliteration, and repetition of key terms and
phrases. Their present-tense verbs, "where it is" and "what is happening," move people to respond emotionally to their call and to
contribute to whatever cause they espouse.

When he met Bill Clinton, Phil became aware of a key ingredient in Clinton's charisma—the ability to narrow his focus and gaze
directly into the eyes of the person with whom he is engaged,
shutting out all else around him. It makes his listener feel special,
chosen—for a full forty-five seconds! Then Clinton's gaze shifts
past that one person to the next eager acolyte: "Good to meet you."
As his hand comes out of a goodbye shake, it slips smoothly into
the hello shake with the next person in line. Blinders go up to
block out the old contact, and he narrows his focus upon the new
contact. Suddenly, someone else is feeling special. Then, like clock-
work, that person's time is up, and Clinton moves on to work the
rest of the room. His time-management skill is central to his charisma. Everyone feels singled out, individuated, special for a frac-
tion of a minute. How else could Clinton and other celebrities
manage to interact with the hordes who want their attention other
than by parceling their precious, limited time into such mini-
moment meaningful contacts? If you think about it, isn't the ability to make others feel special under your gaze central to intimacy,

to being seen as charming—although the time you spend is longer than forty-five seconds.

The ability of powerful men to slip into a totally present-hedonistic persona can also have a downside. For instance, it makes some of them vulnerable to the temptation of casual sexual gratification, as we have seen in politicians at every level of government as well as in clergy. We can expect future leaders to suffer from similar weaknesses, the product of the poor time management and failures of conscience that are associated with present hedonism. Evolutionary psychologist David Buss tells us that in the mating game, over endless eons, the males of most species have opted for as many sexual conquests as they could manage, and alpha males get the pick of the harem. In contrast, females are always more future-oriented than males because their evolutionary plan is to select for mating with those males who would be the best providers for their offspring and offer the best genes for their success.[23] For the same reasons, young attractive women seek out older, even unattractive men for sex if they are rich and have resources that are associated with status. Former secretary of state Henry Kissinger, when he was questioned by the media about his attractiveness to so many beautiful women (given his appearance), offered the enduring remark "Power is the ultimate aphrodisiac."

Certain leaders' ability to charm goes far beyond attracting sexual partners, offering an attraction that captivates followers, according to the analysis of Jean Lipman-Blumen in *The Allure of Toxic Leaders*. Lipman-Blumen shows how and why we follow destructive bosses, like Enron's Kenneth Lay and Jeffrey Skilling, and those from WorldCom, Tyco International, Sunbeam, and other similarly corrupted corporations. She explores the reasons that we believe phony TV evangelists, are captivated by in-your-face media personalities, and are susceptible to the hypnotic allure of mass motivators and murderers like Adolf Hitler. To one degree or another, all fulfill a number of our basic psychological needs, and they are invariably people of action now, without concern for later consequences. Their appeal is the call of absolute power—and too many of us are fascinated by its dangerous allure.[24]

ENTREPRENEURSHIP

According to the management guru Peter Drucker, innovation is not just capturing lightning in a bottle. Innovation can be systematically pursued and found—if you know where to look. In *Innovation and Entrepreneurship*, Drucker tells us where to look,[25] identifying and ranking seven sources of innovation and entrepreneurial opportunity. First on his list was the unexpected. From Drucker's perspective, the unexpected occurs when the future doesn't turn out the way you thought it would. The unexpected can signal unexpected success or unexpected failure. Of the two types, unexpected success offers more opportunity, but unexpected failure also has its virtues. Louis Pasteur, the inventor of pasteurization, wrote that "Chance favors the prepared mind." When the unexpected chance event happens, it is more likely that future-oriented folks will understand what it means and how to capitalize on it, because they have already invested in education and have learned to focus on contingencies and causal thinking. They can quickly go from "Aha" to "So that's it," because they are prepared to take the new and put it in familiar old molds or create new ones that fit better.

Innovation Is Time's Baby

You've undoubtedly heard an invention described as "the best thing since sliced bread."[26] What you may not have done is to stop and think why the term is used. After all, what's so great about sliced bread? It didn't exist until 1928, and people seemed to get along fine without it. Slicing our own bread actually seems to be making something of a comeback, so it couldn't be that wonderful, could it?

If we do stop to think about what makes sliced bread so great, we find that it has two of the hallmarks of great inventions. First, sliced bread saves time. It's not a lot of time, but it is time that most people are happy to save. There is not much intrinsically rewarding about slicing bread. The second is more subtle: Slicing bread is an inexact science. When you do it yourself, you may wind up with parts of each slice that are paper-thin and other parts that are too thick. Slicing bread is so difficult to do that even if we gave you as much time as you wanted, you could probably never slice bread as well as a machine does. So, not only has sliced bread saved you the amount of time that you would have devoted to slicing bread, it has also saved you the considerable amount of time that you could have futilely devoted to slicing the bread perfectly. Sliced bread allows you to have something you could not have before—perfectly sliced bread.[27]

In allowing us to do new things, inventions take their toll on time. As we can do more and more new things, the toll becomes higher and higher. If the new things that we can do were always better than the old things, this might be acceptable. But they are not. As Stephen Covey has pointed out, urgent items on our to-do list push less urgent items down the list no matter how relatively important they are. Similarly, the ability to do new things pushes old things down the list—no matter how important or enjoyable those things were. Future goals can help us avoid the urgent-new trap. Once we've determined whether we want fame, fortune, happiness, excitement, quiet, comfort, some, or all of the above, then we can decide how best to spend our time achieving them.

TIME TRAPS

Some inventions allow us to do what we could not do before, or to do old things better, faster, more cheaply. Most of the time, this is good, but innovation and technology can have negative effects as well. For example, what if you loved to slice bread? Would you do it as frequently as you did before sliced bread became available? Probably not. There would probably be occasions when saving time would be more urgent than the pleasure derived from slicing it yourself. However, each of us has a fixed amount of time. Doing something new means doing less of something old. If this something old was not enjoyable, that is good. If the something old was enjoyable, that is not so good.

Inventions and technology can save us time, but they can consume it as well. It takes time to learn to use new technology, and it takes time to use it. That time could be spent on other activities.

For some, the time demands of technology are acceptable, even enjoyable. For others, technology is a useful tool whose time demands must be controlled. For still others, technology is an unnecessary distraction from what they love to do in the old-fashioned way.

As you read the following description of typical days in the lives of three very successful people, think about how they control technology, how technology controls them, and then please reflect on how technology fits in your life.

A Typical Workday for Musician Wynton Marsalis

In His Own Words[28] (artistic director, Jazz at Lincoln Center)

I have to do a lot of other work besides playing and composing—like speeches and fund-raising—but everything is for jazz. Even if I'm talking about American culture or American people, it's really about jazz. So it all goes to what my skill set is. I'm really not an organized person. For me, my philosophy is "Just do it all, all the time."

I've never sent an e-mail. I have a computer but haven't plugged it in. I do have a cell phone. I just learned how to text on it. I do everything longhand or talk it out with my staff, and then they type it.

The music is about improvising and being able to create new things at the spur of the moment with other people. There's not a long line of people who can do that in the context of a groove. To find a groove means practice, practice, and more practice. I'm very serious about this. We have the same system of understanding, the music, and a love between each other. It's a flow.

A Typical Workday for Executive Bill Gross

In His Own Words[29] *(chief investment officer, Pimco)*

I get up about four-thirty A.M. and check out the markets. I have a Bloomberg and a Telerate and some other machines downstairs. Bloomberg is the most important: You can get a review of the most recent New York play, or you can get a fifty-year currency history of the Brazilian real. It's amazing what you can access.

I check out Japan and Europe. I make myself some breakfast and then head off to work about five-forty-five A.M. and get into the office about six. The first hour or two are used for acclimating to the markets and various economic data releases. Lots of big, macro numbers—GDP, the unemployment number, other employment statistics—typically come out around five-thirty A.M. Pacific time.

For a portfolio manager, eliminating the noise is critical. You have to cut the information flow to a minimum level. You could spend your whole day reading different opinions. For me, that means I don't answer or look at any e-mails I don't want to. Other than for my wife, I'll only pick up the phone three or four times a day. I don't have a cell phone; I don't have a BlackBerry. My motto is "I don't want to be connected; I want to be disconnected."

The most important part of my day isn't on the trading floor. Every day at eight-thirty A.M., I get up from my desk and walk to a health club across the street. I do yoga and work out for probably an hour and a half, between eight-thirty and ten. I'm away from the office, away from the noise, away from the Bloomberg screens.

After about forty-five minutes of riding the exercise bike and maybe ten or fifteen minutes of yoga, all of a sudden some significant lightbulbs seem to turn on. I look at that hour and a half as the most valuable time of the day.

A Typical Workday for Executive Marissa Mayer

In Her Own Words[30] (vice president, search products and user experience, Google)

I don't feel overwhelmed with information. I really like it. I use Gmail for my personal e-mail—fifteen to twenty e-mails a day—but on my work e-mail, I get as many as seven to eight hundred a day, so I need something really fast. I do marathon e-mail catch-up sessions, sometimes on a Saturday or Sunday. I'll just sit down and do e-mail for ten to fourteen hours straight.

I'm very speed-sensitive. With TiVo, for example, I just seem to spend too much of my life looking at the PLEASE WAIT sign. I adore my cell phone, but there's just a second of delay when you answer it: Hello, hello?

I've been trying to figure out how to make time that was previously unproductive productive. If I'm driving my car somewhere, I try to get a call in to my family and friends then. Or during dead time when I'm waiting in line, I will hop on my cell phone and get something done.

In an average week, I'm getting scheduled into about seventy meetings, probably ten or eleven hours a day. On Friday, around six, I go up to San Francisco and do something interesting.

Each of these people is at the top of his/her profession. It's hard to imagine how any of them could be more successful. Yet the manner in which they live their lives and their attitudes toward time are very different. Which person do you feel uses time most wisely? Whose day does your typical day most resemble? Whose day would you most like to have? How does this make you feel? Your answers are telling.

If you are future-oriented, we expect that Marissa Mayer's description resonates best with you. Her life is the epitome of an American success story. She has gotten where she is through talent and hard work. She wears her e-mail load and long hours working as badges of pride. She describes her day in terms of numbers: numbers of e-mails received, numbers of hours worked, and numbers of seconds waited. Her weeks, days, minutes, and seconds are planned. Every second counts. For her, unproductive time is wasted time. The old time-and-motion man Frederick Winslow Taylor would be proud of Marissa.

If you are present-oriented, we expect that you identified most strongly with Wynton Marsalis, who is an American success story as well, though one who succeeded not because of his ability to work long hours in pursuit of future goals but because of his ability to lose himself completely in the music of the present. Wynton describes his day in terms of his passion—jazz. As in jazz, much of his life is im-provised. He just does it, all of the time. He is so immersed in the flow of his craft that he has not bothered to learn the tools of future orientation, such as computers, e-mail, and scheduling. However, his talent polished by long hours of practice has put Wynton in a posi-tion where he can hire others to deal with his appointments, e-mails, and the other sundry future-oriented details of everyday life.

Bill Gross's attitudes toward time are a pragmatic cross between Wynton's and Marissa's. Like Marissa, Bill works long hours and describes his day in terms of numbers. However, unlike Marissa, Bill very consciously takes time to disconnect himself from "the matrix" so that he, like Wynton, can get into the flow through yoga. For Bill, technology is a necessary and extremely useful tool, but he recognizes that it can take him only so far. Technology—and de-voting time to it—is a means, not an end.

Life and business are marathons. Like the first Greek marathon runner, all people and many businesses die at the end of the race. However, between now and the end, because you can do new things does not mean that you should or must do them. Evaluate how you use your time in terms of both present and future goals. What do you want today, what do you want tomorrow, and how can you best balance the two? Quarterly earnings do matter, but so does staying out of jail. Focusing solely on the present may lead us to our own personal bankruptcy. Focusing solely on the future may encourage us to put the new and the novel before simple enjoyment and happi-ness. Recall those successful middle managers we introduced in

Chapter Five who said that despite their status and material wealth, their personal lives were empty. Who wants that written on his gravestone? Ask yourself what you want to do today. How do you want to spend this weekend? Don't ask what tasks you have to do today or what obligations you must meet before you can take time to enjoy yourself. Continually ask the big questions: What do I really want out of my life? What am I doing to get what I want? What is the best way to get from here to there?

THE POLITICS OF TIME

As a society, we largely avoid political discussions in polite conversation, reserving them for relationships that can withstand a knock-down-drag-out fight—or with people whom we are actively working to alienate. If you're like us, you learned this lesson slowly and still forget it occasionally. You have also undoubtedly left an animated political "discussion" thinking two things about people at the other end of the political spectrum. The first is: Can they really believe that? The bad thinking behind others' beliefs often dismays us. How can they be so blind to the obvious? Their beliefs are clearly not rational, not logical, and perhaps not even sane.

We also think: How can they fail to see the logic and morality inherent in my position, which I elaborated so cogently? If someone laid out the evidence as clearly for us—we think—we would have to adopt his or her political opinions. And we would do it gratefully! In the end, we are surprised by our antagonists' naïveté if not outright stupidity when they remain unimpressed by the brilliance and rightness of our position. Of course, they are thinking the same thing about us.

Why are political discussions so consistently unproductive? Although there is little research on this topic, we think that time has an unrecognized effect on political issues and political debate. Understanding this effect allows us insight into our own and others' political positions and may offer opportunity for resolving conflict.

Conflicting time perspectives lie at the heart of the political process. In 1979 the psychologists Daniel Kahneman[31] and Amos

Tversky published a simple but interesting finding about how views of the present and expectations of the future influence choice. To illustrate their theory—which they called Prospect Theory—they asked participants to imagine losing a bet for a hundred dollars on the flip of a fair coin. You chose heads, and the coin came up tails. The friend to whom you lost the bet offers you a second bet—double or nothing on the flip of the same coin. If you accept the bet and you call the coin incorrectly, you will owe your friend two hundred dollars. If you accept the bet and call the coin correctly, you will owe your friend nothing. You have a 50 percent chance of owing two hundred dollars and a 50 percent chance of owing nothing if you accept the second bet. The expected utility of the second bet is thus minus a hundred dollars,[32] which is exactly what you owed your friend after the first bet. Because the expected outcome of accepting and not accepting the second bet is the same (minus a hundred), you should be as likely to accept the new bet as you are to reject it. In theory, you should be indifferent to accepting or refusing the second bet. In practice, you are not indifferent. You are very likely to accept the second bet. You are more likely to accept the risk of owing two hundred dollars rather than accept the certain loss of a hundred dollars.

In this example, the present is framed as a loss from the first bet. You lost a hundred dollars. The future contains two possible outcomes, each of which has an equal probability of occurring. Kahneman and Tversky showed that people prefer to take risks rather than accept certain losses. In Kahneman and Tversky's words, people are risk-seeking in the domain of losses.

Now let's imagine that you won the first hundred-dollar bet. Your friend who lost the bet then asks you to bet double or nothing. If you accept the second bet now, there is a 50 percent chance that you will win two hundred dollars and a 50 percent chance that you will win nothing. The expected possible outcome of the bet is again equal, a hundred dollars. Because the expected utility of the new bet equals the value of the bet that you previously won, you should be as likely to accept the new bet as you are to reject it. In theory, you should be indifferent to accepting or rejecting the second bet.

In practice, once again, you are not indifferent. You are likely to reject the second bet.

In this example, the present is framed as a gain from the first bet. You won a hundred dollars. The future is framed as containing two possible outcomes. Again, each outcome has an equal probability of occurring. Kahneman and Tversky showed that people are generally risk-aversive in the domain of gains. This means that people avoid risk after having secured a sure gain.

In their study, Kahneman and Tversky created an artificial situation in which people had an almost perfect understanding of the present and the future, i.e., they knew they had just won or lost a hundred dollar.[33] "Winners" and "losers" then faced a choice regarding an uncertain future. Despite the uncertainty, people knew the exact probability of the only two possible future outcomes: heads or tails. They also knew the consequences of these outcomes. If they rejected the bet, their state would not change. If they accepted the bet, they would end up a hundred dollar richer or poorer than they started.

In life, decisions are seldom this clear. One day we feel like a winner and are willing to take risks; the next day we feel like a loser and avoid taking more risks—even though our objective circumstances may not have changed. Our present state depends on how we reconstruct the past, interpret the present, and construct the future. Through the lens of time perspective, we frame the present around us. Through time perspective, we frame ourselves. As a result, we may frame a decision as a loss one day and as a gain the next.

The future in the researchers' study is also very different from the future in life. Seldom are we faced with the simple choice of accepting or declining an offer; seldom are there only two possible outcomes of our decision; and seldom do we know the exact probability of these outcomes occurring. In life, even simple decisions have more than two possible outcomes. We are forced to construct the future on our own. We may have vague ideas about probabilities, but we almost never know them. In life, the way we reconstruct the past, interpret the present, and construct the future affects the way we frame the present as well as the expectations that we form for the future.

Experienced voters know that casting a ballot is all too similar to betting on the flip of a coin. Unlike Kahneman and Tversky's studies, where participants had perfect knowledge of the present and the future, we are faced with election decisions that are complicated and clouded by emotion, propaganda, disinformation, and uncertainty. Politicians, political parties, and special-interest groups are not sympathetic to the voter's plight. In an effort to manipulate voters, they complicate what is already a complex task.

When we are engaged in the political process, the first step is to frame the present as a gain or a loss. When politicians want to frame it as a gain, they talk about how much better things are now than they used to be. Framing the present as a gain increases the likelihood of a vote for the status quo favoring those who are supposedly responsible for these gains. This tactic appeals most to past-oriented voters. To frame the present as a loss, on the other hand, politicians talk about how much worse things are now than they used to be. Framing the present as a loss increases the likelihood of a vote for change and for the party that is not responsible for the losses. This tactic appeals most to present- and future-oriented voters.

The second step is to manipulate the probability and certainty of the future. Greater uncertainty increases the threat of risk and enhances risk aversion. Uncertainty increases the likelihood of a vote for the status quo. Greater certainty decreases risk as a threat and enhances risk-seeking. Certainty increases the likelihood of a vote for change.

The majority party and incumbents seek to frame the present as a gain and to point out the uncertainty of the future as it will be if their opponents seize control. They want people to view a vote for incumbents as ensuring gain and a vote for challengers as a risky move with potentially disastrous consequences. Scare tactics increase the threat of the potentially disastrous consequences. The minority party and challengers seek to frame the present as a loss and to point out the certainty of a bright future with them at the helm. They want people to view a vote for the incumbents as ensuring loss and a vote for challengers as a low risk worth taking.

Table 1: Prospect Theory, Politics, Time, and Strategy

		Time Zone		Likely Vote
		Present	Future	
Candidate	Incumbent	Frame as gain	Stress uncertainty	For status quo
	Challenger	Frame as loss	Stress certainty	For change

Bill Clinton won the 1992 presidential election with the campaign slogan "Don't stop thinking about tomorrow." George W. Bush won the 2004 presidential election in part by appealing to voters' needs for consistency, for maintaining his party's status quo in fighting "the global war on terrorism." Various speeches echoed the theme of the foolishness of changing horses midstream. His opponent, John Kerry, was depicted as inconsistent, as "flip-flopping" on various issues. Kerry never managed to offer a viable frame for a future that would be brighter with him running the show than his adversary's.

Consider the basis for the impact that President John F. Kennedy's appeal to his nation's citizens had: Stop asking what the government can do for you, and start asking what you can do for your government. It shifted the focus of the election from the present to the future. It moved people away from complaining about inequities and injustice and the inadequacy of the welfare system toward envisioning the ways that their personal actions could create a better future for their country. It mobilized many young people to join the Peace Corps, just as the powerful "I have a dream" speech of Martin Luther King, Jr., inspired young and old with the vision of a future that they could help create filled with brotherhood, compassion, and human dignity.

Environmental Politics

Conservation of limited natural resources is an issue of global concern, yet often people fail to see the need to protect the environment for future generations. Instead, they selfishly exploit and exhaust it. We authors believe that the world's most precious resource is actually not oil for energy but water for drinking. There is simply not enough of it, and, as population explodes in many countries, there will be conflicts over the ownership of and access to water.

A recent study in Mexico highlights the contrasting roles of present versus future orientation in regard to water conservation. Three hundred Mexican citizens completed the ZTPI and reported on how frequently they engaged in various water conservation practices.

The results are in line with what you would predict. Those who had past orientations did not engage in or concern themselves with water conservation. Pro-environmental practices were significantly and positively related to future orientation. Presents were least likely to practice water conservation. Future orientation increased with number of years of schooling and for people over age eighteen.[34] However, in many countries around the world, education is limited, and the demographics favor a population of youth over the elderly, which makes for a dominant present orientation and failure to conserve natural resources. Addressing this issue may require the development of new and different conservation appeals designed to target present-oriented citizens.

LEARNING TIME PERSPECTIVE THE PRUSSIAN WAY

Each of us filters political information and disinformation through our own time perspective: the information and disinformation are created partly by an educational system whose development was instigated by politicians and continues to be dominated by governments. Consequently, the great circle of time perspective is complete. Governments create institutions that teach time perspective. People then vote in ways that sustain the government and the institutions that it created.

It has not always been so. In 1852 the Massachusetts governor Edward Everett recognized an emerging need to teach children to be productive members of a rapidly industrializing society. For advice, Everett turned to a lawyer named Horace Mann, secretary of the Massachusetts Board of Education. Mann had traveled the world evaluating educational systems and recommended implementing the Prussian educational system, which consisted of eight years of compulsory education centering on academics and character. Academic subjects included reading, writing, and arithmetic. Character lessons focused on discipline, morality, and obedience. Although generations of American schoolchildren have grown to loathe Mann's recommendation, it was brilliant for its time.

Everett's goal was not to educate generations of freethinkers but rather to prepare America's huddled masses for a lifetime of factory work. Chief among the skills required for successful factory work are punctuality, obedience, and a remarkable tolerance for monotony and boredom. The Prussian educational system produced these "skills" with military precision.

When they enter school, most children go from a free-form day, where they can play and think as they wish, to having a teacher, class schedule, and work. Schedules and time begin to rule their lives. They learn that being late is bad, that they can have fun only some of the time, that recess is only twenty minutes long, and that they must go home every day at the same time. They also learn that no matter how quickly or slowly they work, they cannot escape days, weeks, and years of schooling. Regimentation is the name of this game, and lessons prepare them for life in a factory. How well these lessons prepare them for life outside of the factory or indeed an almost factoryless society is another story.

The primary function of our educational system is the domestication of present-hedonistic children and transformation of them into future-oriented adults ready to assume their place on the factory line. School breaks present-hedonistic children from their "wild" sense of time and replaces it with a more civilized future orientation that ensures their behavior can be predicted and controlled in line with the rest of society's. Education today is as much about what children forget about playfulness and spontaneity as it is about what they learn. Stay in your seat, don't talk, don't play, don't act out, delay gratification, obey authority, and tolerate boredom. These are some of the main lessons ingrained by traditional schooling.

For many, our educational system works. Most people learn future orientation and become productive members of society. They show up for work on time, pay bills on time, and plan for retirement. For others, the system does not work. They rebel against the boring tasks and the regimentation. Without future orientation to temper their desires, they revert to the present hedonism of childhood. The perils of present orientation lure them into drugs, alcohol, unsafe sex, unwanted pregnancy, risk-taking, bankruptcy, and crime.

The problems associated with not learning a future orientation are obvious, but the solutions to them are not. To begin with, people who suffer from excessive present focus often neither identify their conditions nor desire treatment of them. Their lives are just the way they are. Futures, in contrast, identify their problems and seek to eliminate the causes. From their future-oriented perspective, the sources of the problems are decisions that have failed to anticipate the possible negative future consequences of behaviors. The answer for them, therefore, is simply to point out the negative future consequences of certain behaviors. Future-oriented groups such as Planned Parenthood spend countless hours and dollars developing educational programs that are designed to teach presents the relationship between their current behavior and its negative future consequences: If you have unsafe sex, then you may have a baby nine months later or a sexually transmitted disease at any time.

The logic of these programs is unassailable, and if a future-oriented person went through them, the programs would undoubtedly have the desired effect. Unfortunately, the people who enter these programs and could benefit most from them are predominantly present-oriented. By definition, they do not have strong future time perspectives. At community schools in San Mateo, California, for instance, we found that students were primarily present-oriented. We taught fifty students a two-week program in mental stimulation, a technical name for mentally rehearsing and visualizing yourself performing an action. In other words, we encouraged these kids to imagine scenarios in which they might act in the future.

Then John visited two classes every day for two weeks and led them in mental simulation exercises. Each selected a personal goal and imagined the thoughts, feelings, and actions that would be associated with reaching that goal. Initially, the goal they chose was to be achieved the next day; on subsequent days, the goal was extended progressively further into the future: next week, next month, six months, one year, five years, ten years, and twenty-five years ahead. A comparison group also learned the mental simulation techniques but did not participate in these daily exercises. Over the course of the two-week program, one student overdosed, one ran away, and one dropped out of school completely.

The changes recorded in those students who had both visualized and rehearsed reaching their goals were profound. Ill-defined and unrealistic goals—becoming a brain surgeon, a rock star, or an NBA superstar—were replaced by specific, well-defined goals that they could reasonably meet, such as getting a GED, staying out of jail, and going back to regular high school. Their estimates of the probability that they would reach three of their chosen life goals were significantly associated with their new future orientation.[35]

We found other, less quantifiable changes in the students' attitudes toward time, such as these touching quotes below taken from a debriefing session after the study. Students wrote: "At first, I did not understand what this mental simulation was about. But it has helped me achieve one of my most important goals, staying out of jail. It has been fun" and "I set a goal and it came true. That never happened before."[36]

Programs that stress the negative future consequences of present actions have minimal impact on presents' behavior because thinking about the future has minimal impact on them. Futures, in contrast, have learned to recognize these connections and thus have not developed the problems of addiction. Applied to futures, the programs are preaching to the already saved.

Traditional programs that are designed to instill future orientation are marginally effective at best. For example, six separate studies that evaluated the long-term success of the Drug and Alcohol Resistance and Education (DARE) program found that children who had gone through the DARE program used drugs and alcohol just as much as children who had not gone through the program.[37] There are two possible ways to improve such programs. The first is to develop behavioral-change programs that are not dependent on participants' possessing a future orientation. These programs would work solely through the present to modify behavior. The absence of these types of programs today probably reflects the future orientation of the people who are likely to create and evaluate behavior-change programs.

The second way is to teach people a future orientation so they become amenable to traditional behavioral-change programs. This does not mean teaching them how to work a nine-to-five job five days a week for the rest of their lives. It does mean instilling a degree of future orientation sufficient for people to understand the negative consequences of common behavior. It means teaching them about contingencies, causalities, and the delay of gratification, as well as planning, goal-setting, and self-rewarding for the achievement of objectives and self-censure for the violation of social norms and moral codes. The program should be a process of socialization that has not been fully internalized by those who are primarily presents.

There will be a need for such public educational programs to address the development of new future consequences—as there was during the 1980s, when the connection between unsafe sex and AIDS was first discovered. For the most part, however, people will learn to make such associations only as they learn to adopt a future time perspective.

Cruel and Unusual Punishments

For people who possess both a present hedonism and a future time perspective, the future acts as a brake on their hedonistic impulses. People who are high on present hedonism and low on future time perspective have all gas and no brake. They break laws, conventions, and expectations because they have no concept of the future. For them there are no if-then relationships, only if relationships. Presents commit crimes because they have never learned a future time perspective, or because, like Lay and Skilling, they have let their future time perspective wither away or hide.

As a society, we impose future-oriented punishments on present-oriented criminals. When people commit crimes, we punish them by taking away time from their futures. We send them to time-outs in prisons. For the future-oriented, the threat of doing hard time is undoubtedly a deterrent. For presents, however, the threat of jail time is unlikely to matter.[38] When a person does not have a concept of the future or believes there is no future for him, the future cannot be taken from him.

Our criminal justice system is ill equipped to deal with presents. Almost all traditional behavioral-change programs suffer from a similar "made by futures for futures" syndrome. We live in a world created by futures for futures, and the devil take the hindmost—the presents.

As a concrete example of how present orientation results in discrimination, consider the effect of welfare and social support time limits. Alameda County, in the San Francisco Bay Area, is considering limiting general assistance payments to six months during any twelve-month period.[39] Thirty-three other California counties already limit support. From a future-oriented perspective, the move makes perfect sense. We authors predict that time limits will have little impact on futures, because the few of them who need assistance get off general assistance as quickly as possible. From a present-oriented perspective, it's clear that the move is likely to hurt those presents who most need help. We predict that such time limits will save the government money, but they will not help presents get themselves off assistance. Because presents are less likely to respond to time limits quickly, we can expect that such governmental programs will have a higher percentage of presents whose assistance will be terminated than futures.

The solution to this problem is obviously much more complex than simply extending assistance benefits indefinitely. A simple first step in solving this and similar problems may be to recognize that presents are more likely to need assistance in the first place. They are less likely to have saved for a rainy day and are therefore more likely to rely on a safety net. A second step may be to recognize that time limits create a situation in which the presents who most need help are the least likely to be well served. In essence, presents are being penalized twice. Their present orientation may have led to their problems in the first place, and the help that they are offered to address their problems targets the motivational style of futures. In short, we must come to realize that one size does not fit all in our public assistance programs or remedial public education campaigns.

Presents may be the invisible men and women of the twenty-first century, whereas futures of both sexes, all races and nationalities live and play by the rules of time. Presents do not. Like Ralph Ellison's "invisible man," the person of color who is ignored by the dominant white society, presents are socially invisible. Futures talk over, under, around, and through the present-oriented denizens of this world. The discrimination faced by presents is pervasive and woven into the fabric of society. For instance, if you asked most American businesspeople whether they would hire someone who was fifteen minutes late for an interview, the vast majority would say no. Yet in many parts of the world, being fifteen minutes late is considered on time. Unlike Ellison's invisible man, presents cannot look to the darker color of their skin for an answer to why they did not get the job. Some presents may not be aware that they are invisible people in a future-oriented society. Time influences our personal, social, business, and political lives. We must begin to acknowledge that and to investigate what we can do to make our attitudes toward time work better for us individually and collectively.

eleven

RESETTING YOUR PSYCHOLOGICAL CLOCK
Developing Your Ideal Time Perspective

Time stays long enough for anyone who will use it.
—Leonardo da Vinci

To achieve great things, two things are needed; a plan, and not quite enough time.
—Leonard Bernstein

Our task in this chapter is to provide guidelines that will help you develop an ideal, balanced time perspective and allow you to live a longer, fuller, more successful, and happier life. Before we begin, you must decide if you really want to change something so basic to your everyday functioning. Changing your attitudes toward time will not be easy. It took years for you to learn your time perspective, and you cannot change it overnight. But you can begin now and make progress.

Our approach is to accentuate the positives and eliminate the negatives. First, we'll show you what an optimally balanced time perspective would look like, and why we think it is fundamental to an effective lifestyle. Then we'll discuss the challenges that you must face when you are trying to modify your perspective. Finally, we'll provide some general strategies and specific tactics for helping you contain the excesses of extreme time perspectives by incorporating some of the best things from the other time perspectives into your own. We'll help you embrace and benefit from the paradox of time.

Before we begin, please understand that we are *not* going to give advice on time management. There are already dozens of self-help books that have as their sole purpose enabling futures to achieve more by better scheduling their limited time. They teach ways in which to do more in less time, stressing goals and subgoals, making to-do lists, checking off the did-thats in tiny boxes on one's day planner or Palm. Presents and pasts do not have to-do lists. They have doing and did lists. So those books are helpful to only a small percentage of people and may actually do more harm than good by encouraging an even greater focus on the future for the future-oriented.

Some time management books suggest that you have to set goals in order to climb the ladder of success. Without a plan, you might reach the top of the ladder and realize that you have your ladder against the wrong wall. We agree that the sooner you can identify personal goals, the better, but we also believe that there is value in climbing for its own sake. You never can tell what you'll be able to see from the top.

Before you manage your time by assigning activities and goals to calendar boxes, you want to understand what to put in those boxes. You need to assess the direction that you want to take and the steps you must take on the path to your goals. Equally important, you need to stop the rush of your daily existence from time to time to determine whether other paths might be better for you.

AN OPTIMAL BLEND OF TIME PERSPECTIVES

Your time perspective biases you. It can put blinders on your eyes, plugs in your ears, and barriers around your mind, depriving you of fully appreciating who you are and what you could become. It causes you to see everything through one lens, which can prevent you from learning from the past, enjoying the present, and planning for the future. On the other hand, a balanced, flexible time perspective that allows you to choose the time perspective most appropriate for each situation can open your eyes to the full range of human experience. Depending on the demands of a particular situation, one time perspective must take precedence, while the others may temporarily recede. When you have work to finish, the future time perspective must come to the forefront. When your work is done and it is time for pleasure, the present-hedonistic time perspective will surface. During the holidays, the past-positive time perspective may be most appropriate for preparing you to enjoy family customs.

Given the research we have done—and acknowledging our inherent bias as residents in the Western world—we believe that the optimal time perspective profile is:

- High in past-positive time perspective

- Moderately high in future time perspective

- Moderately high in present-hedonistic time perspective

- Low in past-negative time perspective

- Low in present-fatalistic time perspective

This blend offers three critical advantages:

A sense of a positive past gives you *roots*. The center of self-affirmation, the past connects you to yourself over time and across place. A positive past grounds you, provides a sense of the continuity of life, and allows you to be connected to family, tradition, and your cultural inheritance.

With a future perspective, you can envision a future filled with hope, optimism, and power. The future gives you *wings* that enable you to soar to new destinations and to be confident in your ability to deal with the unexpected challenges that you might encounter on the way. It equips you to escape the status quo, the fear inherent in straying from the safe, known ways, the well-traveled roads to your destination.

A hedonistic present gives you *energy* and joy about being alive. That energy drives you to explore people, places, and self. Present hedonism is life-affirming, in moderation, for it opens the senses to appreciation of nature and the pleasure of human sexuality.

The ideal time perspective is low on past-negative and present-fatalistic time perspectives. Our research suggests that nothing good comes out of them. New research makes evident that time-perspective biases emphasizing a negative past or a fatalistic present put people at risk for both mental and physical illness. A study of Dutch-speaking young adults compared a psychiatric group in clinical treatment with normal participants who did not receive treatment. All completed the ZTPI along with a battery of standard personality and other tests. Psychiatric patients were significantly more likely than normal people to be high on past-negative and present-fatalistic time perspectives. Patients were also lower on the past-positive time perspective. These time perspectives "appear to be fairly good predictors" of problems, according to the research investigator,[1] including neuroticism, lack of self-control and personal responsibility, and difficulty with interpersonal relationships. As with present fatalism, the past-negative time perspective was also a significant predictor of suicide and the tendency toward suicidal thinking.

A British study found these two time orientations to be similarly linked to a low sense of self-actualization, low levels of positive outlook and expectations, and high levels of negative outlook and expectations.[2] On the other side of the Atlantic, recent research on how patients adapt to live with the chronic illness Type 1 insulin-dependent diabetes also indicates the influence of time-perspective factors.[3] Anxiety, depression, and anger of the mostly female participants were also associated with negative past perceptions and present fatalism. Patients who adapted well had positive perceptions of the present and an expanded view of the future. They actively avoided negative thoughts about the present and their situation. Patients who can work on their negative perceptions of the past and present and adopt more of a future time orientation cope more successfully with their medical conditions.

Later on, we will present some ways to convert negative perceptions of the past into more neutral or even positive views. Before exploring how you can make such constructive changes, we want to tell this personal story.

"Going South"

It was common during the late 1960s and early 1970s in California to see young hippies hitchhiking at intersections. Part of the rock-and-roll flower-child generation, they would hold up hand-lettered signs indicating where they wanted to go, and usually, they would be picked up and transported some or all the way there. Most signs asked for short rides to the next town, but some were more ambitious—CANADA, ANYONE? or MEXICO, AMIGO?

One day, on his hour-long journey from San Francisco to Stanford, Phil picked up a young man whose sign read simply GOING SOUTH. Here is the rest of the story in Phil's words:

"Mo," short for Moses, jumped into the front seat of my Mercedes-Benz convertible; his huge backpack and equally huge Labrador retriever filled the tight backseat. He had stopped out of a local community college to check out the "happening action." After we talked a bit, Mo asked if he could smoke. "Sure, why not?" I replied, not realizing that meant smoking a joint. I politely turned down the generous offer to share the smoke, but I was curious about where he was going.

"How far are you headed? I only go to Palo Alto," I said.

"That'll do me fine," replied Mo.

"Going to Santa Cruz?"

"No, just south."

"All the way to Los Angeles?"

"No, just south."

"Are you going as far as Mexico? I hope to go there someday."

"Nope, only headed south."

I realized I was getting upset by these evasive answers from someone who claimed he wanted to live his life transparently, like an open book. When we got to the Stanford exit on Highway 101, I told my passenger to "just get out here."

"Hey, man, why are you being so uncool?"

"Look, I let you smoke dope, for which I could get in trouble; gave you and your dog a ride; and you refuse to tell me where you are going, and—"

"Oh, now I get it. You think I'm going *somewhere,* and you don't understand that I'm just going anywhere, as long as it's going south. I'm not headed to any destination, to any particular place, because I might not get rides to take me there. Then I'd be frustrated, and who wants to carry that mental load around? Not me. So by going only in a general direction, I am never upset if I get only a short ride, as long as it's headed south. You've made my day already by taking me this far. If I got no farther, I'd be happy, because now I am where I was headed—south, you see?"

"Yeah, I see," I said, "but out anyway!"

"Mister, thanks for the ride and your time. Have a good life, starting today."

Afterward, as I reflected on the deeper meaning of this experience, I realized that in my excessively future-oriented world, I went only to specific places, to standard destinations, for particular purposes. I could not imagine heading out without a travel plan, without having made reservations in advance. My irritation actually shifted to envy of this kid who could just up and go, who could just "waste time" without any plan in hand. Then I felt admiration for a person who was able to enjoy the trip fully by not fixating on getting to a given destination. He was all about *process.* I also acknowledged that I myself had stopped taking the time to smell the proverbial roses because I never even noticed them anymore. I found myself longing to be a kid again, to put off appointments, to dump my to-do lists, and mark all my many commitments as "later."

The aftermath of this revelation was the hypnotherapy session described in Chapter Five that allowed Phil to experience being in the expanded present and to allow future and past concerns to be distant and remote. He followed up on his personal experience with formal research on liberating behavior from time-bound controls. Both personally and academically, he showed that someone who is future-oriented can become more present-oriented. Before giving other examples of this kind of successful change, we will add another from Phil.

From that day three decades ago, whenever I get uptight thinking of all my obligations, I close my eyes, touch my thumbs to forefingers, and say, "I am going south." That simple gesture puts things in balance and perspective. It reminds me to take time out of my endless quest for The Next—to get a massage, call an old friend, enjoy a cappuccino in a local café, or prepare a candlelit dinner at home.

Changing Time Perspectives

Not everyone agrees with our belief that time perspectives are learned and therefore modifiable. Some psychologists argue that the ability to conceptualize the future is genetically determined and difficult or impossible to change.[4] A similar point of view has been expressed by the old elitist we met in Chapter Four, Edward Banfield, who labeled the present orientation of the poor "pathological." If Banfield is right, we have all been pathological at one point: when we were present-hedonistic children. Banfield does not think that anything can save the poor from poverty, because their chronic present orientation is tantamount to an immutable life sentence.[5]

We are more optimistic about the possibility of changing attitudes toward time as well as the behaviors associated with them. Phil's research on curing shyness in adults and adolescents, and his extensive writing on social influence and attitude change, lead us to believe that most people can change their attitudes and behavior when they are sufficiently motivated to do so and are taught or shown how. Remember the present-oriented kids in the last chapter who learned mental simulation to help them become future-oriented. Also called visualization and in some cases affirmation, this can be a highly effective method of change.[6]

RESETTING YOUR TIME PERSPECTIVE CLOCK

Moderating Future Intensity

Much that is good about being future-oriented becomes negative when you overuse it. Are you endlessly competitive? Have you willingly sacrificed your circle of friends, family, and neighbors to success in the future? Are you locked in to an ever more compressed time crunch that is squeezing the juice out of life? If so, you are overinvested in the future.

Here are some tips for balancing your time perspective.

First, you need to do *less*, not more. When a pollster calls to ask you how busy you are, we want you to be able to say, "Less busy this year than last." That means practicing saying, "No, thanks. I can't take that on." It also means that when you make your to-do list, you discard all those things at the bottom of the list and do not add anything new until you are rid of one or more of the old.

You make conscious choices about what you *must* do and decide what is really so important that it cannot be put on the back burner. Your aim is to slim down your commitments and obligations. Eliminate as much as you can until you are in a comfort zone. The pruning may influence your sense of self, which you no doubt established in grade school, as a high performer, but you can use your skills and talents well when you do not stretch them too thinly across myriad activities. Start to do more by doing less. Throw out the trash. Clean your closets of worn-out working garments. Stop going to events you don't like.

Ralph Keyes, in his analysis of the hectic life, *Timelock*, informs us that "Trying to increase one's menu of possibilities contributes to overchoice, a key source of timelock. Reducing the range of options makes it possible to narrow one's focus and concentrate better."[7]

As a future, you should practice giving and graciously receiving the *gift of time*. Time is your most precious possession, so give it to others, especially those you care about, when they can most appreciate it. And give some of that precious time to yourself as downtime, play time, fun time, exercise time, indulgence time, being-a-kid-again time. Try to reserve at least one weekend day as a workless day. Don't forget to disconnect once in a while.

On an ordinary day, try to minimize the intrusion of work into your home life. Work carried around in 24/7 portable portfolios can devour your time. Keyes reminds us of an obvious truth that most futures ignore: "We chose to rush and be busy. We can choose to slow down and cut back. This is in our power. But making such a choice is not easy."

Start simply: Do not drive in the fast lane. Take the time to say, "Hello, goodbye, ciao, good morning, lovely day, and enjoy the holiday." Listen to what people say in reply. Look at yourself in the mirror and vow to balance what is best in your future orientation with what is good in a revived positive-past and vibrant present-hedonistic perspective. When you do work, find the *flow* within the activity, the pleasure of intrinsic motivation that transforms what you *have* to do into what you *want* to do.

Moderating Present Intensity

Your present energy is wonderfully contagious. Others love to be around you. However, unfocused energy disrupts discipline and organization and is often wasted. Your adventurous nature leads you to venture everywhere and to take risks that others avoid. You rush in where angels fear to tread. Then you die or go broke.

If ever moderation is a virtue, it is surely so for hedonists. Turning down the volume allows you to hear the lyrics. Developing the cerebral muscle you need to resist temptation grants you immunity from mindless, seductive actions. Learning that the house always wins may help you to temper your attraction to gambling. If you live fast and die young, your corpse is unlikely to be good-looking, despite what you may have heard.

As a successful hedonist, you are a role model for overextended futures and stagnant pasts. You demonstrate the virtues of sensuality, emotion, and curiosity. Tempering your hedonism with a dose of the holistic present will put you in touch not only with your feelings but also with your inner wisdom. Your focus on the here and now needs to be broadened to incorporate the there and then. Embrace periods of boredom as times to look within and create new fantasies and imagine scenarios of possible roles you might play in the future drama of your life. Finally, being a leading actor is good, but becoming a director or scriptwriter is better. It puts you in charge of the whole show and allows you to design a happy ending.

Reconstructing Past Negative

If you suffer recurrent depression, you may have a past-negative time perspective, which attributes global significance to the negative events in your life. You blame yourself for everything. You do not identify the specific events that caused you pain but, rather, find failure and impossible hurdles everywhere. Your negative past focus makes you vulnerable to depressive ruminative cycles.

You want to reconstruct past negative experiences and either neutralize them or discover some hidden positive elements in them. Whenever you find yourself replaying the familiar old slides of past negative experiences, make yourself take out those slides and insert new slides into your memory tray. These new slides can come from your recollection of recent positive events and emotions that you also experienced. Practice viewing your new positive-only personal slide show to flood the dreary old past with a bright light of optimism. By doing this, you provide yourself with an encouraging perspective on current experiences that will lead to a better future.

In this time-perspective reconstruction therapy, you don't just recall some good experiences to offset the bad ones. You are reweaving your past from the vibrant fabric of the present. You mentally alter the past to be what you would have liked to happen, what should have been, or might have been.

For example, one woman has difficulty trusting men or male authorities because encounters with men remind her of childhood rejection by her father. Did her father really always reject her (a global attribution), or did the rejection occur only on occasion? Might those painful occasions have been when she was eager to jump on his lap and tell him what happened to her that day, and instead of being welcoming, he said, "Honey, I am just too tired now, maybe later." In her memory of the past, that simple explanation was translated into "I am never interested in you." But how might she reconstruct it now? She can see that her father was fatigued by his long commute and stressful job and create a new memory to take its place: "He did give me a good-night hug and kiss later."

Remind yourself that a good deal of research has shown that memories of past events are fragile and unreliable and can easily be distorted.[8] Ashleigh Brilliant, who was skeptical of the truth in recovered memories of childhood abuse that appeared after decades, said, "Some of the things that will live longest in my memory—never really happened."

That observation recalls George Orwell's description in *1984* of the political party's power to change the past:

> It's necessary to re-arrange one's memories to remember that events "really" happened in the desired manner. Not in their originally experienced form. All that was needed was an unending series of victories over your own memory.[9]

You can create your own victories over negative memories in order to give yourself a more positive present and future. Because past-positive time perspective is associated with good outcomes and a healthy lifestyle, you want to adopt it as your own. Forget about whether you had less love, success, and good fortune than others early in your life. That's over and done with. Decide to become positive about your past and start afresh.

BECOME MORE FUTURE-ORIENTED

If you have been engulfed by the present or buried in the past, here are some things you can do to increase your future orientation.

- Do the exercise in Chapter Five.

- Wear a watch, even if it doesn't work.
- Write an important future date on the back of your hand.

- If you are young, visit the Death Clock (www .deathclock.com).

- Practice delaying gratification. Put out a bowl of some inviting chocolates, nuts, and cherries, or anything you really like. Now mentally frame it, saying, "Later for you."
- Avoid alcohol.

- Set a few reasonable goals that you would like to reach today, then tomorrow, then within the month. Write them down on your to-be-accomplished list. Keep this list with you and review it regularly.
- Chart your progress toward a goal.
- Practice mental simulation, mental rehearsal, and visualization. Progressively extend the distance of your visualization into the future. Build a sequence of visions for your future.
- Make to-do lists; rank them from most to least important; check off completed ones; give yourself some reward for each task you complete; try to discover what is blocking completion of the rest.
- Decide in advance the moment when you will allow yourself to take *one*.

- Stop thinking of the world as divided into black or white. Think gray. Consider the many possibilities between the extremes. Think contingencies, options, cost-benefit analyses, and probabilities.

- Say no to temptations.

- Work toward long-term bigger rewards instead of settling for short-term quick ones.

- Read good science fiction, especially novels set in the future.

- Create stability in your personal life so that you can anticipate your future with a degree of certainty

- Get an appointment book and calendar and make appointments for medical, dental, vision checkups.
- Make flossing your teeth a daily ritual.
- Hang out with futures to get a sense of what their world looks like (and take from them the good and not their excesses).

BECOME MORE PRESENT-ORIENTED

Here are some things you can do to increase your present orientation if you are engrossed in the future or buried in the past.

- Do the exercise in Chapter Four.

- Practice relaxation exercises, meditation, yoga, and self-hypnosis.

- "Go South."
- Plan for periods of spontaneity. Set aside a weekend day and make absolutely no plans for it. Decide what you will do when the day arrives.

- Go to a comedy club.
- Practice telling jokes.

(For advanced hedonism:
Let someone else decide
what to do and still
enjoy it.)

- Don't wear a watch.

- Go to Las Vegas.

- Drink alcohol in moderation.
- Buy a pet.

- Practice mindfulness.

- Go to an amusement park.

- Listen to live jazz.
- Play with a child. Cooperate
  with him or her to make up
  a game.
- Learn something new.

- Learn improvisation skills;
  get involved in improv
  sports.
- Work at wasting time. Fly
  kites, blow bubbles, toss Fris-
  bees, be silly whenever you
  feel too serious and too
  grown up.
- Go for a hike and enjoy
  nature.
- Go to a karaoke bar—and
  sing, even off-key!
- Practice sensual pleasures;
  get regular massages, go to a
  spa, soak in a hot tub, sweat
  in a sauna, and take a long
  shower.
- Allow yourself to laugh out
  loud and to cry.
- Try a new restaurant.
- Say yes to most invitations.

- Adopt a pet from your local
  shelter.
- Associate with other hedonists.

BECOME MORE PAST-POSITIVE-ORIENTED

Here are some things that you can do to increase your past-positive
orientation.

- Do the exercise in Chapter Three.
- Attend a traditional cultural event.

- Atone for past sins.

- Call an old friend.

- Tell your parents that you love them.

- Look through your high school yearbook.
- Make a scrapbook of all your past mementoes. Include everything you can find about yourself, family, and friends: photos, letters, and report cards. Write down your reflections of each stage of your life.
- Tape an oral history of your family. Start with those who are oldest and work backward down to the youngest. Do the taping in a comfortable private setting. Make the process an enjoyable, relaxing, and nonevaluative session, as though you were an interested cultural anthropologist. As the recorder, you can also ask the people whom you interview what they remember about a particular event, or something special they recall about your youth.
- Offer to help plan family reunions, and participate in their organization and execution.
- Remind your parents, grandparents, special relatives, and close friends of your gratitude for what they did for you. Express your gratitude

- Take a trip back to your hometown.

- Start a diary and reread it occasionally.
- Place pictures of happy times in your home.

in a note, call, card, or even e-mail, but do it and see how good it makes them and you feel.
- Watch old movies, read historical novels and biographies, and listen to golden oldies and classical music.
- Spend time with past-positive people; avoid negative ones.

EMBRACE YOUR NEW BALANCED TIME PERSPECTIVE

Those who embrace a balanced time perspective are better off for doing so and are likely to be happier than others. A recent British study defined a balanced time perspective as scoring above average on all three positive time perspectives—past positive, future, and present hedonistic—and below average on the past-negative and present-fatalistic perspectives. The 150 people who matched this profile were significantly high on many measures of well-being. They were satisfied with their past, their present, and their future prospects and had lots of positive personality characteristics. Most important, these time-balanced people were significantly more self-actualized—more successful in work and career and happier in relationships with family and friends.[10] Similar findings have emerged from another study of balanced time perspective and well-being that used Scottish participants.

Continuity and *balance* of time perspective are also associated with high-functioning people who have a sense of well-being.[11] Continuity, for instance, has been shown to correlate with intelligence, achievement, strong identity, self-actualization, and purpose with a positive perception of time. A significant relation between a productive time orientation and adult well-being has also been found in a comparative study of Americans and Yugo-slavians.[12]

Related to our conception of a balanced time perspective is the idea that time competence is a necessary component of a self-actualizing personality. The Time Competence Scale attempts to measure both balance and continuity in an individual's time perspective.[13] The two concepts are complementary.

> The self-actualizing person is primarily Time Competent and thus appears to live more fully in the here-and-now. Such a person is able to tie the past and the future to the present in meaningful continuity; appears to be less burdened by guilts, regrets and resentments from the past than is a non-self-actualizing person, and aspirations are tied meaningfully to present working goals. There is an apparent faith in the future without rigid or over-idealistic goals.[14]

Work hard when it's time to work. Play hard when it's time to play. Enjoy listening to Grandma's old stories while she is still alive. Meaningfully connect with your friends. View children through the eyes of wonder with which they see the world. Laugh at jokes and life's absurdities. Indulge your desires and passions. Save for a rainy day, and save enough to spend when it is sunny. Recognize the way in which your social and sexual behavior complements your rational self. Take fuller control of your life. These are all the benefits of learning to achieve a balanced time perspective and are key to unlocking personal happiness and finding meaning in life despite the relentless, indifferent ticking of life's clock.[15]

The single most important thing that you can do to enhance the quality of your life is to trade in an old, biased time perspective for a new, optimally balanced one. Change is never easy, but the gains you make will be worth the temporary pain. Once you find balance, you will be free to take the best from the past, the present, and the future to construct a new, better you.

twelve

OUT OF TIME
Making Your Time Matter

The whole life of man is but a point of time; let us enjoy it,
therefore, while it lasts, and not spend it to no purpose.
—Plutarch[1]

In our opinion, Samuel Beckett's *Waiting for Godot*[2] may be the most actionless play ever written. As the name implies, the "action" of the play consists in the two main characters—tramps Vladimir and Estragon—waiting day after day along a desolate road for the mysterious Godot. The waiting is agonizing and nearly unbearable—for Vladimir, for Estragon, and for the audience.

Hints throughout the play suggest that we are not to view *Waiting for Godot* in the usual way. For example, both acts of the play end with the same odd sequence. Vladimir and Estragon have waited an entire day. Godot has not come. They resign themselves to the fact that he will not come that day and turn toward the hope that he will come tomorrow. Vladimir and Estragon despondently decide to abandon their post and to seek shelter from the night that is rapidly settling upon them.

Estragon: Well, shall we go?
Vladimir: Yes, let's go.
[They do not move.]

How do they "go" without moving? They do not "go" in the way that you may think. They do not "go" through physical space but through time. Beckett distills human experience down to its bare essence within the confines of a small, barren stage. He strips away conventional ideas of progress and time and exposes the true nature of our existence. At this most fundamental level, Becket eliminates physical space and movement through it, but he does not stop time.

The lives of Vladimir and Estragon are not unlike our own. As they wait, they tell stories and jokes. They meet new people. They laugh and cry. They do pointless exercises and get bored. They help each other and ask for help when they need it. For Vladimir and Estragon, as for us, time passes more slowly when they are bored. Time flies when they are having fun. But no matter what they do, Vladimir and Estragon notice that time passes just the same. It is a fundamental law of the universe: Time Passes. It passes for actors, it passes for audiences, and it passes for all those who stayed at home.

LIFE IS SHORT—WHAT ARE YOU WAITING FOR?

On consecutive days, Vladimir and Estragon encounter Pozzo, a man who claims to own the land upon which they wait, and his servant, Lucky. The first day Pozzo orders Lucky to entertain Vladimir and Estragon with an impromptu speech. Although the meaning of the speech is unclear, Lucky's soliloquy is elegant and articulate. When the four meet the following day, Pozzo does not remember their earlier meeting. Morever, Lucky is dumb, and Pozzo is blind. Vladimir asks when Lucky became dumb, and Pozzo becomes irate.

Pozzo: [Suddenly furious.] Have you not done tormenting me with your accursed time! It's abominable! When! When! One day, is that not enough for you, one day like any other day, one day he went dumb, one day I went blind, one day we'll go deaf, one day we were born, one day we shall die, the same day, the same second, is that not enough for you? [Calmer.] They give birth astride of a grave, the light gleams an instant, then it's night once more.[3]

Although Beckett cannot stop the passage of time, he can change the speed at which it passes. Years seem to have passed in a single day. This, too, is not unlike our lives. In time, only three days really matter: yesterday, today, and tomorrow. Yesterday is all of the days that have come before today. Tomorrow is all of the days that will come after today. Three days are all that we have in which to live our lives.

Beckett was not the first to lament the meaninglessness and brevity of human existence. He will not be the last. Three hundred years before Beckett wrote, Shakespeare's Macbeth said:[4]

Tomorrow, and tomorrow, and tomorrow
Creeps in its petty pace from day to day
To the last syllable of recorded time;
And all our yesterdays have lighted fools
The way to dusty death. Out, out, brief candle!
Life's but a walking shadow, a poor player
That struts and frets his hour upon the stage,
And then is heard no more. It is a tale
Told by an idiot, full of sound and fury,
Signifying nothing.

A long line of brilliant thinkers has sought meaning in human life. Some found meaning. Others found absurdity and nothingness. Yet wherever they looked, even when they did not find meaning, they found time. Time lies at the heart of what it is to be human. For Plutarch, whose words introduced this chapter, life is short, but there may be some purpose in the spark of life. Discovering what that purpose is and where it is to be found is what life is all about.

MAKING TIME MATTER

Our time is brief, and it will pass no matter what we do. So let us have purpose in spending it. Let us spend it so that our time matters to each of us, and matters to all those whose lives we touch. The question then becomes how you can make time matter. If you know why the time allotted you matters, consider yourself lucky and be prepared to find new purpose tomorrow. If you do not have purpose right now, wait a moment, for it may change.

Where can you find purpose? Like success and happiness, our purpose exists in the present, and we constantly strive toward the future to maintain it. What it is for which we strive is up to each of us. The important thing is that we strive toward something. Societal expectations matter little; personal expectations matter tremendously. Vladimir and Estragon's simple purpose is waiting in a fatalistic present. They are waiting for Godot, whom no one seems to know. Estragon and Vladimir describe him variously as an acquaintance, as a man whom they hardly know, as one whom they would not recognize if they saw him.[5] Despite their inability to know Godot, they have chosen to trust him with their time. They could entrust him with nothing more valuable.

What are *you* waiting for? What are you waiting for to bring purpose, clarity, and direction to your life? While you are waiting for your Godot, time is passing. Don't let it slip by unnoticed. Embrace time fully while you recognize that it is fleeting.

Depending on whom you ask, time is money, time is love, time is work, time is play, time is enjoying friends, time is raising children, and time is much more. Time is what you make of it. Life is what you make of it. *You* can make your time matter. Now is not the time to wait. Now is the time to act. Now is the time to make the most of the time of your life. Yesterday was too early. Tomorrow will be too late. Today is the day of reckoning for each of us.

Finding purpose is a personal quest. Only you will know when you have arrived. We cannot accompany you, but we can suggest a simple starting point, which we call the Golden Rule of Time. It reads, "Use your time as you would like others to use theirs." Would you like others to work hard so they can use the talents that they possess and you and they can benefit from them? Would you like them to be able to reflect warmly on the success their talents have brought them? Would you like them to immerse themselves in the pleasure of the moment? If your answers to these questions were yes, you should do the same yourself.

A First Simple Step Toward Making Time Matter

The Golden Rule of Time is obviously our variation on the traditional Golden Rule, traditionally phrased as "Do unto others as you would have them do unto you." The rule makes sense, and the world would be a better place if we all lived by it. If we look closely, however, we see that it is a rule that applies only some of the time. We spend much of our lives not doing anything to others. Others spend much of their time not doing anything to us. Much of the time, we are just minding our own business. At these times, the Golden Rule does not seem to apply. If we rephrase the Golden Rule in terms of time, however, it applies no matter what we are doing. Even when we are alone, time is passing. Think of how much better the world would be if we all lived by the Golden Rule of Time.

The Golden Rule is common to many religions, as is a focus on using time wisely. As you read the paragraph below, try to guess from which religion it came:

> Sometimes when I meet old friends, it reminds me how quickly time passes. And it makes me wonder if we've utilized our time properly or not. Proper utilization of time is so important. While we have this body, and especially this amazing human brain, I think every minute is something precious. . . . So, we need to make the best use of our time. I believe that the proper utilization of time is this: if you can, serve other people, other sentient beings. If not, at least refrain from harming them. I think that is the whole basis of my philosophy.[6]

A declaration of purpose does not get much simpler. If you can, help other people. If you cannot, at least don't hurt them. These are the words of the Dalai Lama, although spokespeople for many religions other than Buddhism would agree with the sentiment he expresses. Whether you adopt this simple purpose, adopt a particular religion in its entirety, or invent your own purpose in life is up to you. No one can give you purpose. No one can make your time matter except you. You can choose not to begin the journey, but remember that time will swirl past you just the same.

No matter what purpose you settle on, time gives you three chances to be happy. A past-positive time perspective allows you to reexperience past happiness whenever you remember it. A present-hedonistic time perspective allows you to immerse yourself in happiness and pleasure in the present. Finally, a future time perspective allows you to plan to be happy in the future and to derive pleasure from the expectation of future happiness. No matter where you find happiness, you must give yourself time to experience it. It takes time to find purpose, and it takes time to be happy. Give yourself the gift of time. If you do not give yourself time to be happy, no one else will.

If you are unsatisfied with your past, present, or anticipated future, do not worry. You can be certain that they will change. Time shapes our lives as a river shapes the banks beside it. We cannot always predict the direction or rate of change, but we can be sure that change will occur. Sometimes small changes aggregate over time and generate large differences. A couple of shovels of dirt can redirect the mighty Mississippi. A few small changes in your attitude toward time can change your entire life. Change does not always appear at the rate you would like, but changes appear in due time.

Think back to the start of this journey you have taken with us. Did you know then that your particular time perspective influences your decisions, and that communal time perspectives have determined the fate of nations? Now that we have pointed to some of these effects, we hope you will harness your new knowledge to shape your destiny and others'.

Although we have shown both the positives and negatives associated with each time perspective, our overarching message is that developing a balanced time perspective will change your life for the better. Moderate levels of future and present hedonism blended with a solid dose of past positive is the ideal we propose. Flexibly shifting among time perspectives in reponse to the demands of situations you find yourself in allows you to get the most from your time.

In the End, It Is All Up to You

Whether you drink alone or are a leader of nations, time passes just the same.[7] Your time matters to you and, in the end, is all that matters. Time is all that you have. You might as well spend it seeking happiness and purpose—whatever they mean to you. Phil and John find purpose turning over interesting stones on the banks of the River Time, surrounded by family, friends, colleagues, and students. We continually seek new knowledge as we balance gratitude for what we found yesterday, awe for what we find today, and hope for what we will find tomorrow. We hope that you have enjoyed what you found under the stones we turned over for you on our journey together. We will have been good stewards of the time you have spent reading this book if in some way we have inspired you to reclaim yesterday, enjoy today, and master tomorrow.

BUSY AND GETTING BUSIER:

New Findings on the Pace of Your Life

by John Boyd and Philip Zimbardo

Much has changed since we finished writing the first edition of this book. The global economy melted down, and the Greenland ice cap appears headed for a similar cataclysmic fate. Ironically, global climate change is but one of the few things upon which we can count. Our conviction that attitudes toward time play a fundamental role in shaping lives and the world also remains firm. No doubt, people's lives and the world are complicated. Physical, psychological, and environmental factors all have a marked effect on us. Nonetheless, personal attitudes toward time are the foundation upon which other psychological processes and attitudes stand—the lens through which people perceive and experience the world. Fortunately, recent research clarifies to how this lens shapes and directs the course of people's daily lives.

HEALTH & HAPPINESS IN AN UNCERTAIN WORLD

First, the good news. Despite the chaos, uncertainty, and angst of today's contemporary world, most people are happy and healthy. In a survey that we conducted in collaboration with *USA Today* in the summer of 2008, 64 percent of more than 2,000 respondents reported that they are "happy" or "very happy".[1] Only 9 percent reported that they are not happy. Similar positive results were found for both self-reported physical and psychological health. Sixty-five percent of respondents reported that they are physically healthy, and an even higher 72 percent reported that they are psychologically healthy. Less than 10 percent reported that they were not physically or psychologically healthy. The survey sample was not random (it was web-based) and the data were self-reported, so we need to be careful how we generalize the results. Nonetheless, the data paint a rosy view of health and happiness, at least of *USA Today* readers. Happiness and health were evenly distributed across the sexes and age groups, although older respondents reported being slightly more psychologically healthy. Time may indeed heal all wounds. Overall, the world may be teetering on the brink around them, but most people remain happy and healthy individually.

Unfortunately, health and happiness are not evenly distributed across time perspectives. Consistent with findings reported in Chapter 9, *USA Today* survey respondents high (the top quartile) on past-positive, future, and transcendental-future time perspectives reported that they are happier and healthier than people who score low (the bottom quartile) on these time perspectives. In contrast, people high in the past-negative and present-fatalistic time perspectives reported that they are less happy and less healthy than low scorers are.

This pattern of results reinforces our belief that the ideal time-perspective profile is high in past-positive, moderately high in future, moderately high in present-hedonistic, low in past-negative, and low in present-fatalistic time perspectives. The relationship between the past-negative time perspective and happiness and health is particularly strong. On average, people who score in the top quartile on the past-negative time perspective are 40 percent less likely to report being happy than those who score in the bottom quartile. High scorers are also 38 percent less likely to report that they are psychologically healthy and 26 percent less likely that they are physically healthy.

BUSYNESS AND THE APPARENT ACCELERATION OF THE PACE OF LIFE

Most People are Busy

While our 2008 *USA Today* survey touched on happiness and health, the bulk of the survey addressed people's attitudes toward time and pace of life. In addition to abridged versions of our time-perspective inventories, the survey included sections related to busyness, activities sacrificed when people are "really" busy, events that make people angry or impatient, and technologies people use to save time. Sixty-nine percent of respondents reported that their lives are "busy" or "very busy." Only 8 percent reported being "not very" or "not at all" busy. Women reported being more busy than men, and busyness appears to peak in middle age. Those under thirty and over sixty years old were substantially less busy. People high in present-fatalistic and past-negative time perspectives reported that they were less busy, while people high in past-positive, future, and transcendental-future time perspectives reported that they were busier.

Most Would Like to Be Less Busy

About half of people would like to be less busy (49 percent), while 37 percent would not like to be less busy. Thirteen percent are unsure. Women were more likely to want to be less busy than men were, and middle-aged people are more likely to want to be less busy than younger and older people are. People over sixty years old do not want to be less busy. People high in past time perspectives would like to be less busy, while people low in present-hedonistic time perspective would like to be busier.

Busier This Year than Last

Responses to the question of whether people's lives are busier this year than last were quite consistent. Only two significant differences were found. People over sixty years old feel "about" as busy this year as last, and people high in past-negative time perspective feel busier this year than last. As noted in Chapter 2, people have always felt as though they are living on the bleeding edge of time, and the feeling that one lives an accelerating pace of life is relatively consistent across both time perspectives and time periods. In that recent 2008 survey, 51 percent of all respondents reported that their lives were busier this year than they were last year. In a parallel study conducted "way back" in 1987, 47 percent of respondents reported that their lives were busier than they had been the year before. (Given some small changes in sampling methodology, this 4 percent difference is easily within the margin of error. In essence, there was no change between 1987 and 2008). While it is possible that our busy lives are accelerating at the same rate in 2008 as they were in 1987, we believe it more likely that our attitude toward the *acceleration* of our lives has not changed. Pace of life has always pressured personal, social, and business lives.

WHAT ARE WE DOING ABOUT IT?

Shortchanging our friends, our families, and ourselves

We found numerous other consistencies between the surveys. In both 1987 and 2008, most people felt busy, most people felt busier this year than last, and many people would like to be less busy. That much hasn't changed. It turns out, however, that many people deal with these consistent feelings in ways that may actually make things worse, may actually reduce the quality and quantity of their lives. Our 2008 survey results suggest that, when people feel too busy, rushed, and stressed, they shortchange their friends, families, and themselves. Most respondents reported sacrificing hobbies (57 percent), sleep (56 percent), household chores (56 percent), and recreation (52 percent). Even worse, many reported sacrificing time with friends (44 percent) and family (30 percent). Some even reported sacrificing work (6 percent). Sacrificing chores makes some sense. Who likes to do them anyway? However, sacrificing sleep, family, and friends can lead to serious physical and psychological health consequences.

Speaking of serious psychological consequences, 40 percent of the people in relationships reported that "Not having enough free time together" causes stress in their relationship. This top relationship stressor was followed in frequency by financial problems (36 percent), deciding how to spend free time (23 percent), dividing household chores (20 percent), sexual problems (19 percent), and deciding how to discipline children (13 percent). That's right! Lack of time causes more stress in relationships than financial and sexual problems! Maybe it's because we never have enough time to discuss money or to have sex since we are all too busy.

When couples somehow do find time to reproduce, their children suffer from their parents' rapid pace of life. One of the most striking differences between our 1987 and 2008 surveys relates to the evening family meal. In 1987, 59 percent of respondents reported that they sat down and ate the evening meal together with their family "every day." By 2008, this number had plunged to 20 percent. That's a 66 percent decrease in twenty years! A daily family tradition is now seldom practiced by anyone in any time perspective, although people high in past-positive, future, and transcendental-future time perspectives are most likely to continue the tradition. It's possible that families have found a better use for the time traditionally spent on the evening meal. Perhaps parents are reading to their children more, families are out in the yard playing catch, or they are indoors playing board games. Perhaps, but we believe it's unlikely. More likely is that the family dinnertime is now split between various practices, errands, homework, chores, video games, and TV shows, likely done separately and not in an old-fashioned "all in the family" style.

People high in the transcendental-future time perspective were the only people who did not report sacrificing anything more frequently than low scorers did. (See Table 1.) People high in transcendental-future time perspective actually report sacrificing vacation and friends *less* than people who score low. People who scored high on all other time perspectives were more likely to shortchange some activities and less likely to shortchange others, often in predictable ways.

Table 1: Time perspective profiles based upon USA Today *survey data (n = 2060)*

High Past-positive	High Past-negative	High Present-fatalistic
• More happy and healthy	• Least happy and healthy	• Less happy and healthy
• Less angry or impatient when waiting in line and caught in traffic	• More angry or impatient when waiting in line, caught in traffic, looking for parking, and waiting for webpages to load, restaurant service, government acts, the bus, a repairperson, and computers to start up	• More angry or impatient when looking for parking, waiting for government acts, webpages to load, a repairperson, the bus, and in line
• Shortchange church, hobbies, dinner parties, and movies out when very busy		• Shortchange charities, vacations, church, cultural events, dinner out, and work
• Do NOT shortchange family		• Use TV shopping to save time
• Use microwaves, voice mail, DVRs, e-mail, mail catalogs, and texting to save time	• Shortchange family, friends, vacation, recreation, dinner out, sleep, movies out, and church when really busy	• Less likely to use house cleaners to save time
• Less likely relationship stress caused by sexual problems	• Use fast food, banking by phone, and texting to save time	• More likely to have relationship stress caused by financial problems, sexual problems, and disciplining kids
	• Less likely to use house cleaners to save time	
	• More likely to have relationship stress caused by sexual problems, financial problems, and household chores	

High Present-hedonistic

- More happy and healthy
- More angry or impatient when waiting in line
- Less angry or impatient when waiting for a doctor
- Shortchange charities, family, vacations, and work
- Use texting, instant messaging, fast food, laundry service, and overnight shipping to save time
- More likely to have relationship stress caused by deciding how to spend free time

High Future

- More happy and healthy
- More angry or impatient when waiting for late people, a repairperson, and a doctor
- Shortchange hobbies, recreation, vacation, and TV
- Do NOT shortchange house chores, work, and sleep
- Less likely to use fast food to save time

High Transcendental-future

- Most happy and healthy
- Less angry or impatient when caught in traffic, waiting for the bus, and computers to start up
- Do NOT shortchange vacation and friends
- Use fast food, microwave, car phones, voice mail, and banking by phone to save time
- Less likely to use instant messaging to save time

For example, people high on the past-positive time perspective were more likely to report sacrificing church, hobbies, dinner parties, and movies out, but were less likely to report sacrificing family. They were also no more likely to sacrifice friends, which suggests that they value time with the select people who matter the most to them.

People who scored high on the past-negative reported sacrificing more activities than any other time perspective, including family, friends, vacation, recreation, dinner out, sleep, movies out, and church. In fact, they sacrifice almost everything that is critical to social and psychological health, which is consistent with the lower happiness and health scores reported earlier. People who scored high in present-fatalistic time perspective were also likely to report sacrificing multiple activities, including charitable activities, vacations, church, cultural events, dinner out, and work. Fully 8 percent of people high in present-fatalistic time perspective reported sacrificing work when very busy. When fate determines one's life and hard work does not matter, work is a logical place to cut. Present-fatalists were, however, no more likely to sacrifice family and friends.

People high in present-hedonistic time perspective also reported sacrificing work, as well as charitable activities, family, and vacations. They did not sacrifice things that are fun, such as recreation or friends. People high in future time perspective reported sacrificing activities that do not interfere with goal achievement, including hobbies, recreation, vacation, and TV. Interestingly, people high in future time perspective also reported that they sacrificed household chores, work, and sleep *less* frequently than people low in future time perspective. Future-oriented people are willing to sacrifice fun, but not their goals.

A question early in the survey asked respondents if they wished that they had more time to spend with family and friends. Fully 89 percent of respondents reported that they did. Later in the survey, we asked how respondents would use an imaginary extra day each week. We were amazed by the answers. Thirty-one percent reported that they would spend the extra day with family, followed by spending it having fun (26 percent), spending it on themselves (26 percent), spending it with friends (8 percent), and spending it catching up on work (8 percent). Overall, this is a reasonable pattern, but it differed substantially according to time perspective.

People high in present-fatalistic time perspective were less likely to spend the time with family and more likely to spend the time on themselves. People high in past-positive time perspective were more likely to spend the time with family and less likely to spend the time on themselves, which is consistent with what they reported sacrificing. People high in transcendental-future time perspective were more likely to spend the time with family and less likely to spend the time on themselves or having fun. They didn't sacrifice time with family, and they would spend the extra day with family when possible. People high in present-hedonistic time perspective were more likely to spend the time having fun, which is again consistent with what they would sacrifice.

HOW TIME MAKES PEOPLE ANGRY AND IMPATIENT

A lot of time-related events made people angry or impatient in both 1987 and 2008. Most people reported becoming angry or impatient when "waiting for late people" (59 percent) and "being caught in traffic" (60 percent). These two familiar frustrations of modern life topped the list in 1987 and 2008. (See Table 2.) While findings were relatively consistent across time perspectives, there are some important differences. People high in past-negative time perspective were the most impatient of the bunch. Just about everything makes them angry, including waiting in line, being caught in traffic, and looking for a parking space, as well as waiting for webpages to load, the government to act, restaurant service, the bus, and repairpeople. People high in present-fatalistic time perspective also reported being relatively impatient. They become angry when looking for parking,

Table 2: What Makes People Angry or Impatient?

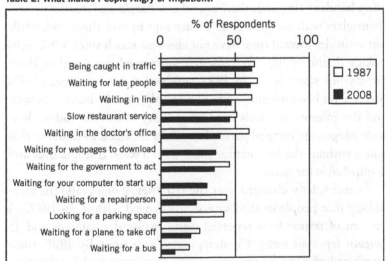

waiting in line, waiting for the government to act, webpages to load, repairpeople, and the bus.

A small subset of similar events irritated the future-oriented. People high in future time perspective are set off by waiting for people. People high in future time perspective are 13 percent more likely than the average person to become angry or impatient when waiting for late people. In contrast, people high in present-hedonistic time perspective are relatively patient. They do become angry or impatient when waiting in line, but they are *less* likely to be upset by waiting for the doctor than people low on present-hedonistic. People high in past-positive and transcendental-future time perspectives do not become impatient or angry when confronted with any of the activities listed. In fact, people high in the past-positive and transcendental-future time perspectives report being *less* angry and impatient when waiting and caught in traffic. It's as if these two time perspectives inoculate people against the frustrations of modern living. That's another point for the optimists.

Avoiding the technology trap

Making sacrifices is one common strategy to beat back the accelerating hands of time, but there are others. People also frequently arm themselves with technology in an attempt to save time, and, while our attitudes toward time have not changed much since 1987, technology definitely has. Technology transformed the world in those twenty-one short years. In 1987, compact disks were new, DVDs had not yet been invented, e-mail was only used by businesspeople, and the Internet was only used by military scientists. Today, these technologies are integral parts of our daily routines, so much so that going without the Internet for more than a week disrupts lives and is impossible for many.[2]

As technology changed over the last twenty-one years, the technology that people used to save time changed with it. In 1987, 64 percent of respondents reported using mail-order catalogs and 15 percent reported using TV shopping to save time. By 2008, these numbers had dropped precipitously to 16 percent and 3 percent respectively, which represents over 75 percent decreases in usage rates over twenty years. What did people do with the time that they had been spending on mail-order catalogs and TV shopping? They found newer, even faster ways to save time. In 1987, less than 20 percent of respondents reported using home computers to save time. Today the number is over 72 percent. Most people now use e-mail (81 percent), ATMs (60 percent), online shopping (56 percent), and fast food (45 percent) to "save" time. (See Table 3.)

The specific technologies used to save time vary by time perspective, often in predictable ways. For example, people high in present-hedonistic time perspective report using text messaging, instant messaging, overnight shipping, laundry services, and eating fast food more than people low in present-hedonistic time perspective. Even the ways that they save time provide immediate gratification. We expected that people high in future time perspective would use the most technologies to save time, but people high in future time perspective were no more likely to use any technology than people low in future time perspective. Surprisingly, people high in past-positive and transcendental-future time perspectives reported using the most technologies to save time. However, people high in future time perspective were less likely to report eating fast food, which is what would be predicted. It may be that future-oriented people plan their days so well that they don't need to save time and can actually afford to do some things more slowly, such as cooking healthy food at home.

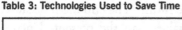

Table 3: Technologies Used to Save Time

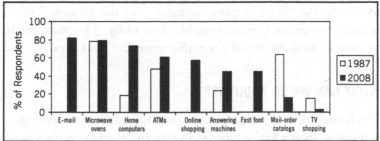

THESE TIME-TESTED STRATEGIES MAY MAKE THINGS WORSE

Sacrificing when really busy may make sense in the short-term. If an hour sacrificed today leads to two hours gained tomorrow, the strategy is sound. A stitch in time can save nine. Self-sacrificing, however, is not a sound strategy when used for years. At some point, it ceases to be a strategy and it becomes a way of life. Especially for those high in past-negative time perspective, typical sacrifices could become unhealthy and maladaptive habits. Sacrificing family, friends, and sleep is no way to go through life.

While technology can save time, it is a double-edged sword and can actually add to our stress, frustration, and anger. Roughly one-third of respondents indicated that waiting for their computers to start up and waiting for webpages to download made them angry or impatient. Computers start up in minutes and webpages download in seconds, yet we still get angry with them because they are too slow! How far we have come from the days when we had to plant a seed in March if we wanted to eat in October! Computers frustrate more people today than looking for a parking space and waiting for a repairperson, two activities that made the list of frustrations in both 1987 and 2008. The technology cure can contribute to a sense of busyness. Paradoxically, unless people recognize this, frustration and anxiety may increase as new "time-saving" technologies are invented.

So why do many people sacrifice today for tomorrow and rely on technology to save time? They do these things to relieve the stress and anxiety that come from attitudes toward time and, specifically, attitudes toward the present and the future. They do them because, for many, the future is more valuable than the present. Unconsciously, tomorrow is more valuable than today. This may not be rational or ideal, but it is the way that many live their lives.

WHAT CAN WE DO ABOUT IT?

If self-sacrifice and technology are not the answers to feelings of time press, then what is? First, recognize and accept that the answer is not to be found in self-sacrifice or in ever more efficient time-management strategies and technology. The answer is to be found inside, in personal attitudes toward time. We cannot change time. We probably cannot even change the perception that it moves increasingly quickly from the future to the past. Nonetheless, we can change our attitudes toward time and our appreciation for it. Here are some more suggestions for how to do this.

Some Timely Prescriptions

The 2008 *USA Today* survey both reinforces previous lessons and suggests new ways to modify attitudes toward time. Some prescriptions apply to everyone, while others target individuals high in specific time perspectives. Overall, there are four steps that you can take to enrich your time perspectives and enhance your happiness and heath.

- **Accept that you feel busy and are likely to feel busier in the future.** These feelings are unlikely to change until you retire, and, on the bright side, busier people tend to report being happier.

- **Learn to relax and be patient.** Relaxation techniques may help you endure the inevitable frustrations in life. Increased patience may also reduce the frequency that you feel "really" busy, which can lead to shortchanging important aspects of your life.

- **Reexamine what you are shortchanging when "really" busy.** It's possible that you are comfortable with the trade-offs that you are making currently, but make sure that they are consistent with your values and the person that you strive to be.

- **Recognize that technology is a double-edged sword.** Technology can save time, but it can also be a new source of frustration. Watch out for the point at which technology ceases to be part of the answer and becomes part of the problem.

While these strategies apply across time perspectives, time perspectives do not contribute equally to happiness and health. The *USA Today* data also point to specific benefits and detriments associated with each individual time perspective.

The past-positive time perspective

The past-positive time perspective is strongly associated with a host of positive attributes. People who are high in the past-positive time perspective are happy, healthy, and patient; they shortchange activities that are not core to physical and psychological health when really busy; and they use technology in ways that do not appear to frustrate them. They also have fewer sexual problems. People who are low in the past-positive would do well to strengthen their positive attitudes toward the past. If you are high in past-positive, keep up the good work—and your positive attitudes.

The past-negative time perspective

As the name implies, the past-negative time perspective is everything that the past-positive is not, and much of it is potentially destructive. People high on the past-negative time perspective are less happy, less healthy, and easily angered by many aspects of modern life, some of which are beyond any individual's control. They shortchange people and activities that contribute to their physical and psychological health. Technology can frustrate them. More so than any other time perspective, people high in the past-negative may benefit from learning relaxation techniques, such as mediation and yoga, to deal with their impatience. They may also benefit from reexamining the people and activities that they shortchange when they are really busy. Sacrificing family, friends, and sleep is likely to be inconsistent with personal values and to lead to isolation and sickness. As noted in the Prologue, many veterans benefit from therapy sessions that focus on Time Perspective Therapy, which emphasizes the problems of having one foot stuck in a negative past. They have to drag that foot out of the muck and get it on more solid footing so that they have a better present and future. They may also have the other foot stuck in the muck of a fatalistic present and they have to move that foot, too, to either more hedonistic or future foundations. Just as these time metaphors work for vets, they may also work for other people experiencing chronic depression.

The present-fatalistic time perspective

People high on the present-fatalistic time perspective are less happy, less healthy, and become angry or impatient relatively frequently. They, too, may benefit from learning and practicing relaxation strategies. They shortchange multiple activities when too busy, but the activities are less central to happiness and health than those shortchanged by people high in past-negative time perspective. People high on the present-fatalistic time perspective need to strengthen their past-positive, present-hedonistic, future, and transcendental-future time perspectives. Strengthening future time perspective specifically may lead to less sacrifice of work.

The present-hedonistic time perspective

People high on the present-hedonistic time perspective fare relatively well in the *USA Today* survey. They are happy, healthy, relatively patient, and calm. They may become impatient when waiting in line, but this may be because they are eager to experience the thrill of the show or event for which they are waiting, not because of anger. They do sacrifice family and work, which may reflect the priorities of fun, of friends and play, over family and work. Finally, deciding how to spend free time in relationships causes them significant stress, and they may benefit from discussing the issue with their partners.

The future time perspective

People high on the future time perspective are happy and healthy, but they become angry or impatient primarily when waiting for people. Relaxation techniques may help here, as may the recognition that not everyone shares their future orientation. They shortchange activities that, when done in moderation, will not compromise quality of life, but they should be vigilant that their short-term sacrifices do not become ways of life, do not become biased future-time perspectives. They may also benefit from exploring how technology can help them save time. And as we have said repeatedly, Futures can always benefit from a healthy dash of hedonism in their daily lives.

The transcendental-future time perspective

While much more research is needed to substantiate this finding, the transcendental-future appears to be the time perspective most strongly associated with happiness and health, based upon the *USA Today* survey data. People high in the transcendental-future time perspective are less likely to become angry or impatient, and they are less likely to shortchange important areas of their lives when really busy. They also use technology, but are not frustrated by it. Whether or not this time perspective is based upon religious beliefs, the data clearly show that it is related to positive life outcomes.

THE ONE "FREE LUNCH" OF TIME PERSPECTIVE: DIVERSIFICATION AND BALANCE

As thoroughly documented in the body of the book, the past-negative and present-fatalistic time perspectives are associated with decreased happiness and health. If you are high on either of these time perspectives, we strongly encourage you to work to strengthen other time perspectives. Remember to take each day at a time. Change takes time. Anticipate setbacks. Lasting quality change seldom happens all at once. In contrast, the past-positive, present-hedonistic, future, and transcendental-future time perspective are associated with happiness and physical and psychological health. If you are high on these positive time perspectives, remember that a little is good, but an exclusive focus on any one time perspective can lead to biases that constrict quality of life. Bias is the enemy of a healthy time perspective. Balance is your friend. Just as it would be foolish to invest all your retirement funds in a single stock, it is foolish to focus exclusively on any one aspect of time.

Time gives you three paths to happiness: the past, the present, and the future. The wise among us will take advantage of all three.

Diversification may be the only "free lunch" in the domain of happiness, just as it is in the domain of investments.[3] During these uncertain times, who can afford to pass up a free lunch?

There is hope for each of us in a balanced time perspective, and there is hope for the world as well. When economic anxiety works to focus time perspective on the present, it is even more imperative to maintain a belief in the future. From the present, we derive motivation and energy to make great changes, and from the future, we gain clarity of purpose and direction. Respect for the past adds an additional source of balance. With a balanced time perspective that learns from the past, draws energy and emotion from the present, and is guided by a clear vision for the future, each of us as individuals and all of us as a world can accomplish great things. In the end, fulfilling the promise of tomorrow is contingent upon today's respect for the past and hope for the future. Our hope for the future includes a balance and harmony of the past, present, and future; of thinking and feeling; of people and nature; and an abundance of happiness and health for all.

Notes

PROLOGUE

1 Kern, M. L. & Friedman, H. S. (2008). Do conscientious individuals live longer? A quantitative review. *Health Psychology* 27, pp. 505–512.

ONE: WHY TIME MATTERS

1 Although this church is less popular than St. Peter's today, in the past people were dying to get in.

2 Franklin, B. (1748). *Advice to Young Tradesmen.* Boston.

3 Shakespeare, W. Sonnet 30. In *The Complete Works of Shakespeare,* 4th ed. Bevington, ed.

4 Van Boven, L., and Gilovich, T. (2003). "To Do or to Have: That Is the Question." *Journal of Personality and Social Psychology* 85, 1193–1202.

5 Einstein, A. (1931). *Relativity: The Special and General Theory.* Lawson, R. W., trans. New York: Crown.

6 As "quoted" by Steve Mirsky in *Scientific American* (September 2002), Vol. 287, No. 3, p. 102. This should hardly be taken as an authentication of the statement as actually Einstein's, as Mirsky cites the original source as being a fictional magazine: "Amazingly, the pretty girl/hot stove quote is actually the abstract from a short paper written by Einstein that appeared in the now defunct *Journal of Exothermic Science and Technology* (1938), Vol. 1, No. 9. Also quoted in Levine's book.

7 Ornstein, R. E. (1970). *On the Experience of Time.* Baltimore, MD: Penguin Books.

8 For an online experiment on how pitch influences perception of duration, see: www.owlnet.rice.edu/~aniko/duration/.

9 Darley, J. M., and Batson, C. D. (1973). "From Jerusalem to Jericho: A Study of Situational and Dispositional Variables in Helping Behavior." *Journal of Personality and Social Psychology* 27, 29–40.

10 Levine, R. (1997). *A Geography of Time: The Temporal Misadventures of a Social Psychologist, or How Every Culture Keeps Time Just a Little Bit Differently.* New York: Basic Books.

11 Possible explanations include the geographic proximity to Mexico and the large immigrant population resident in Los Angeles.

12 Orwell, G. (1949). *1984.* New York: Harcourt Brace Jovanovich.

13 Becker, E. (1973). *The Denial of Death.* New York: Free Press, p. ix.

TWO: TIME

1 Sagan, C. (1977). *The Dragons of Eden: Speculations on the Evolution of Human Intelligence.* New York: Ballantine.

2 According to Gordon Moore's "Moore's Law." Moore, Gordon E. (1965). <ftp://download.intel.com/museum/Moores_Law/Articles_Press_Releases/Gordon_Moore_1965_Article.pdf>. Electronic Magazine <http://en.wikipedia.org/wiki/Electronics_%28magazine%29>.

3 This example conveniently ignores the massive parallel processing capacity of the human brain.

4 Libet, B. (2004). *Mind Time: The Temporal Factor in Consciousness.* Cambridge, MA: Harvard University Press.

5 Fiske, S., and Taylor, S. (1991). *Social Cognition,* 2nd ed. New York: McGraw-Hill.

6 See Tversky, A. and Kahneman, D. (1974). "Judgment Under Uncertainty: Heuristics and Biases." *Science* 185, 1124–1131, or Kahneman, D. and Tversky, A. (1984). "Choices, Values, and Frames." *American Psychologist* 39, 341–350.

7 From "Why War?" (1932), a letter from Sigmund Freud to Albert Einstein. See *Character and Culture* (1963), Macmillan, for the full text of the letter. As translated by Bruno Bettelheim in his book *Freud and Man's Soul* (1984), p. 99.

8 Hobbes, T. (1955). *Leviathan or the Matter, Forme, and Power of a Common Wealth Ecclesiastical and Civil.* Oxford: Basil Blackwell (originally published 1651).

9 Douglas, K. (March 18, 2006). *New Scientist.* Also see Colapinto, J. (April 16, 2007). "The Interpreter: Has a Remote Amazonian Tribe Upended Our Understanding of Language?" *The New Yorker* (www.newyorker.comreporting/2007/04/16/070416fa_fact_colapinto?currentPage=all).

10 Event time is analogous to ordinal data, while clock time is analogous to interval data.

11 Similar stories are related by Katie Barnett Curhan in her honor's thesis, *New Zealand Maori Selfways* (1996). Stanford University.

12 Landes, D. S. (2000). *Revolution in Time: Clocks and the Making of the Modern World,* revised and enlarged ed. Cambridge, MA: Belknap Press.

13 Dohrn-van Rossum, G. (1996). *History of the Hour: Clocks and Modern Temporal Orders.* T. Dunlap, trans. Chicago: University of Chicago Press.

14 Taylor, F. W. (1911). *The Principles of Scientific Management.* New York: Harper & Brothers.

15 Bell, D. (1975). *The Clock Watchers: Americans at Work.* Time Magazine Bicentennial Essay. The original article can be found here: www.time.com/time/printout/0,8816,917797,00.html

16 U.S. Bureau of Labor Statistics: 100 Years of U.S. Consumer Spending: Data for the Nation, New York City, and Boston. From *The Valley Times* (Pleasanton, CA), June 25, 2006.

17 Ball State University (2005). Middletown Media Studies, Center for Media Design. See www.bsu.edu/middletown.

18 Ramirez, J. (August 21, 2006). "Watchers: Time May Run Out." *Newsweek.* www.newsweek.com/id/46413.

19 The Oxford English Dictionary, http://news.bbc.co.uk/1/hi/uk/5104778.stm.

20 The Oxford English Dictionary, http://news.bbc.co.uk/2/hi/uk_news/5104778.stm.

21 In the end, the statistics are not in our favor. Ninety-nine percent of all species that have ever lived on earth are now extinct.

22 Bennis, W., and Slater, P. (1998). *The Temporary Society*, rev. ed. San Francisco: Jossey-Bass.

23 Gleick, J. (2000). *Faster: The Acceleration of Just About Everything*. New York: Vintage.

24 See these works: Toffler, A. (1970). *Future Shock*. New York: Random House; Toffler, A. (1980). *The Third Wave*. New York: Morrow; Toffler, A. (1990). *Powershift: Knowledge, Wealth, and Violence at the Edge of the 21st Century*. New York: Bantam.

25 Van Doren, C. (1991). *The History of Knowledge: The Pivotal Events, People, and Achievements of World History*. New York: Ballantine, p. 4.

26 Macaulay, Lord Thomas Babington. *History of England*, vol. i, chap. i.

27 See Wikipedia for a summary of Timothy Leary's work and social influence: http://en.wikipedia.org/wiki/Turn_on,_tune_in,_drop_out.

28 In *The Complete Works of Shakespeare* (1992), 4th ed. D. Bevington, ed.

29 James, W. (1890). *The Principles of Psychology*, vol. 1. New York: Dover Press.

30 Lewin, K. (1942). "Time Perspective and Morale," in *Resolving Social Conflicts*. G. W. Lewin, ed.

31 Lewin, K. (1920). "Socializing the Taylor System," in *The Complete Social Scientist* (1999). M. Gold, Washington, D.C.: American Psychological Association (APA) Books.

32 Some psychologists did make time central to their work, and to them we owe a tremendous debt of gratitude. For a partial list of early contributors to the field, see: DeVolder, M., and Lens, W. (1982). "Academic Achievement and Future Time Perspective as a Cognitive-motivational Concept." *Journal of Personality and Social Psychology* 42, 566–571; Fraisse, P. (1963). *The Psychology of Time*. J. Leith, trans. Greenwood Press; Hulbert, R. J., and Lens, W. (1988). "Time Perspective, Time Attitude, and Time Perspective in Alcoholism: A Review." *International Journal of the Addictions* 23 (3), 279–298; Levine, R. V. (1990). "The Pace of Life," *American Scientist* 78, 450–495; Levine, R. V. (1997). *A Geography of Time: The Temporal Misadventures of a Social Psychologist, or How Every Culture Keeps Time Just a Little Bit Differently*. New York: Basic Books; Lewin, K. (1942). "Time Perspective and Morale," in G. Watson, ed. *Civilian Morale: Second Yearbook of the S.P.S.S.L.* Boston: Houghton Mifflin; McGrath, J. E., and Kelly, J. R. (1986). *Time and Human Interaction: Toward a Social Psychology of Time*. New York: Guilford Press; Nuttin, J. (1964). "The Future Time Perspective in Human Motivation and Learning." *Acta Psychologica* 23, 60–82; Nuttin, J. R. (1985). *Future Time Perspective and Motivation: Theory and Research Method*. Hillsdale, N.J.: Lawrence Erlbaum; Strathman, A., Gleicher, F., Boninger, D., and Edwards, C. (1994). "The Consideration of Future Consequences: Weighing Immediate and Distant Outcomes of Behavior." *Journal of Personality and Social Psychology* 66, 742–752; Strathman, A., and Joireman, J. eds. (2005). *Understanding Behavior in the Context of Time: Theory, Research, and Applications*. Mahwah, N.J.: Lawrence Erlbaum Associates; Zaleski, Z. (1994). "Towards a Psychology of the Personal Future." In Z. Zaleski, ed., *Psychology of Future Orientation*, 10–20. Lublin: Towarzystwo Naukowe KUL.

33 Greater detail on the scale can be found in our JPSP article: Zimbardo, P. G., and Boyd, J. N. (1999). "Putting Time in Perspective: A Valid, Reliable Individual-differences Metric." *Journal of Personality and Social Psychology* 77 (6), 1271–1288.

34 See our website for more information about the ZTPI and its uses: www.time perspective.com.

35 Ross, L., and Nisbett, R. E., (1991). *The Person and the Situation: Perspectives of Social Psychology*. New York: McGraw-Hill.

36 Freud, S. (1990). *Beyond the Pleasure Principle*. New York: W. W. Norton.

37 Rothspan, S., and Read, S. J. (1996). "Present Versus Future Time Perspective and HIV Risk Among Heterosexual College Students." *Health Psychology* 15, 131–134.

38 Alvos, L., Gregson, R. A., and Ross, M. W. (1993). "Future Time Perspective in Current and Previous Injecting Drug Users." *Drug & Alcohol Dependence* 31, 193–197. See also Keough, K. A., Zimbardo, P. G., and Boyd, J. N. (1999). "Who's Smoking, Drinking, and Using Drugs? Time Perspective as a Predictor of Substance Use." *Journal of Basic and Applied Social Psychology* 21, 149–164.

39 Zimbardo, P. G., Keough, K. A., and Boyd, J. N. (1997). "Present Time Perspective as a Predictor of Risky Driving." *Personality and Individual Differences* 23, 1007–1023.

40 Hutton, H. H., Lyketsos, C. G., Hunt, W. R., Bendit, G., Harrison, R. B., Swetz, A., Treisman, G. J. (1999). "Personality Characteristics and Their Relationship to HIV Risk Behaviors Among Women Prisoners." Unpublished manuscript, Johns Hopkins Hospital.

41 Gurarnio, A., DePascalis, V., and Di Chiacchio, C. (1999). "Breast Cancer Prevention, Time Perspective, and Trait Anxiety." Unpublished manuscript, University of Rome.

42 Levine, R. V. (1997). *A Geography of Time: The Temporal Misadventures of a Social Psychologist, or How Every Culture Keeps Time Just a Little Bit Differently*. New York: Basic Books.

43 Greene, B. (2005). *The Fabric of the Cosmos: Space, Time and the Texture of Reality*. New York: Vintage.

THREE: THE PAST

1 Santayana, G. (1905). *The Life of Reason*, vol. 1. New York: Scribner's.

2 Inge, W. (1929). *Assessments and Anticipations*. London: Cassell and Company.

3 Adler, A. (1956). *The Individual Psychology of Alfred Adler*. H. Ansbacher and R. Ansbacher, eds. New York: Basic Books.

4 Khayyám, O. (1946). *The Rubiyat of Omar Khayyám*. London: George G. Harrap.

5 For an outstanding review of Freud's work and contributions, see Gay, P. (2006). *Freud: A Life for Our Time*. New York: W. W. Norton.

6 Freud, S. (1963). "Reflections on War and Death," in *Character and Culture*. New York: Macmillan.

7 Freud, S. (1960). *The Ego and the Id*. J. Strachey ed. New York: W. W. Norton.

8 Freud, S. (1961). *The Future of an Illusion*. J. Strachey, trans. New York: W. W. Norton. (Originally published 1927.)

9 Freud, S. (1969). *An Outline of Psychoanalysis*. J. Strachey, trans. New York: W. W. Norton.

10 Breuer, J., and Freud, S. (1893). *Studies on Hysteria*. J. Strachey, trans., p. 308.

11 Skinner, B. F. (1948). *Walden Two*. New York: Macmillan.

12 Phil Zimbardo remains an honorary member of the behaviorists based upon his graduate years spent running rats at Yale (1954–59).

13 Watson, J. (1913). "Psychology as the Behaviorist Views It." *Psychological Review* 20, 158–177.

14 Skinner, B. F. (1987). *Upon Further Reflection*. Englewood Cliffs, N.J.: Prentice-Hall.

15 Loftus, E., and Palmer, J. (1974). "Reconstruction of Automobile Destruction." *Journal of Verbal Learning and Verbal Behavior* 13, 585–589.

16 Braun, K., Ellis, R., and Loftus, E. (2002). "Make My Memory." *Psychology and Marketing* 19, 1–23.

17 Loftus, E. (1997). "Creating False Memories." *Scientific American* 277, 70–75.

18 Loftus, E. (1993). "The Reality of Repressed Memories." *American Psychologist* 48, 518–537.

19 See here: www.brown.edu/Departments/Taubman_Center/Recovmem/.

20 Anderson, M. C., Ochsner, K. N., Kuhl, B., Cooper, J., Robertson, E., Gabrieli, S. W., Glover, G. H., and Gabrieli, J. D. (January 9, 2004). "Neural Systems Underlying the Suppression of Unwanted Memories." *Science* 303, 232–235.

21 Middleton, De Marni Cromer, and Freyd, J. (Sept. 2005). "Remembering the Past, Anticipating a Future." *Australian Psychiatry* 13(3), 223–232.

22 Williams, L. (1994). "Recall of Childhood Trauma: A Prospective Study of Women's Memories of Child Sexual Abuse." *Journal of Consulting and Clinical Psychology* 62, 1167–1176.

23 Bass, E. and Davis, L. (1988). *The Courage to Heal: A Guide for Woman Survivors of Child Sexual Abuse*. 3rd ed. New York: HarperCollins. www.fmsfonline.org.

24 See www.fmsfonline.org/about.html.

25 From the False Memory Syndrome Foundation website.

26 See, for example, Garcia, J., and Koelling, R. (1966). "Relation of Cue to Consequence in Avoidance Learning." *Psychonomic Science* 4, 123–124.

27 See the description of the Cambridge Sommerville study in Ross, L., and Nisbett, R. E. (1991). *The Person and the Situation: Perspectives of Social Psychology*. New York: McGraw-Hill.

28 Seligman, M. (2004). *Authentic Happiness: Using the New Positive Psychology to Realize Your Potential for Lasting Fulfillment*. New York: Free Press, p. 67.

29 Martial (A.D. c. 40–A.D. c. 104). *Epigram* x. 23, 7.

30 Freud, S. (1961). *The Future of an Illusion*. J. Strachey, trans. New York: W. W. Norton. (Originally published 1927.)

31 Speech to the Virginia Convention, March 1775.

32 Karniol, R. (1996). "The Motivational Impact of Temporal Focus: Thinking About the Future and the Past." *Annual Review of Psychology* 47, 593–620.

33 Goldberg, J., and Maslach, C. (1996). "Understanding the Connections Between the Past and Future." Paper presented at the annual convention of the Western Psychological Association in San Diego, CA.

34 The Dalai Lama and Cutler, H. C. (1998). *The Art of Happiness: A Handbook for Living*. New York: Riverhead.

FOUR: THE PRESENT

1 Lamm, H., Schmidt, R. W., and Trommsdorff, G. (1976). "Sex and Social Class as Determinants of Future Orientation (Time Perspective) in Adolescents." *Journal of Personality and Social Psychology* 34(3), 317–326.

2 Banfield, E. C. (1970). *The Unheavenly City: The Nature and the Future of Our Urban Crisis.* Boston: Little, Brown, p. 54.

3 Levine, R. (1997). *A Geography of Time: The Temporal Misadventures of a Social Psychologist.* New York: Basic Books.

4 Dolci, D. (1981). *Sicilian Lives.* New York: Pantheon, pp. 20–21.

5 There are notable exceptions to this Sicilian time perspective. Phil is one of them, as you will see later in the chapter.

6 For more information about discounting see the work of George Loewenstein on intertemporal choice. An early review can be found in: Loewenstein, G., and Prelec, D. (1993). "Preferences for Sequences of Outcomes." *Psychological Review* 100, 91–108. And also later relevant articles: Frederick, S., Lowenstein, G., and O'Donoughe, T. (2002). "Time Discounting and Time Preference: A Critical Review." *Journal of Economic Literature,* 40, 351–401; and Sanfey, A., Lowenstein, G., McClure, M., and Cohen, D. (2006). "Neuroeconomics: Crosscurrents in Research on Decision-Making." *Trends in Cognitive Sciences,* 10, 108–116. Also review Stern, M. L. (2006). "Edogenous Time Preference and Optimal Growth." *Economic Theory,* 29, 49–70.

7 Loewenstein, G., and Thaler, R. H. (1989). "Intertemporal Choice." *Journal of Economic Perspectives* 3, 181–93; see also Loewenstein, G., and Elster, J. (1992). *Choice over Time.* Russell Sage Foundation.

8 These data and those following are taken from research that we conducted at the College of San Mateo, California, on 205 students, reported in our article: Zimbardo, P. G., and Boyd, J. N. (1999). "Putting Time in Perspective: A valid, Reliable Individual-differences Metric." *Journal of Personality and Social Psychology* 77, 1,271–1,288.

9 Johnson, A. (April 19, 2007). "Gunman Sent Package to NBC News." MSNBC. Retrieved on April 19, 2007. (www.msnbc.msn.com/id/18195423/).

10 Johnson, B. J. (August 20, 2006). "Rise in Youth Killings." *San Francisco Chronicle,* pp. A1, 4.

11 A good sourcebook on the basics of hypnosis is found in: Bowers, K. (1983). *Hypnosis for the Seriously Curious.* New York: W. W. Norton.

12 The data reported here and more can be found in: Zimbardo, P. G., Marshall, G., and Maslach, C. (1971). "Liberating Behavior from Time-bound Control: Expanding the Present Through Hypnosis." *Journal of Applied Social Psychology* 1, 305–323.

13 Quoted in Cohen, J. (1967). *Psychological Time in Health and Disease.* Springfield, Ill.: Charles C. Thomas.

14 Ryan Madson, Patricia (2005). *Improv Wisdom: Don't Prepare, Just Show Up.* New York: Bell Tower, p. 21.

15 Csikszentmihályi, M. (1975). "Beyond Boredom and Anxiety." San Francisco: Jossey-Bass; also Csikszentmihályi, M. (1996). *Creativity: Flow and the Psychology of Discovery and Invention.* New York: HarperPerennial.

16 Zimbardo, P. G., and Warren, M. L. (2008). *Time to Create: Investigating the Dis-*

positional and Situational Determinants of Creativity. Unpublished ms., Stanford University.

17 Zimbardo, P. G., Keough, K. A., and Boyd, J. N. (1997). "Present Time Perspective as a Predictor of Risky Driving." *Personality and Individual Differences* 23, 1007–1023. Also see: Keough, K. A., Zimbardo, P. G., and Boyd, J. N. (1999). "Who's Smoking, Drinking, and Using drugs? Time Perspective as a Predictor of Substance Use." *Basic and Applied Social Psychology* 21, 149–164.

18 Petry, N. M., Bickel, W. K., and Arnett, M. (1998). "Shortened Time Horizons and Insensitivity to Future Consequences in Heroin Addicts." *Addiction* 93, 729–738.

19 Willis, T. A., Sandy, J. M., and Yaeger, A. M. (2001). "Time Perspective and Early-onset Substance Abuse: A Model based on Stress-coping Theory." *Psychology of Addictive Behavior* 15, 118–125.

20 For a closer look at the pros and cons of the DARE program, check out these websites: www.dare.com; http://en.wikipedia.org/wiki/D.A.R.E., and www.drcnet. org/DARE/. The research-based conclusion that DARE does not work is found in: Rosenbaum, D. P., and Hanson, Gordon S. (1998). "Assessing the Effects of School-based Drug Education: A Six-year Multilevel Analysis of Project D.A.R.E." *Journal of Research in Crime and Delinquency* 35, 381–412.

21 Information about sexual abstinence programs for children and teens can be found at: www.moz.org/Kids_and_Teens/Teen_Life/Sexuality/Abstinence/ and also www .teenpregnancy.org/resources/data/pdf/abstinence_eval.pdf. Contrary evidence regarding its effectiveness can be found at: www.mathematica-mpr.com/abstinence report.asp and also at: www.advocatesforyouth.org/publications/stateevaluations/ index.htm. See also Laura Bell's recent *New York Times* article "House Takes Up Abstinence Program Funding." July 18, 2007, p. A7.

22 Harber, K. D., Boyd, J. N., and Zimbardo, P. G. (2003). "Participant Self-selection Biases as a Function of Individual Differences in Time Perspective." *Journal of Experimental Social Psychology* 25, 255–264.

23 French, H. W. (March 5, 2000). "Japanese Teens Pick Nightlife over Class." *San Francisco Chronicle,* p. A13.

24 Veechio, Rick. "On Their Own Time." *Psychology Today* (July/August 2007), p. 31.

FIVE: THE FUTURE

1 These ideas were first developed by Max Weber, the brilliant German sociologist-economist, in his 1905 book, *The Protestant Ethic and the Spirit of Capitalism.* They were expanded with a greater focus on the influence of Calvinist thought on capitalism in the classic work by R. H. Tawney, *Religion and the Rise of Capitalism* (1998). Edison, N.J.: Transaction Publishers.

2 D'Alesio, M., Guarino, A., De Pascalis, V., and Zimbardo, P. G. (2003). "Testing Zimbardo's Stanford Time Perspective Inventory (STPI)—Short Form, an Italian Study." *Time & Society* 12, 333–347.

3 Holman, A., and Zimbardo, P. G. (In press). *The Social Language of Time: Exploring the Time Perspective–Social Network Connection.*

4 Harber, K. D., Boyd, J. N., and Zimbardo, P. G. (2003). "Participant Self-selection Biases as a Function of Individual Differences in Time Perspective." *Journal of Experimental Social Psychology* 25, 255–264.

5 Landes, D. S. (1983). *Revolution in Time: Clocks and the Making of the Modern World*. Cambridge, MA: Belknap Press.

6 Zimbardo, P. G., and Maslach, C. (1992). "Cognitive Effects of Biased Time Perspective." *International Journal of Psychology* 27, 167. Abstract of presentation at XXV International Congress of Psychology, Brussels, July 1992.

7 Webly, P., and Nyhus, E. K. (2006). "Parents' Influence on Children's Future Orientation and Saving." *Journal of Economic Psychology* 27, 140–164, 160.

8 Epel, E. S., Bandura, A., and Zimbardo, P. G. (1999). "Escaping Homelessness: The Influences of Self-efficacy and Time Perspective on Coping with Homelessness." *Journal of Applied Social Psychology* 29, 575–596.

9 Personal online communication to PGZ from Sarah Pobereskin, March 25, 2005.

10 Harber, K. D. (1996). Washington University. Unpublished data. For a review of Hope literature, see Snyder, C. R., Harris, C., Anderson, J. R., Holleran, S. A., Irving, L. M., Sigmon, S. T., Yaoshinbou, L., Gibb, J., Langelle, C., and Harney, P. (1991). "The Will and the Ways: Development and Validation of an Individual-Differences Measure of Hope." *Journal of Personality and Social Psychology* 60, 570–585.

11 A good source for research and creative ideas about hope is found in: Synder, C. R. (1994). *The Psychology of Hope: You Can Get There from Here*. New York: Free Press. Also see Synder, C. R. (2000). "The Past and Possible Futures of Hope." *Journal of Social and Clinical Psychology* 19, 11–28.

12 See Zimbardo's views on these rehabilitation issues in his article: Zimbardo, P. G. (2003). "Enriching Psychological Research on Disability." In F. E. Menz and D. F. Thomas, eds., *Bridging Gaps: Refining the Disability Research Agenda for Rehabilitation and the Social Sciences—Conference Proceedings*, pp. 19–32. Menomonie: University of Wisconsin–Stout, Stout Vocational Rehabilitation Institute, Research and Training Centers.

13 Hardin, G. (1968). "The Tragedy of the Commons." *Science* 162, 1243–1248.

14 Milfont, T. L., and Gouveia, V. V. (2006). "Time Perspective and Values: An Exploratory Study of Their Relations to Environmental Attitudes." *Journal of Environmental Psychology* 26, 72–82.

15 Taylor, S. E., Pham, L. B., Rivkin, I. D., and Armor, D. A. (1998). "Harnessing the Imagination: Mental Simulation, Self-regulation, and Coping." *American Psychologist* 53, 429–439.

16 *USA Today* weeklong series on the Time Crunch, August 1989.

17 Rifkin, J. (1987). *Time Wars: The Primary Conflict in Human History*. New York: Holt.

18 See article in *International Herald Tribune* (April 18–19, 1992). "Topless Bars Go for the Pinstripe Crowd," p. 14.

19 McCarthy, Barry, and McCarthy, Emily (2003). See *Rekindling Desire: A Step-by-Step Program to Help Low-Sex and No-Sex Marriages*. New York: Brunner-Routledge.

SIX: THE TRANSCENDENTAL FUTURE

1 www.bibleontheweb.com/Bible.Bible.com.asp.

2 Al-Qur'an: The Book of Guidance for All Mankind www.al-bukhari.org.

3 2006 Dalai Lama www.go2nepal.com/d-lama.html.

4 2004 Stanford Encyclopedia of Philosophy Alan Hájck. http://plato.stanford.edu/entries/pascal-wager.

5   Charles Darwin, 1809–1882, from *Life and Letters*. (1897). New York: D. Appleton and Company.

6   He is commonly known as the tailor of death. See http://en.wikipedia.org/wiki/ Suicide_bombers.

7   www.israelinsider.com/channels/security/articles/sec_0049.htm.

8   Atran, S. (2003). "Genesis of Suicide Terrorism." *Science* 299, 1534–1539.

9   Hassan, N. (November 2001). "An Arsenal of Believers: Talking to the Human Bombs." *The New Yorker*. http://academic2.american.edu/~dfugel/HassanAn ArsenalofBelievers.html.

10 Sageman, M. (2004). "Understanding Terrorist Networks," available at www.fpri. org/enotes/20041101.middleeast.sageman.understandingterrornetworks.html. Also see Shermer, M. (January 2006). "Murdercide: Science Unravels the Myth of Suicide Bombers," *Scientific American*, p. 33.

11 Safire, W. (June 4, 2001). "Arafat's Arsenal of Missiles." *The New York Times*. http://query.nytimes.com/gst/fullpage.html?res=9907E7D8153FF937A35755C0A 9679C8B63;scp=2tamp;sq=safire+arafat%27s+arsenal+of+missles+amp;st=nyt.

12 According to *The American Heritage Dictionary*.

13 Atran, S. (2003). "Genesis of Suicide Terrorism." *Science* 299.

14 Merari, Á. (2006). "Psychological Aspects of Suicide Terrorism," *Psychology of Terrorism*, B. Bongar, L. M. Brown, L. Beutler, J. Breckenridge, and P. G. Zimbardo, eds. (New York: Oxford University Press), pp. 101–115.

15 As cited by Scott Atran in his *Science* article.

16 www.newyorker.com/fact/content/articles/011119fa_FACT1?011119fa_FACT1.

17 Pape, R. (September 2006). "The Growth of Suicide Terrorism." *Chicago Tribune*.

18 Hassan, N. (Nov 19, 2001). An Arsenal of Believers: Talking to the "Human Books" www-news.uchicago.edu/citations/06/060911.page-ct.html. www.new yorker.com/fact/content/articles/011119fa_FACT1?011119fa_FACT1.

19 Freud, S. (1962). "Thoughts for the Times on War and Death: Our Attitude Towards Death." In J. Strachey, ed. and trans., *The Standard Edition of the Complete Psychological Works of Sigmund Freud*, vol. 14, pp. 289–300. London: Hogarth Press. (Originally published 1915.) 289, 296.

20 Hout, M., and Fisher, C. (June 2005). *Religious Diversity in America, 1940–2000*. "Percentage of American Adults (25 and Older) Who Believe in Life After Death by Year and Education." Source: Gallup Polls: General Social Survey. From Chapter 7, "How Americans Prayed: Religious Diversity and Change." *USA: A Century of Difference*. Berkeley, CA: Russell Sage Foundation. See http://ucdata.berkeley.edu:7101/.

21 Lindsay, D., and Gallup, G. (2000). *Surveying the Religious Landscape: Trends in U.S. Beliefs*. Harrisburg, PA: Morehouse Publishing.

22 Boyd, J. N., and Zimbardo, P. G. (1997). "Constructing Time After Death: The Transcendental-future Time Perspective." *Time and Society* 6, 5–24.

23 All of our samples are from the U.S. If we were to collect parallel data in other parts of the world, specifically the Middle East and Asia, we may find different patterns.

24 Nuttin, J. R. (1985). *Future Time Perspective and Motivation: Theory and Research Method*. Hillsdale, N.J.: Lawrence Erlbaum.

25 Hassan, N. (November 2001). "An Arsenal of Believers: Talking to the Human Bombs." *The New Yorker*. http://academic2.american.edu/2dfagel/HassanAn ArsenalofBelievers.html.

26 Marx, K. (1970). *Critique of Hegel's Philosophy of Right*. A. Jolin & J. O'Malley, trans, J. O'Malley, ed. London: Cambridge University Press. (Originally published 1844, p. 131.)

27 Kearns Goodwin, D. (2001). *The Fitzgeralds and the Kennedys: An American Saga*. New York: Simon & Schuster.

28 Edwards, A. & Orr, D. (2005). *The Sustainability Revolution: Portrait of a Paradigm Shift*. Gabriela Island, BC (Canada): New Society Publishers. Or see Wikipedia for an overview: http://en.wikipedia.org/wiki/Sustainability.

29 www.longnow.org/.

30 Harris, S. (2004). *The End of Faith: Religion, Terror, and the Future of Reason*. New York: W. W. Norton, p. 26.

31 Taylor, S. (1989). *Positive Illusions: Creative Self-deception and the Healthy Mind*. New York: Basic Books.

SEVEN: TIME, YOUR BODY, AND YOUR HEALTH

1 Farber, P. L. (2000). *Finding Order in Nature: The Naturalist Tradition from Linnaeus to E. O. Wilson*. Baltimore: Johns Hopkins University Press.

2 See Todes, D. (2000). *Ivan Pavlov: Exploring the Animal Machine*. New York: Oxford University Press.

3 Watson, J. (1913). "Psychology as the Behaviorist Views It." *Psychological Review* 20, 158–177.

4 Skinner, B. F. (1958). "Diagramming Schedules of Reinforcement." *Journal of the Experimental Analysis of Behavior* 1, 67–68.

5 Dunlap, J. (January 22, 1999). *Cell* 96, 271–290.

6 Klein, D., Moore, R., and Reppert, S. (1991). *Suprachiasmatic Nucleus: The Mind's Clock*. New York: Oxford University Press.

7 While circadian rhythms are the best known, other human biological processes correspond to shorter and longer periods. For example, a resting human heart beats at approximately sixty beats per minute, or once per second. Women's menstrual cycles occur on roughly monthly cycles.

8 Kryger, M., Roth, T., and Dement, W. C. (2005). *Principles and Practice of Sleep Medicine*. Philadelphia: Saunders.

9 Dement, W. C., and Vaughan, C. (1999). *The Promise of Sleep: A Pioneer in Sleep Medicine Explores the Vital Connection Between Health, Happiness, and a Good Night's Sleep*. New York: Delacorte Press.

10 Czeisler, C. A., Duffy, J. F., Shanahan, T. L., Brown, E. N., Mitchell, J. F., Rimmer, D. W., et al. (June 25, 1999). "Stability, Precision, and Near-24-hour Period of the Human Circadian Pacemaker." *Science* 284, 2,177–2,181.

11 Coren, S. (1996). "Daylight Savings Time and Traffic Accidents." *New England Journal of Medicine*. Also see www.mcmaster.ca/inabis98/occupational/coren0164/two.html.

12 See the NASA Z-Team website here: http://human-factors.arc.nasa.gov/zteam/.

13 J. Risberg and J. Grafman, eds. (2006). *The Frontal Lobes: Development, Function and Pathology*. New York: Cambridge University Press.

14 Fuster, J. M. (May 2001). "The Prefrontal Cortex—An Update: Time Is of the Essence." *Neuron* 30, 319–333.

15 See the Nobel Prize Organization's website here: http://nobelprize.org/nobel_prizes/medicine/laureates/1949/index.html.

16 El-Hai, J. (2007). *The Lobotomist: A Maverick Medical Genius and His Tragic Quest to Rid the World of Mental Illness.* Hoboken, NJ: John Wiley & Sons.

17 Aristotle (1991). *The Art of Rhetoric.* (H. C. Lawson-Tancred, trans.) London: Penguin Books.

18 Ekman, P. (1993). "Facial Expression and Emotion." *American Psychologist* 48 (4), 384–392. Also see Ekman, P. (1994). "Strong Evidence for Universals in Facial Expressions: A Reply to Russell's Mistaken Critique." *Psychological Bulletin* 115 (2), 268–287. And: Ekman, P., Friesen, W. V., O'Sullivan, M., and Chan, A. (1987). "Universals and Cultural Differences in the Judgments of Facial Expressions of Emotion." *Journal of Personality & Social Psychology* 53 (4), 712–717.

19 Aristotle (1991). *The Art of Rhetoric.* H. C. Lawson-Tancred, trans. London: Penguin Books.

20 Holman, E. A., and Silver, R. C. (1998). "Getting 'Stuck' in the Past: Temporal Orientation and Coping with Trauma." *Journal of Personality & Social Psychology* 74, 1146–1163.

21 Spiegel, D. (1997). "Trauma, Dissociation, and Memory." *Annals of the New York Academy of Sciences* 821, 225–237.

22 Beiser, M. (1999). "Strangers at the Gate: The 'Boat People's' First Ten Years in Canada." Toronto: University of Toronto Press. Also see: Beiser, M. (1980). "Coping with Past and Future: A Study of Adaptation of Social Change in West Africa." *Journal of Operational Psychiatry* 11 (2), 140–159. And: Beiser, M. (1988). "Influences of Time, Ethnicity and Attachment on Depression in Southeast Asian Refugees." *American Journal of Psychiatry* 145, 46–51.

23 Stetson, C., Fiesta, M. P., Eagleman, D. M. "Does Time Really Slow Down During a Frightening Event?" *Nature Neuroscience,* under review. PLoS ONE 2(12): e1295 .doi:10.1371/journal.pone.0001295.

24 Shakespeare, W. (1992). "The Rape of Lucrece," in *The Complete Works of Shakespeare,* 4th ed. D. Bevington, ed.

25 Monod, J. (1971). *Chance and Necessity: An Essay on the Natural Philosophy of Modern Biology.* New York: Alfred A. Knopf, p. 149.

26 Dodd, M., and Bucci, W. (1987). "The Relationship of Cognition and Affect in the Orientation Process." *Cognition* 27, 53–71, p. 53.

27 Damasio, A. (2006). *Descartes' Error.* New York: Vintage.

28 As quoted on p. 74 of Melges, F. T. (1982), *Time and the Inner Future: A Temporal Approach to Psychiatric Disorders.* New York: John Wiley & Sons, p. 614.

29 Shakespeare, W. *Hamlet.* Act I, Sc. 5. In a graduate class on Shakespeare and mental illness, John Boyd diagnosed Hamlet as clinically depressed with a brief psychotic episode. The brief psychotic episode would explain his belief that time was out of joint.

30 http://en.wikipedia.org/wiki/Seasonal_affective_disorder.

31 www.neurosurvival.ca/ClinicalAssistant/scales/clock_drawing_test.htm#shulman.

32 Melges, F. T. (1982). *Time and the Inner Future: A Temporal Approach to Psychiatric Disorders.* New York: John Wiley & Sons, p. 177.

33 Melges, F. T. (1982). *Time and the Inner Future: A Temporal Approach to Psychiatric Disorders.* New York: John Wiley & Sons.

34 Nolen-Hoeksema, S. (1991). "Responses to Depression and Their Effects on the Duration of Depressive Episodes." *Journal of Abnormal Psychology* 100, 569–582.

35 Ward, A., Lyubomirsky, S., and Nolen-Hoeksema, S. (2003). "Can't Quite Commit: Rumination and Uncertainty." *Personality and Social Psychology Bulletin* 29, 96–101.

36 Because of its current importance and ongoing controversy, we felt it important to provide our readers with an extended set of references on both sides of this issue, so that they might explore it further on their own. See: Begley, S. (2003) "Is Trauma Debriefing Worse Than Letting Victims Heal Naturally?" *The Wall Street Journal,* September 12, 2003; Devily, G. J., Gist, R., and Cotton, P. (2006). "Ready! Aim! Fire! The Status of Psychological Debriefing and Therapeutic Interventions: In the Workplace and After Disasters." *Review of General Psychology* 10, 318–345; Everly, G. S., and Mitchell, J. T. (1983). *Critical Incident Stress Management (CISM): A New Era and Standard of Care in Crisis Intervention.* Ellicott City, M.D.: Chevron; Foa, E. B., and Meadows, E. A. (1998). "Psychosocial Treatments for Posttraumatic Stress Disorder: A Critical Review," *Annual Review of Psychology* 48, 449–480; Gray, M. J., Maguen, S., and Litz, B. T. (2004). "Acute Psychological Impact of Disaster and Large-scale Trauma: Limitations of Traditional Interventions and Future Practice Recommendations." *Prehospital and Disaster Medicine,* Web publication http://pdm.medicine.wisc.edu; McNally, R. J., Bryant, R. A., and Ehlers, A. (2003). "Does Early Psychological Intervention Promote Recovery from Posttraumatic Stress?" *Psychological Science in the Public Interest* 4, 45–79; Mitchell, J. T. "When Disaster Strikes . . . The critical incident stress debriefing process." *Journal of Emergency Services* 8, 36–39; Raphael, B., Meldrum, L., and McFarlane, A. C. (1995). "Does Debriefing After Psychological Trauma Work?" *British Medical Journal* 310, 1479–1480; Ruzek, J. I., Maguen, S., and Litz, B. (2007). "Evidence-based Interventions for Survivors of Terrorism." In B. Bongar, L. Brown, L. Beutler, J. Breckenridge, and P. G. Zimbardo, eds. *Psychology of Terrorism.* New York: Oxford Press, pp. 247–272; Tuckey, M. R. (2007). "Issues in the Debriefing Debate for Emergency Services: Moving Research Outcomes Forward." *Clinical Psychology Science & Practice* 14, 106–116.

37 Quote from a schizophrenic patient, p. 133, in *Time and the Inner Future.*

38 Quote from a schizophrenic patient, p. xix, in *Time and the Inner Future.*

39 Huxley, A. (1954). *The Doors of Perception.* New York: Harper and Brothers, p. 21.

40 Steele, C. M., and Josephs, R. A. (1990). "Alcohol Myopia: Its Prized and Dangerous Effects." *American Psychologist* 45, 921–933.

41 A personal communication to John Boyd and several thousand others on January 28, 2006, at the KCBS Health Etc. Event.

42 An early version of the ZTPI contained a question that related to gambling: "I like to gamble." We removed it because gambling was largely illegal in California, where the scale was developed, and we thought that only a moderate percent of respondents would have had the experience with gambling required to provide a valid answer.

43 MacKillop, J., Anderson, E. J., Castelda, B. A., Mattson, R. E., and Donovick, P. J. (2006). "Convergent Validity of Measures of Cognitive Distortions, Impulsivity,

and Time Perspective with Pathological Gambling." *Psychology of Addictive Behaviors* 20, 75–79.

44 Sapolsky, R. M. (1994). *Why Zebras Don't Get Ulcers: A Guide to Stress, Stress-Related Diseases and Coping.* New York: W. H. Freeman.

45 Sapolsky, R. (1996). "Why Stress Is Bad for Your Brain." *Science* 273, 749.

46 Matthews, K. A. (November 2005). "Psychological Perspective on the Development of Coronary Heart Disease." *American Psychologist*, 60, 783–796.

47 See Whitehall Study I here: www.statistics.gov.uk/STATBASE/Source.asp?vlnk= 1326&More=Y.

48 Levine, R., (1997). *A Geography of Time: The Temporal Misadventures of a Social Psychologist, or How Every Culture Keeps Time Just a Little Bit Differently.* New York: Basic Books.

49 Melges's book is dedicated to his mother, who twice gave him life, once by giving birth to him and the second time by giving him a kidney.

50 Melges, F. T. (1982). *Time and the Inner Future: A Temporal Approach to Psychiatric Disorders.* New York: John Wiley & Sons, p. 290.

EIGHT: THE COURSE OF TIME

1 Shoda, Y., Mischel, W., and Peake, P. K. (1990). "Predicting Adolescent Cognitive and Self-regulatory Competencies from Preschool Delay of Gratification." *Developmental Psychology* 26, 978–986. See also: Mischel, W. (2007). "Delay of Gratification Ability over Time: Mechanisms and Developmental Implications." Paper presented at the Association for Psychological Science Convention, Washington, D.C., May 26, 2007.

2 Block, J. (1995). "On the Relationship Between IQ, Impulsivity, and Delinquency." *Journal of Abnormal Psychology* 104, 395–398.

3 Carstensen, Laura L., Isaacowitz, Derek M., Charles, Susan T. (1991). "Taking Time Seriously: A Theory of Socioemotional Selectivity." *American Psychologist* 54, 165–181.

4 Carstensen, Laura L., Fung, Helene H., Charles, Susan T. (2003). "Socioemotional Selectivity Theory and the Regulation of Emotion in the Second Half of Life." *Motivation and Emotion* 27, 103–123.

5 Lang, Frieder R., Carstensen, Laura L. (2002). "Time Counts: Future Time Perspective, Goals, and Social Relationships." *Psychology and Aging* 17, 125–139.

6 Ersner-Hershfield, Hal, Mikels, Joseph A., Sullivan, Sarah J., Carstensen, Laura L. (2008). "Poignancy: Mixed Emotional Experience in the Face of Meaningful Endings." *Journal of Personality and Social Psychology* 94, 158–167.

7 Carstensen, Laura L. (2006). "The Influence of a Sense of Time on Human Development." *Science* 312, 1913–1915.

8 Mather, Mara, Carstensen, Laura L. (2005). "Aging and Motivated Cognition: The Positivity Effect in Attention and Memory." *Trends in Cognitive Sciences* 9, 496–502.

9 Löckenhoff, Corinna E., Carstensen, Laura L. (2004). "Socioemotional Selectivity Theory, Aging, and Health: The Increasingly Delicate Balance Between Regulating Emotions and Making Tough Choices." *Journal of Personality* 72, 1395–1424.

10 For more details on the notion of life convoys, see: Antonucci, T. C. (1989). "Understanding Adult Social Relationships," In Kreppner, K., Lerner, R. L., eds., *Family Systems and Lifespan Development*, pp. 303–317. Hillsdale, N.J.: Erlbaum.

11 Webly, P., and Nyhus, E. K. (2006). "Parents' Influence on Children's Future Orientation and Saving." *Journal of Economic Psychology* 27, 140–164.

12 Goleman, D. (1995). *Emotional Intelligence*. New York: Bantam Books. See also Kagan Structures for Emotional Intelligence; Dr. Spencer Kagan, Kagan Online Magazine, Fall 2001. [www.kagononline.com/KaganClub/FreeArticles/Ask14 .html].

13 Although Boyd never saw the gunman alive, he talked to several coworkers who did. Their amazing stories shed light on how our brains seek to make sense of the extraordinary. For example, one male coworker passed the gunman as he exited the elevator. The coworker was a hunter, and he related that his first reaction was to say, "Hey, nice gun!" Another woman who was initially held hostage by the gunman asked whether he wanted something to drink. He did, and he let her leave his side to get him a drink. While on her way to the break room, the woman ran into the SWAT team. She had to be physically restrained from returning to the gunman with his drink. Finally, a coworker who had been hiding in a cubicle and ultimately directed the SWAT team to the gunman reported that it sounded like he had been shot twice. Actually, twenty rounds were fired from the SWAT team's submachine guns. Thirteen of the rounds struck the gunman. The remaining rounds broke through an eighteenth-floor window above Boyd's house. The window had been replaced by the time people returned to work.

14 The group stopped on the eleventh floor because they were tired and because one bank of building elevators ran from floors one to eleven, and a separate bank ran from twelve to fourteen. The gunman was known to have taken the elevators up to the eighteenth floor, and we doubted that we would switch elevators so we could reach the eleventh floor.

15 Zajonc, R. B. (1980). "Feeling and Thinking: Preferences Need No Inferences." *American Psychologist* 35, 151–175.

16 Contemporary researchers call mental events that are not conscious "nonconscious" events, instead of the more familiar "unconscious," in an attempt to avoid confusion with the Freudian concept of the unconscious.

17 Bargh, J. A., and Chartrand, T. L. (1999). "The Unbearable Automaticity of Being." *American Psychologist* 54, 462–479.

18 Franklin, B. (1748). *Advice to a Young Tradesman*.

19 Burton, J. (Dec. 3, 2006). "Taking the Long View: Time in the Stock Market, Not Timing the Market, Brings Greater Rewards." *CBS MarketWatch*. See here: www .marketwatch.com/news/story/story.aspx?guid={C7CBFB9F-357B-4880-80ED-3292CBCB6966}&dist=rss).

20 Zagorsky, J. L. (2007). "Do You Have to Be Smart to Be Rich? The Impact of IQ on Wealth, Income, and Financial Distress." *Intelligence*. doi:10.1016/j.intell .2007.02.003.

21 See these two investment classics for expert advice on how to invest wisely: Malkiel, B. (2007). *A Random Walk Down Wall Street: The Time-Tested Strategy for Successful Investing*. 9th ed. New York: W. W. Norton; and Bogle, J. C. (2007). *The Little Book of Common Sense Investing: The Only Way to Guarantee Your Fair Share of Stock Market Returns (Little Book Big Profits)*. New York: J. Wiley and Sons.

22 Center for Disease Control Birth Statistics: www.cdc.gov/nchs/data/statab/t941x01 .pdf.

23 Personal communication to Phil Zimbardo, July 26, 2007, Leon from Texas.

24 See Snyder, M., and Omoto, A. M. (1992). "Who Helps and Why?" In Spacapaan S., and Oskamp, S. eds., *Healing and Being Healed: Naturalistic Studies*. Newbury Park, CA: Sage, pp. 213–239.

25 Also see: Schroeder, D. A., Penner, L. A., Dovidio, J. F., and Piliavin, J. A. (1995). *The Psychology of Helping and Altruism*. New York: McGraw-Hill.

26 Rodin, J. (1986). "Aging and Health: Effects of the Sense of Control." *Science* 233, 1,271–1,276. Also see: Langer, E. J., and Rodin, J. (1976). "The Effects of Choice and Enhanced Personal Responsibility for the Aged: A Field Experiment in an Institutional Setting." *Journal of Personality and Social Psychology* 34, 191–198.

NINE: LOVE AND HAPPINESS

1 Bettelheim, B. (1984). *Freud and Man's Soul*. New York: Knopf.

2 Taylor, P., Funk, C., and Craighill, P. (February 13, 2006). *Are We Happy Yet?* Pew Research Center. See here for the full article: http://pewresearch.org/pubs/301/are-we-happy-yet.

3 Lyubomirsky, S. (2008). *The How of Happiness: A Scientific Approach to Getting the Life You Want*. New York: Penguin Press.

4 For reviews of the psychology of happiness, see Seligman, M. (2004). *Authentic Happiness: Using the New Positive Psychology to Realize Your Potential for Lasting Fulfillment*. New York: Free Press. Or see Gilbert, D. (2006). *Stumbling on Happiness*. New York: Alfred A. Knopf.

5 A personal communication from Amos Tversky.

6 Covey, S. R., Merrill, A. R., and Merrill, R. R. (1994). *First Things First: To Live, to Love, to Leave a Legacy*. New York: Simon & Schuster.

7 Dalai Lama and Cutler, H. (1999). *The Art of Happiness: A Handbook for Living*. New York: Riverhead Books, p. 37.

8 Adapted from Lyubomirsky, S. (2008). *The How of Happiness: A Scientific Approach to Getting the Life You Want*. New York: Penguin Press.

9 Langer, E. J. (1990). *Mindfulness*. Reading, MA: Addison, Wesley.

10 See Laberge, S. (1991). *Exploring the World of Lucid Dreaming*. New York: Ballantine. Mindfulness helps you be aware of your current state, whether that state is happiness, sadness, pain, or even dreaming. Lucid-dreaming expert Stephen LaBerge teaches people to lucid-dream by first teaching them to be mindful. His students learn to ask themselves, "Am I dreaming?" frequently throughout the day. The question requires people to reflect on their present state. After people thoroughly master the habit, they begin to ask themselves the same question at night while they are dreaming. Mindfulness, it seems, carries over from waking to sleeping states. Most of the time when people ask themselves, "Am I dreaming?" the answer is no. When people are dreaming, the answer yes makes them mindful not of their physical world but of their dream world. They can take conscious control of their dreams.

Why would anyone want to take conscious control of his or her dreams? you may ask. Stephen LaBerge responds to this question with a question of his own: "Have you ever seen the holodeck on *Star Trek: The Next Generation?*" Invariably, people say yes. He then follows up: "If you had access to a holodeck, would you use it?" Invariably, people say yes. "Lucid dreaming can do the same thing for you. Once you become conscious in your dreams, your mind becomes a holodeck."

11 See: www.coachwooden.com/.

12 Wooden, J. (2003). *They Call Me Coach*. New York: McGraw-Hill.

13 Dalai Lama and Cutler, H. (1999). *The Art of Happiness: A Handbook for Living*. New York: Riverhead Books. p. 63.

TEN: BUSINESS, POLITICS, AND YOUR TIME

1 Enron news release. See here: www.enron.com/corp/pressroom/releases/2001/ene/15-MostInnovative-02-06-01-LTR.html.

2 Remember that earnings per share and price per share are very different things.

3 McLean, B., and Elkind, P. (2003). *Smartest Guys in the Room: The Amazing Rise and Scandalous Fall of Enron*. New York: Penguin Books.

4 As quoted in "Debating the Enron Effect: Business World Divided on Problems and Solutions," by Steven Pearlstein, February 17, 2002, *The Washington Post*.

5 http://archives.cnn.com/2002/LAW/01/14/enron.letter/index.html.

6 Swartz, M., and Watkins, S. (2003). *Power Failure: The Inside Story of the Collapse of Enron*. New York: Random House.

7 Was it a coincidence that a woman wrote the letter to Kenneth Lay expressing anxiety over Enron's future? We think not. Women consistently have higher future time perspectives than do men. Future time perspective allows people to see future consequences. Enron's decision-makers were engrossed in the present, possibly because men tend to be higher in present hedonism. At Enron, Watkins's pleas to recognize the future were not heard by its present-oriented decision-makers.

8 Call to resist Anglo-American model of "short-termism." *Financial Times*, April 26, 2007, p. 2.

9 Adams, G. B., and Balfour, D. L. (2004). *Unmasking Administrative Evil*. New York: M. E. Sharpe.

10 Taylor, F. W. (1967). *The Principles of Scientific Management*. New York: W. W. Norton.

11 See Gold, M., ed. (1999). *The Complete Social Scientist: A Kurt Lewin Reader*. Washington, D.C.: American Psychological Association Press.

12 Schumpeter, J. A., (1950). *Capitalism, Socialism, and Democracy*. New York: Harper.

13 Schumpeter, J. A. (1939). *Business Cycles: A Theoretical, Historical, and Statistical Analysis of the Capitalist Process*. New York: McGraw-Hill.

14 As quoted in Cornish, E. (2004). *Futuring: The Exploration of the Future*. World Future Society, p. 11.

15 Bennis, W. G., and Slater, P. (1998). *The Temporary Society*. San Francisco: Jossey-Bass.

16 McKenna, R. (1999). *Real Time: Preparing for the Age of the Never Satisfied Customer*. Boston: Harvard Business School Press.

17 Galbraith, J. K. (1958). *The Affluent Society*. Boston Houghton Mifflin.

18 From James Burke's Connections video series. (1978). BBC.

19 We've chosen a number greater than 50 percent, because the general direction of the market is up. Therefore, if an adviser picked every stock to rise, he or she is likely to be correct over 50 percent of the time.

20 For a fascinating discussion of how statistics are consistently abused and ignored, see Taleb, N. N. (2007). *The Black Swan: The Impact of the Highly Improbable*. New York: Random House.

21 Bogle, J. C. (2007). *The Little Book of Commen Sense Investing: The Only Way to Guarantee Your Fair Share of Stock Market Returns (Little Book Big Profits)*. New York: J. Wiley and Sons.

22 Malkiel, B. G. (2007). *A Random Walk Down Wall Street: The Time-Tested Strategy for Successful Investing*. 9th ed. New York: Norton.

23 Buss, D. M. (1994). *The Evolution of Desire: Strategies of Human Mating*. New York: Basic Books.

24 Lipman-Blumen, J. (2005). *The Allure of Toxic Leaders: Why We Follow Destructive Bosses and Corrupt Politicians—and How We Can Survive Them*. New York: Oxford University Press.

25 Drucker, P. F. (1993). *Innovation and Entrepreneurship*. New York: Collins.

26 See the Wikipedia entry for the history of sliced bread: http://en.wikipedia.org/wiki/Sliced_bread.

27 By these criteria, the prepaid time cards would be better than sliced bread.

28 Adapted from a "How I Work" gallery on http://money.cnn.com. Murphy, C. (March 16, 2006). "Secrets of Greatness: How I Work, E-mail and Voicemail; Yoga and Personal Assistants; Structure and Grooving: A Dozen Accomplished People Tell What Works for Them." *Fortune* on CNNMoney.com. See here for the entire article: http://money.cnn.com/popups/2006/fortune/how_i_work/frameset.exclude.html.

29 Adapted from a "How I Work" gallery on http://money.cnn.com. Murphy, C. (March 16, 2006). "Secrets of Greatness: How I Work, E-mail and Voicemail; Yoga and Personal Assistants; Structure and Grooving: A Dozen Accomplished People Tell What Works for Them." *Fortune* on CNNMoney.com. See here for the entire article: http://money.cnn.com/popups/2006/fortune/how_i_work/frameset.exclude.html.

30 Adapted from a "How I Work" gallery on http://money.cnn.com. Murphy, C. (March 16, 2006). "Secrets of Greatness: How I Work, E-mail and Voicemail; Yoga and Personal Assistants; Structure and Grooving: A Dozen Accomplished People Tell What Works for Them." *Fortune* on CNNMoney.com. See here for the entire article: http://money.cnn.com/popups/2006/fortune/how_i_work/frameset.exclude.html.

31 Daniel Kahneman won the 2002 Nobel Prize in economics for prospect theory, despite the fact that he is a psychologist. Amos Tversky likely would have shared in the award if he had not died several years earlier. See Kahneman, D., and Tversky, A. (1973). "On the Psychology of Prediction." *Psychological Review* 880, 237–251. Also see: Kahneman, D., and Tversky, A. (1994). "Choices, Values, and Frames." *American Psychologist* 39, 341–350. And: Kahneman, D., and Tversky, A. (1979). "Prospect Theory: An Analysis of Decision Under Risk." *Econometrica* XLVII, 263–291.

32 $((0.5 \times -\$200) + (0.5 \times -\$0) = \$100))$

33 In Kahneman and Tversky's studies, the past was largely ignored.

34 Corral-Verdugo, V., Fraijo-Sing, B., and Pinheiro, J. Q. (2006). "Sustainable Behavior and Time Perspective: Present, Past, and Future Orientations and Their Relationship with Water Conservation Behavior." *Revista Interamericana de Psicología/Interamerican Journal of Psychology* 40, 139–147.

35 Taylor, S. E., Pham, L. B., Rivkin, I. D., and Armor, D. A. (1998). "Harnessing the Imagination: Mental Simulation, Self-regulation, and Coping." *American Psychologist* 53, 429–439.

36 Boyd, J. N., and Zimbardo, P. G. (1995). *The Affect of Cognitive Training on Atti-*

tude Change, Self-Esteem, and Time Perspective of Juvenile Delinquents. (Boyd, Master's thesis, Stanford University.)

37 A GAO Report (January 15, 2003). *Youth Illicit Drug Use Prevention: DARE Long-term Evaluations and Federal Efforts to Identify Effective Programs,* GAO-20 03-172R. For the full report, see here: www.gao.gov/new.items/d03172r.pdf.

38 See Phil's *The Lucifer Effect* for an example of how prisons can distort time perception and increase present orientation. Zimbardo, P. (2007). *The Lucifer Effect: Understanding How Good People Turn Evil.* New York: Random House.

39 Steffens, S. (October 4, 2007). "Aid Cutoff Looms for Poor." *The Valley Times,* p. 1.

ELEVEN: RESETTING YOUR PSYCHOLOGICAL CLOCK

1 Van Beck, W. (2007). *Time Orientation and Personality Problems.* (In preparation.)

2 Boniwell, I., and Linley, P. A. (2007). *Time Perspective and Well-being.* University of East London, UK. (In preparation.)

3 Livneh, H., and Martz, E. (2007). "Reactions to Diabetes and Their Relationship to Time Orientation." *International Journal of Rehabilitation Research* 30, 127–136.

4 Herrnstein, R., and Murray, C. (1995). *The Bell Curve.* New York: Free Press.

5 Banfield, E. (1974). *The Unheavenly City Revisited.* Boston, MA: Little, Brown, p. 236.

6 Zimbardo, P. G., and Leippe, M. (1991). *The Psychology of Attitude Change and Social Influence.* New York: McGraw-Hill.

7 Keyes, R. (1991). *Timelock: How Life Got So Hectic and What You Can Do About it.* New York: HarperCollins, pp. 202, 215.

8 Loftus, E. F. (2005). "Planting Misinformation in the Human Mind: A 30-year Investigation of the Malleability of Memory." *Learning & Memory* 12, 361–366.

9 Orwell, G. (1948). *1984.* New York: Harcourt Brace, p. 32. See also: Zimbardo, P. G. (2005). "Fictional Concepts Become Operational Realities in Jim Jones' Jungle Experiment." In *On Nineteen Eighty-Four: Orwell and Our Future.* Gleason, A., Goldsmith, J. Nussbaum, M., eds. Princeton: Princeton University Press, 127–154.

10 Boniwell, I., and Linley P. A. (2007). *Time Perspective and Well-being.* University of East London, UK. (In preparation.)

11 Rappaport, H., Sandy, J. M., and Yaeger, A. (1985). "Relation Between Ego Identity and Temporal Perspective." *Journal of Personality and Social Psychology* 48, 1609–1620.

12 Litvinovic, G. (1999). "Perceived Change, Time Orientation and Subjective Well-being Through the Lifespan in Yugoslavia and the United States." Doctoral dissertation, University of North Carolina, Chapel Hill.

13 Boyd-Wilson, B. M., Walkey, F. H., and McClure, J. (2002). "Present and Correct: We Kid Ourselves Less When We Live in the Moment." *Personality and Individual Differences* 33, 691–702.

14 Shostrom, E. L. (1974). *Manual for the Personal Orientation Inventory.* San Diego, CA: Educational and Industrial Testing Service. See also: Shostrom, E. L. (1968). *Man, the Manipulator: The Inner Journey from Manipulation to Actualization.* New York: Bantam Books/Abingdon Press.

15 Boniwell, I., and Zimbardo, P. (2004). "Balancing Time Perspective in Pursuit of Optimal Functioning," in Linley, P. A., and Joseph, S., eds., *Positive Psychology in Practice.* New Jersey: John Wiley & Sons.

TWELVE: OUT OF TIME

1 Plutarch (circa 46–127). *Of the Training of Children.*
2 Beckett, S. (1955). *Waiting for Godot,* in *Samuel Beckett: The Complete Dramatic Works.* London: Faber and Faber.
3 Ibid.
4 Shakespeare, W. (1992). *Macbeth,* in *The Complete Works of Shakespeare.* 4th ed. D. Bevington, ed.
5 Beckett, S. (1955). *Waiting for Godot.*
6 Dalai Lama and Cutler, H. (1999). *The Art of Happiness: A Handbook for Living.* New York: Riverhead Books, 63–64.
7 This has, of course, been "repurposed" from Sartre. See: Sartre, J. P. (1956). *Being and Nothingness: An Essay on Phenomenological Ontology.* New York: Philosophical Library.

EPILOGUE

1 www.usatoday.com/news/health/2008-08-04-time-paradox-happiness_n.htm.
2 www.usabilitynews.com/news/article1940.asp.
3 www.madmoneystocks.com/jim-cramer.aspx?id=2/6/2007&seg=4.

Acknowledgments

Writing a book like this takes time. You undoubtedly expect that of the authors, but what you may not expect is that countless other people also generously gave their time and energy. Without their efforts, this book would not have been possible.

Early on, Christina Maslach and Gary Marshall worked with Phil on his first time-related publication. That was more than thirty years ago. In the mid 1980s, Alex Gonzalez helped Phil develop the first Stanford Time Perspective Inventory. Some ten years later, George Parrott introduced John to Phil and to a new world of psychological time. The rest is, as they say, history.

At Stanford University we have had the privilege of collaborating with many outstanding researchers on time-related publications, including Kent Harber and Kelli Keough. Students in numerous time-perspective seminars also contributed to our thinking.

Researchers at other schools have also shaped our work. Robert Levine has been an invaluable friend, mentor, and collaborator. Alan Strathman, Jeff Joireman, Alison Holman, and Ilona Boniwell have published works that have moved the field—and thus the thinking in this book—forward. More recent, Anna Sircova of the State University of Moscow and many other young researchers around the world have used our measure to generate a host of important findings about human nature. Because of the collective action of this dedicated group of researchers, we believe that the future of time in psychology is a bright one.

We are deeply indebted to our stellar literary agent, Gillian MacKenzie, for helping shape our initial proposal and refining our message; to our intrepid editor, Leslie Meredith, for providing keen advice, wise constructive criticism, and an unusually sensitive editing of our final manuscript; to her talented and patient assistant, Donna Loffredo, for enabling our manuscript to flow over the many publishing hurdles in timely fashion; and, finally, to Dr. Rose Zimbardo, for rendering an early draft into readable English prose.

To all of those who gave their time to make this book what it is, thank you. We hope that you believe your contribution—and this book—worth your time.

Index

Page numbers in *italics* refer to illustrations and tables.

Illustration Credits

1. The Crypt of the Capuchin Monks, Santa Maria della Concezione: Photo from Stanthejeep/Wikipedia.com
2. The Crypt of the Capuchin Monks, Santa Maria della Concezione: Photo from Tessier/Wikipedia.com
3. The Crypt of the Capuchin Monks, Santa Maria della Concezione: Photo from Tessier/Wikipedia.com
4. Keeping Watch: The Transformational Power of Time: Public domain
5. A Future-Product Painting of a Basket of Flowers: Courtesy of Phil Zimbardo
6. A Present-Process Painting of a Basket of Flowers: Courtesy of Phil Zimbardo
7. Another Present-Process Painting of a Basket of Flowers: Courtesy of Phil Zimbardo
8. A Present-Product Painting of a Basket of Flowers: Courtesy of Phil Zimbardo
9. Time by Moments: A Sundial at Howard Castle, England: Courtesy of Phil Zimbardo
10. The Clock Drawing Test: Clocks Drawn by People Suffering from Dementia: Courtesy of John Boyd
11. A Joe Euclid Treatise: A Retrospective Prediction of the Future: Courtesy of John Boyd

About the Authors

PHILIP ZIMBARDO is professor emeritus of psychology at Stanford University and has also taught at Yale University, New York University, and Columbia University. He is currently teaching clinical graduate students at the Pacific Graduate School of Psychology in Palo Alto and also at the Naval Postgraduate School (Monterey). He is the coauthor of *Psychology and Life* and the author of *Shyness* and *The Lucifer Effect*, which together have sold millions of copies. Zimbardo has been president of the American Psychological Association and is now director of the Stanford Center on Interdisciplinary Policy, Education, and Research on Terrorism (CIPERT). He also narrated the award-winning PBS series *Discovering Psychology*, which he helped create. In 2004 he acted as an expert witness in the court-martial hearings of one of the American army reservists accused of criminal behavior in the Abu Ghraib prison in Iraq. His informative website www.prisonexperiment.org is visited by millions every year. Visit the author's personal website at www.zimbardo.com, and visit this book's website at www.lucifereffect.com.

JOHN BOYD received his Ph.D. in psychology in 1999 from Stanford University, where he studied with Zimbardo. A frequent contributor to the scientific literature on time perspective, he was instrumental in the construction of the Zimbardo Time Perspective Inventory (ZTPI) and was the first to identify the transcendental-future time perspective. His more recent academic work has explored the interaction of thoughts and feelings through time. Boyd brings a strong record of translating science into practice through his current role as research manager at Google and his previous roles as director of research at Yahoo! and director of scientific affairs at Alertness Solutions, a boutique international consulting firm specializing in human performance management. Please visit the website John developed to complement this book: www.thetimeparadox.com.